CHANGE LEADERSHIP IN DEVELOPING COUNTRIES

In *Change Leadership in Developing Countries*, Franca Ovadje offers readers a comprehensive and integrative model for the design, implementation and evaluation of organizational change. This unique book embodies an African perspective, discussing the specific needs and issues associated with leading change within the institutional, economic, social, and cultural contexts of developing economies. Based on extensive research, as well as on the first-hand experiences of managers who have led change initiatives in Africa, this book envisions a change leadership model based on conscious decision-making, rather than taking a prescriptive approach. With examples and case studies drawn from African organizations, this book is a vital tool for students and managers who are based in, or interact with, emerging economies.

Franca Ovadje, PhD, has a doctorate in Business Administration from IESE Business School, Spain. She leads sessions in human resource management, leadership and organizational change in both local and international programs. She is an active consultant to industry. Her current research interests include change management, knowledge management, and human resource management and performance. Dr. Ovadje was a recipient of the African Management Scholar Award in 2005. She is a pioneer member of faculty of the Lagos Business School, Nigeria.

CHANGE LEADERSHIP IN DEVELOPING COUNTRIES

Franca Ovadje

Routledge
Taylor & Francis Group

NEW YORK AND LONDON

First published 2014
by Routledge
711 Third Avenue, New York, NY 10017

and by Routledge
2 Park Square, Milton Park, Abingdon, Oxon OX14 4RN

Routledge is an imprint of the Taylor & Francis Group, an informa business

© 2014 Taylor & Francis

The right of Franca Ovadje to be identified as author of this work has been asserted by her in accordance with sections 77 and 78 of the Copyright, Designs and Patents Act 1988.

Library of Congress Cataloging-in-Publication Data
Ovadje, Franca.
Change leadership in developing countries / Franca Ovadje.
pages cm
Includes bibliographical references and index.
1. Organizational change—Africa. 2. Organizational change—Developing countries. 3. Leadership—Africa. 4. Leadership—Developing countries.
I. Title.
HD58.8.O933 2014
658.4'092091724—dc23
2013038034

ISBN: 978-0-415-81922-0
ISBN: 978-0-415-81923-7
ISBN: 978-0-203-57645-8

Typeset in Bembo
by Cenveo Publisher Services

To Mum, Anne Ererebue Ovadje, who exemplifies leadership and taught her twelve children what really matters.

CONTENTS

Cases

ACKNOWLEDGEMENTS

An African proverb says: 'if you want to run fast, run alone; if you want to run far, run with others'. I began this journey with many others. Some of them taught me and others encouraged me. They all ran with me all the way. We have been able to run far. I am grateful to all of them.

My special thanks to Charo Basterra for her encouragement and support. I was privileged to tap into her wealth of experience in Africa. She has also been an enthusiastic cheerleader. I thank my siblings, nieces, nephews, and in-laws. They have all been a great support. I am very grateful to my family for helping me remain focused on the fundamentals and for the sacrifices they made during my sabbatical year. It is indeed a great blessing to be a member of this family. You are awesome.

Conducting the research was a truly enriching experience for me. Thanks to the dozens of managers I interviewed for the case studies and to hundreds of others who shared their personal insights with me. Without them this book would not exist. Thanks also to my research assistants over the years: Elohor Ovadje, Eva Okolie, Amaka Ihejieto, and Ruky Esharegaran.

I shared the model presented in this book with hundreds of executives at the Lagos Business School and the Strathmore Business School in Nairobi. I am particularly grateful to the participants of the Chief Executive Programmes, Advanced Management Programmes, the Executive MBA programmes and the MBAs for their comments. I thank them for sharing their stories and frustrations with me and for spurring me on to write this book.

IESE Business School provided me with access to library resources and an intellectually stimulating environment. Nuria Chinchilla opened the doors of IESE to me during my sabbatical year. I am especially grateful to her for her strong support over the years. Thanks also to Mireia Las Heras of the IESE

International Centre for Work and Family. I am grateful to the Dean of IESE, Jordi Canals, for believing in this book and for the encouragement he gave me. Thanks to Brian Leggett who has been a great support in my professional life since my doctoral student days in IESE.

My stay in Barcelona would not have been so fruitful and enjoyable without the friendship of the Monforts, Chus Joner, Ana Gavira, Maria Salud Tora, Beula D'Souza and many others. I look forward to offering all of you African hospitality.

I am particularly grateful to the anonymous reviewers who contributed a great deal to improving the quality of this book. Among others who helped improve the quality of the manuscript, two people deserve special mention. Thanks to Imelda Wallace for her honest feedback and for encouraging me when the going was tough and Esther Ojo for her patience in editing parts of the book.

Finally, special thanks to John Szilagyi, Sharon Golan, and Manjula Raman of Routledge for their feedback and support throughout the editorial process.

INTRODUCTION

In today's changing world, organizations must be both adaptive and flexible. The macroeconomic environment, technology, globalization and a host of other factors are driving radical changes in organizations and entire industries. Managers must not only anticipate these changes, they must respond quickly and effectively if they are to survive let alone thrive. The development of the capacity for change and for institutional learning must be a permanent feature of organizations (Schein 1990, in Blunt and Jones 1992).

Many developing countries are privatizing the public sector; globalization is threatening their indigenous companies, the telecommunications revolution has opened up new vistas for organizations in Africa. The high levels of uncertainty, due in part to the instability of government policies, and the macroeconomic environment, demand adequate responses from organizations if they are to stay alive. Change competence is increasingly a requirement of every manager.

Africa is at a key inflection point (Teagarden 2009: 139). The continent is on the brink of profound change. According to Babarinde (2009: 327), 'sub-Saharan Africa is poised for change and growth in the twenty-first century'. If these changes are to be successful, African leaders need change models that guide them through the maze: models that, while not being prescriptive, do highlight critical decisions to be made and hurdles to be overcome.

Today's managers lack robust change models to guide their organizations through change. Existing models do provide insights especially in the area of overcoming resistance to change. However, many of the existing models are not comprehensive (they do not include all the relevant variables) and are often overly prescriptive. In a rapidly changing and complex environment, prescriptions may not be very useful. Managers (in both private and public sectors) need models that they can use to guide change without taking away the power of choice; they need models that highlight the important strategic design and implementation choice opportunities without telling them what to do.

Managers in African organizations lack local examples of successful change. Most published works are based on research on American companies. The African press rarely carries stories of successful change and great leadership, yet there are examples of successful transformations both in the private and public sectors in Africa, from which managers can learn.

Research suggests that planning is necessary for successful change (Kotter and Schlesinger 1979). Stewart and Kringas (2003) noted that the reason change efforts fail may not be resistance but change strategies that are not well thought through. A change model that helps managers develop a coherent plan for change (transformation or otherwise) may be the key to successful change. Such a model must also be comprehensive; it should include the key choices that should be made in developing a good plan. Without a flight plan, the captain is not likely to arrive at the desired destination. Change is complex enough; those who try to lead change without a plan may be flying blind.

This book presents a model of change leadership which is based on the experience of managers in both the private and public sectors in Africa. It also draws on decades of research on change leadership from other contexts. The model is comprehensive – it includes the relevant variables.

Using the notion of choice (a decision-making perspective), we present an integrated model of change which brings together the critical choice opportunities in the design, implementation and evaluation of a change programme. We argue that the success of a change initiative depends to a large extent on the ability of change strategists and agents to make the right decisions and the consistency of the choices made: how well they fit each other.

The model presented in this book is a framework for decision making in change situations; it is a model of planned change. It should guide managers as they lead change in their organizations. Change is difficult to implement. Unplanned change leads anywhere. The destination should be known and a roadmap for getting to the end state must be developed. Change is too important today to be left to chance. To give up this power of choice is to put one's organization in a worse competitive position than those organizations that recognize this power (Burnes 2004).

Underlying the framework presented in this book is decision making: choice. Conceptualizing and implementing change involves making choices. According to Simon (1976), decision-making processes hold the key to understanding organizational phenomena. Decision making is an important managerial role (Mintzberg 1990). Change creates immense opportunities for choice. Should the organization adapt itself to the environment or influence the environmental constraints? Choices have to be made on – among other things – what to change, how to change and when to change.

Why This Book?

Change models in the literature have provided both researchers and practitioners with useful frameworks for understanding change. There is, however, a need for more comprehensive models of change. This is especially relevant in turbulent environments where disruptive change is the norm. Existing change models exclude important strategic choices. Change is a complex phenomenon. Pettigrew (1985) warns researchers to avoid simplistic explanations of organizational change.

Second, some of the change models in the literature are prescriptive. In a turbulent environment, managers need models that can be used to guide change without taking away the power of choice – they need models that highlight the important choice opportunities without telling them what to do. While present change models have provided both researchers and practitioners with useful frameworks for understanding and implementing change, there is a need for more comprehensive and integrative models. Such models should help managers better understand the change issues, strategies, etc. Leading change is much more than selling a vision and overcoming barriers to change.

This book offers a number of advantages to managers. It provides an integrated framework for planning, implementing and institutionalizing change. It also facilitates discussions around the change and therefore ensures that change strategists and agents are on the same page. The model also enables change actors to bring to consciousness their underlying assumptions, to make conscious choices regarding elements of the model. The framework presented in this book is a learning model; it is open to the environment and encourages learning by change actors as they plan for and implement change.

Finally, the change model is grounded in research and the experience of scores of managers who have been involved in leading change initiatives in Africa. If you are leading change in your organization, or you tried in the past and failed and have been wondering what went wrong, you will find the lessons from the cases presented in this book useful.

Leading change is a difficult journey but it can also be exciting as dreams are realized. This book provides you with a way of thinking about change. Leading change is about making decisions. As all managers know too well the quality of decisions matter but the ability to implement them determines success as a leader of change. The book should help you do both: improve the quality of your decisions and your change execution capacity. It is our hope that you enjoy reading this book as much as we enjoyed writing it.

A Model of Planned Organizational Change

The model of planned change begins with the perception of a need for change. This need usually arises from a performance gap (Zaltman and Duncan 1977), a difference between current performance and a desired or preferred state

(Katz and Kahn 1978). Unless this gap is perceived, the need for change may go unnoticed by the organization.

Drivers of Change

Change may be driven by the internal environment, such as inefficient processes, movement along the organization life cycle, or by the external environment, the macroeconomic and socio-political environment in which the organization operates. As the external environment changes, a mismatch occurs between the firm's internal environment and the changing external environment. A need for change may arise. This need must be perceived otherwise no effort to change will be initiated.

If change strategists and agents feel the need for change, they are then faced with many choice opportunities all of which are summarized in the paragraphs below.

The Vision

The decision to change leads to the need for a definition of the change vision. Irrespective of the nature of the change, every change initiative requires a vision. The vision is a description of the end of state: what the organization or subsystem will look like when the change is implemented.

The choice of vision is critical as all other choices in the model (as we will see) have to be consistent with the vision. To say that a change initiative has been successful is to say that the vision has been actualized. Vision provides purpose and direction for the change.

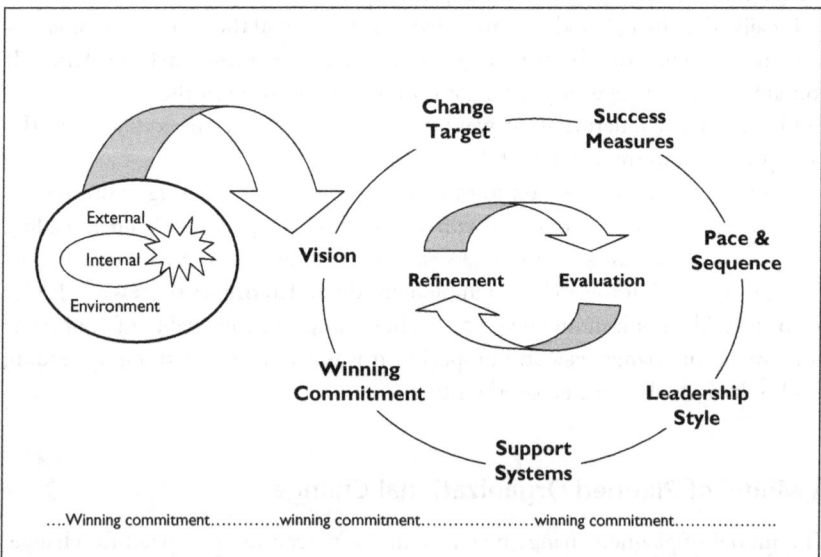

FIGURE 0.1 A model of planned organizational change

The Change Target(s)

Having made a choice of vision, the next choice opportunity is what to change: the change target. Change strategists must identify the targets of the change. Targets answer the question: what should be changed to realize the vision? The change target could be the culture, structure, business process, rewards systems, technology, physical setting, etc. Targets must be consistent with the vision such that if the targets are successfully changed, the vision will be realized.

Choice of Success Measures

Another decision opportunity is the choice of success measures. During the planning stage, change strategists decide how the success of the change will be evaluated. If these measures are not agreed upon during planning and then tracked during implementation, the change initiative will probably drift. What is measured is important because it influences behaviour.

Choice of Pace and Sequence of Change

Change agents also have to make decisions regarding the pace and sequence of the change. They have to decide whether or not the whole organization or only a part will be changed at a time. If a sequential approach is to be followed, the particular sequence to be followed is chosen. The pace at which the change will be introduced is another strategic decision. There are advantages to a fast as well as a slow pace.

Choice of Leadership Style

Another key choice opportunity is the choice of how the change will be introduced (the change leadership style that will be used). The wrong choice can de-motivate employees who would otherwise have championed the change. Leadership style varies from more authoritarian to participative and engaging styles. Different styles may be used in the planning and execution of the initiative.

Choice of Support Systems

If change is to be institutionalized, some support systems and structures are necessary. Change agents must decide on the systems and processes which they will use to support the change. The choice of support systems will vary depending on a number of factors such as the nature of the change targets.

Winning Commitment to Change

Another choice opportunity for change strategists and agents is winning the commitment of stakeholders to the change. Winning commitment to change is such a critical strategic choice in the design and implementation of change that change actors are encouraged to consider the challenge of winning commitment at each choice opportunity in the model. If a change initiative is to be successful, change recipients must accept the change and be willing to actualize the vision. Winning commitment to change involves overcoming resistance to change. Change agents must decide on strategies to identify and deal with resistance.

Evaluation and Refinement

The last choice opportunity in the model is the evaluation and refinement of the change. Choices here are related to how performance will be tracked and monitored, how often evaluation will be done, etc. Evaluation and refinement facilitate learning and action-taking during the change process. Due to the rapidly changing environment and the uncertainties therein, it may not be reasonable to expect that the best change plans will be implemented without the need for modifications, whether minor or major.

Choices made here have to be consistent with choices in all the other elements of the model. Evaluation and refinement during change implementation ensure that change strategists and agents are attuned to the environment and the changes that may be occurring therein.

Summary and Conclusion

A few comments about the model: first, underlying this model is the belief that human action is purposeful. Change agents seek to effect change. Very often they were employed to do precisely that, to bring about changes in the organization. Whether the change is transformation or transitional (involving only minor adjustments in the organization), managers guide the change towards a desired outcome. One does not employ a pilot or ship captain and allow him or her to let the crew evolve a destination and flight plan on their own. We expect the pilot to be involved in the process and to guide the people towards the expected outcome. This is the reality of organizational life. The CEO churn we see in corporate organizations is often due to their inability to deliver on expected outcomes.

In line with the change literature, we distinguish among three change actors: change strategists, agents and recipients. Change strategists are ultimately responsible for the change. They are usually the CEO and the top management. They take major decisions around the change and appoint the change agents. The latter are responsible for implementing the change. They may also have power to make decisions around the change. The change recipients are those who are expected to carry out the change: to change their behaviour, adopt new processes, systems, etc. All change actors are to some extent change recipients.

It is important to consider winning commitment to change at each decision point. For example, while considering possible alternatives regarding change targets, change agents should consider how they will win stakeholder commitment to the change. The availability of resources and the organization's readiness for change are other considerations that change strategists and agents should bear in mind as they plan for and implement changes in their organizations.

Consistency among decisions in all the above elements is critical for change success. All decisions must be aligned with the vision of the change and further its actualization. Decisions must also be consistent among themselves. For example, the choice of change targets must be consistent with choices regarding leadership style, pace and sequences of change, etc.

Organization of this Book

Each of the following chapters is dedicated to one choice opportunity, one element of the model. The first chapter provides the context of this book. It introduces the African macroeconomic, socio-political and cultural characteristics. Attention is drawn to the changes in most African countries in recent times and their implications for business managers.

In the second chapter, we explicate the drivers of change and the decision to initiate change. In subsequent chapters we elucidate the choices in the model: vision, change targets, success measures, pace and sequence of change, leadership style, support systems, winning commitment and evaluation and refinement.

The book ends with a summary and a practical and useful section on the peculiar challenges of an expatriate who is charged with leading organizational change in Africa.

1

ORGANIZATIONAL CHANGE IN THE AFRICAN CONTEXT

The African Socio-economic and Cultural Context

Introduction

Africa economies have seen steady growth rates in over a decade and there are good prospects for future growth. Foreign Direct Investments (FDIs) to Africa has grown and the sources of these investments are changing with China becoming a big investor in Africa.

Multinational Corporations are looking at their African subsidiaries to deliver much needed profits. McKinsey estimates Africa's growth opportunity to be worth $2.6 trillion annual revenues by 2020.[1] To take advantage of these opportunities, organizations in Africa must adapt to changes in the economy; they need to implement changes in their organizations. Some African organizations are doing just that and they are growing and becoming international. GTBank, for example, which was set up in 1990 in Nigeria, has subsidiaries in five African countries. Zenith Bank, United Bank for Africa, Oando plc, and Sahara Energy have all gone international. Equity Bank in Kenya also has subsidiaries in Southern Sudan and Rwanda among others. MTN, a South African telecommunications firm, has operations in 21 African countries and the Middle East. The increasingly competitive environment makes change an imperative.

If Africa's growth is to be sustained, organizations in Africa must take advantage of the increased opportunities in the continent while responding to the challenges in the environment. To do this successfully, they require change models that can effectively guide them through change.

Not much research has been done on organizational change in Africa. In fact, there is a paucity of research on Africa in general. Organizational change models which exist and are taught in African business schools were developed in Western countries. It is becoming increasingly clear that these models may not be universally applicable (Hempel and Martinson 2009). Western countries are different in many respects from other parts of the world, especially developing countries.

Hempel and Martinson (2009) show, in their Chinese study, that context is important for organizational change. Context influences the choice of the objective of the change, the content of the change, and the change process. They argue that even when the same change initiative is implemented in another context, the enacted change may be different from that which was contemplated at the beginning. For example, in certain contexts some change objectives may be more important than those considered important in say the headquarters of a Multinational Corporation (MNC). The subsidiary may be more interested in maintaining its reputation than in the efficiency gains which are the change objective. Thus, implementing a change initiative according to a template developed by the headquarters of an MNC across subsidiaries may not lead to successful change in all subsidiaries. Local contexts may dictate different leadership styles, pace, communication mechanisms, etc.

If context is so important that it influences several aspects of an organizational change initiative, it is important to identify the distinctive contextual characteristics of developing (African) economies compared to Western contexts (especially USA) where extant change models were developed. Context provides the external and internal drivers of change. In a developing country context for example, capital markets are not a significant driver of organizational change. This is because capital markets are relatively underdeveloped in these economies. Share prices may not drive management actions as much as they do in developed economies (Foster and Kaplan 2001). In the absence of a strong capital market pull, other factors are likely to drive change in the African context. According to Hemper and Martinson (2009), the socio-economic and cultural environment are contextual variables likely to influence organizational change.

The Socio-economic Context of Africa

Wanasika *et al.* (2010: 234) argued that 'many cultural and historical similarities exist among [Africa] countries that allow us to treat them as a single entity'. They add that African countries share a common historical experience that includes ethnic and tribal loyalties, colonial dominance and exploitation of rich natural resources, etc. Africa is therefore not only an economic region but also a cultural and social region.

Africa is home to 1 billion people. Almost all the 54 countries (including South Sudan) were colonized. In the 1960s, many of them gained independence. In the 1960s and 1970s, African countries showed positive growth rates (Table 1.1) though these were lower than growth rates in developed (high income) countries.

In the 1980s and 1990s, many developing countries adopted more market oriented economic policies including Structural Adjustment Programmes as

TABLE 1.1 Annual Per Capita Income Growth 1961–2005 (% per year)

	1961–70	1971–80	1981–90	1991–2000	2001–05
High income	4.1	2.6	2.4	1.9	1.4
East Asia and Pacific	2.5	4.5	5.8	7.1	7.3
Europe and Central Asia	—	—	—	−0.9	5.1
Latin America and Caribbean	2.6	3.2	−0.9	1.7	1.0
Middle East and N. Africa	2.8	2.3	0.0	1.8	2.1
South Asia	2.0	0.7	3.4	3.2	4.7
Sub-Saharan Africa	**2.3**	**0.8**	**−1.0**	**−0.3**	**2.0**
World	3.3	1.9	1.4	1.4	1.5

Source: Bigsten and Durevall 2008:17

a condition to access World Bank or International Monetary Fund loans. However, in many countries, economic performance was disappointing (Easterly 2001). Growth rates were negative during this period. Since 2001, per capita income growth in Africa has exceeded that of the developed countries.

Today, Africa is bubbling. According to the McKinsey Report on the progress and potential of African economies,[2] real GDP rose 4.9 per cent per year from 2000 to 2008, more than twice its pace in the 1980s and 1990s. While the prospects for the global economic growth have been adjusted downward (from 4.1 per cent to 3.6 per cent in 2013),[3] the economic outlook for Africa remains very good. In fact, it is one of the fastest growing regions in the world.[4] Real GDP growth is expected to be 5.3 per cent in 2012 and in 2013 (Table 1.2). Even the non-oil exporting countries are showing a lot of resilience.

Future prospects in Africa are driven by 'both external trends in the global economy and internal changes in the continent's societies and economies'.[5] Hostilities in many African countries have ceased. Many African economies have attained a level of macroeconomic stability and implemented a number of economic reforms. This has created an enabling environment for growth. African governments have 'lowered inflation, trimmed their foreign debt', privatized state-owned enterprises and strengthened regulatory and legal systems.[6] Nigeria privatized more than 116 enterprises between 1991 and 2006,[7] 28 governments in Sub-Saharan Africa (of the 46 they studied) implemented at least one regulatory

TABLE 1.2 Sub-Saharan Africa: Real GDP Growth (% change)

	2004–08	2009	2010	2011	2012	2013
Sub-Saharan Africa total	6.5	2.8	5.3	5.2	5.3	5.3
World	4.6	−0.6	5.1	3.8	3.3	3.6

Source: Regional Economic Outlook Sub-Saharan Africa. World Bank & Financial Surveys. IMF

reform between June 2011 and June 2012 and Rwanda has implemented 26 regulatory reforms since 2005.[8]

One consequence of these changes is the emergence of a vibrant private sector. The fastest growing sectors between 2002 and 2007 were tourism, banking and telecommunications.[9] Another consequence of the reforms by African governments was the creation of an attractive environment for Foreign Direct Investments (FDI). FDI into Africa increased from $9 billion in 2000 to $62 billion in 2008 – relative to GDP almost as large as the flow into China. These inflows were not only into the more traditional sectors (oil and gas and mining) but into banking, tourism, textiles, construction, telecommunications, and other sectors.[10]

According to the McKinsey Report, the continent has more than 1,400 publicly listed companies (though its capital markets are underdeveloped). It boasts more than 100 companies with revenue greater than $1 billion. Telecom firms have signed up more than 316 million new mobile phone subscribers on the continent since 2000 – more than the total US population. Banking and retail are flourishing as household incomes climb.

Social and demographic trends are propelling and sustaining the economic growth rates of the continent. Two important demographic trends are: the rise of the middle class and increased urbanization. AfDB estimates that 34 per cent of the African population is middle class (about 313 million people).[11] This number is expected to rise. The middle class has disposable income to spend and therefore can drive further economic growth.

According to the McKinsey Report (2010), in 1980, 28 per cent of Africans lived in cities. In 2008, 40 per cent of Africans were urban dwellers. Thus, more people left the villages (and farming) to seek jobs in the cities. As more of them became employed, they got access to disposable income most of which was spent on food and housing, fuelling the growth of these sectors of the economy.

Challenges

The growth in African economies has not been without challenges. Poverty levels remain high. Poverty headcount ration at $2 a day in Sub-Saharan Africa was 69.2 per cent of the population in 2008. In 2010, 48.5 per cent of the population in 2010 lived on $1.25 a day. Increased urbanization has come with huge infrastructural challenges. Governments will have to provide access to water, electricity and other services to the teeming urban population.

Education remains a challenge. Literacy rate was 72 per cent in 2010. The quality of education especially in some African countries is still poor. There is a large and growing labour force but a challenge for business organizations is the lack of skilled personnel. A number of organizations (mainly large organizations) have training and development programmes for new hires in order to fill the gaps and prepare the new hires to perform. Many small and medium firms (the large majority of business organizations in Africa) are not able to do this. Access to quality hires remains a major challenge for organizations.

The extended family is the social security of many Africans. It is common for a clan or village to sponsor the education of a child with the hope that with his improved income he will sponsor other people in the village.

To summarize: African governments have introduced regulatory and other changes in the environment. For example, they privatized state-owned enterprises and enabled the emergence of a dynamic private sector. There have been some social and demographic changes in the African context which makes it more attractive for investment and accounts for Africa's sustained growth in the last several years. One of these changes is the emergence of the middle class (about 85 million households in 2008). The others are increased urbanization and the growing labour force.

However, some challenges remain. Poverty levels remain high in the continent. While the population of those of working age is growing, many lack the requisite skills to perform in organizations.

The Impact of the Socio-economic Context on Organizational Change

One characteristic of developing economies is their relatively underdeveloped capital markets. Very few companies are quoted on the stock exchange. Variations in the stock price are not a major driver of change in organizations in Africa. This is because senior managers in this context are not under the same pressure as those in the developed nations to run their organizations with a view to impacting the stock price in a very short time.

A major driver of change in the developing country context may be government and its regulations. Government regulations, especially changes in government policies, are a major driver of change. As we shall see in the next chapter, these changes have been many and frequent. The policies affect the business climate and make it necessary for organizations to change if they are to survive and grow.

The improved economic environment of Africa in a world in economic crisis has attracted foreign direct investment to Africa. A number of MNCs have entered the African market. This has increased competition not only for customers but also for talent. The limited pool of talented individuals commands a premium for their services. Organizations have had to re-think their employee value propositions and retention strategies to keep talented people. Some of them have also developed training and development programmes to bring new hires up to speed. Thus, industry dynamics, especially new entrants and increased competition, are propelling change in organizations in developing countries.

Change in Some African Organizations

Some organizations in Africa are taking advantage of the improved socio-economic environment. Standard Bank, which is headquartered in South Africa, has grown in leaps and bounds since the end of apartheid. It now has operations in 18 African countries and a presence in several Asian markets. It is quoted on the Johannesburg Stock Exchange. In 2012, it had total assets of over $170 million. It is the largest bank on the continent.

MTN, a telecommunications firm, became international soon after it was set up in 1994 in South Africa. It is also listed on the Johannesburg Stock Exchange. In less than 20 years, MTN is operating in 21 countries in Africa and the Middle East and has a customer base of 182.7 million.

Equity Bank was set up in 1984 in Kenya to cater to the financing needs of the nwananchi (the ordinary folk in Kenya). It has undergone a major turnaround and several changes. It has adapted to several changes driven by the Central Bank of Kenya and the election crisis of 2008/2009. While maintaining its focus on the bottom of the pyramid, Equity Bank has grown its customer base to 7.8 million. It has operations in Uganda, Tanzania, Southern Sudan and Rwanda. In 2012, Equity Bank's total assets were about $2,900 million. In the same year, the Managing Director of the Bank, James Mwangi, was named Forbes Africa Person of the Year. He also won the Ernst & Young World Entrepreneur of 2012.

Seven Seas Technologies is arguably one of the most prominent firms in the ICT Industry in Kenya. It is a provider of integrated business and technology solutions. It was incorporated in 1994. Taking advantage of the greater openness of the Kenyan government to liberalization and market forces, the firm grew within Kenya and set up offices in Ethiopia, Zimbabwe, Zambia and, more recently, in Nigeria. In 2008, SST sold 21 per cent of its shares to a private equity firm, Aureous, for $5 million.

GTBank was set up in 1990 after the liberalization of the Nigerian banking industry. It has gone through a number of changes. For example, in 2006, GTBank made a major strategic change by going into retail banking. From a focused corporate bank it became a universal bank. It later disposed of its non-banking activities following a change in government regulation. Like Equity Bank Kenya, GTBank has maintained its focus on customer excellence and professionalism. It has become an international bank with subsidiaries in Ivory Coast, Gambia, Ghana, Liberia, Sierra Leone and the United Kingdom. In 2012, GTBank employed over 5000 people.

To summarize: in the last several years, Africa has grown steadily. A number of businesses (both foreign and local) are taking advantage of the improved economic environment to introduce changes in their organizations. In a number of cases, these change initiatives have been successful. We use some of these cases to illustrate the change model presented in this book.

The African Cultural Context

The most recent study of African culture is the Global Leadership and Organizational Behavior Effectiveness Project (GLOBE). The study conducted by House *et al.* (2004) included five African countries – Nigeria, Namibia, Zambia, Zimbabwe and South Africa (black sample). These authors found that African countries were high in power distance and in in-group collectivism and have a humane orientation.

High power distance is evident in the power relationships in organizations and in the respect for the elderly and those in positions of authority. There is therefore, deference to authority. Authority figures may be recognized by the group as having the right answers (Jackson 2004: 128). According to Hofstede (1994) followers in high power distance cultures expect an autocratic or paternalistic decision making style. Decisions are not challenged by subordinates; they are challenged by people with higher authority (Trompenaars 1993: 116).

Another characteristic of the African culture is high in-group collectivism (Wanasika *et al.* 2010: 237). Group members usually belong to the same clan or extended family. They take pride in the group and are ready to sacrifice for the group. The interests of the clan are deemed more important than personal interests. Group members are therefore willing to sacrifice personal goals to achieve the goals of the collective. This is perhaps related to the humane orientation of Africans.

The GLOBE study also showed that Africans have a humane orientation, that is, they are sensitive to the needs of others and are caring. Perhaps this characteristic is the most distinguishing factor between Africa and Western countries. Jackson (2004) argues that humanism is central to an understanding of the cultural context of African organizations. He uses the concept of locus of human value to distinguish between 'an instrumentalist view of people in organizations which perceives people as a means to an end, and a humanistic view of people which sees people as having a value in their own right' Jackson (2004: 26). The instrumentalist view of the person is typical of Western countries while the humanistic view is African.

Jackson (2004) argues that because most African countries were colonized by European countries, African management systems may have been influenced by Western styles and perceptions. This may account for the moderate score of humane orientation in Africa (compared to the scores for all countries) and the desire for more humane orientation by Africans.

Africans value people in themselves. Relationships are not instrumental. While the organization is instrumental towards achieving the workers' goals and those of their group (Jackson 2004: 26), people are valued in themselves and are not instruments for gain. This orientation has been identified with the Ubuntu philosophy. According to Wanasita *et al.* (2010: 239), 'Ubuntu, prominent throughout history in sub-Saharan Africa, is based on respect for the dignity of the people, reciprocity in social relations, and a desire for tolerance and forgiveness'.

TABLE 1.3 Cultural Practices ('As Is') in the Anglo and Sub-Saharan African Contexts

	Africa	*Anglo*
Power Distance	A band (high)	B band (moderate)
In-group Collectivism	5.31	4.3
Humane Orientation	4.42	4.20
Performance Orientation	4.13	4.37
Institutional Collectivism	4.28	4.46
Gender Egalitarianism	3.29	3.40

Source: Culture, Leadership, and Organizations by House *et al.* (2004)

Compared to other GLOBE countries, the performance orientation of Africans, future orientation, institutional collectivism, gender egalitarianism and uncertainty avoidance were moderate.

So does the US context differ significantly from the African context? Would change models developed in the US or Western environment be applicable in the African context? In Table 1.3 we compare results from the GLOBE study for Sub-Saharan Africa and what House *et al.* (2004) call the Anglo countries. The latter include: US, Canada, Australia, New Zealand, England, Ireland and South Africa (white sample).

Table 1.3 shows that people in Sub-Saharan African are very different from those in the Anglo region in several cultural dimensions: power distance, in-group collectivism, humane orientation and even performance orientation and institutional collectivism. While Africans are high in power distance, Anglo countries are moderate. There is a big difference between the contexts in terms of in-group collectivism. The African feels very much part of the clan or in-group and is ready to sacrifice for the betterment of the in-group and its members. This is less so in the Anglo context. Both contexts are also different in their view of the human person. Africans have a more humane orientation than do people in the Anglo context. One African country, Nigeria, had the highest score in humane orientation in the entire sample. These findings are important for organizational change in Africa. In the next section, we examine some of the implications of these differences.

The Impact of the African Cultural Context on Organizational Change

Cultural characteristics have implications for the kind of leader that followers will accept and for leader effectiveness. People have expectations of leaders. These expectations are influenced by cultural factors. For example, in the African culture which is characterized by high power distance and a humane orientation, paternalistic and humane leadership styles may be more effective. The humane leader is concerned about the good of the followers. He or she takes decisions but pursues the good of all. Humane leaders may be more effective change leaders in this cultural context. They are expected to be 'considerate, forgiving and supportive of followers' welfare and development and maintain good relationships' (Wanasika *et al.* 2010: 235).

Cultural characteristics may also influence the purpose of the change and the impact of change on people. Africans may be more resistant to change if the purpose is purely financial and the change initiative has a negative impact on people. For example, a change initiative which will result in many people losing their jobs, their livelihoods, may be resisted vigorously. In a continent where poverty levels remain high and the salaried individual has obligations not only to his or her immediate family but also to the extended family, this is to be expected. It is likely to be difficult to win the commitment of Africans to these change efforts.

Change agents could use some of the cultural characteristics of the African context to advantage. If the organization is seen as a clan, as an in-group, and leaders demonstrate a humane orientation and are paternalistic, it is likely that change in such organizations will be easier to initiate, implement and sustain. Organizational members are ready to sacrifice for the in-group (the organization) knowing that they are contributing to a greater good for all.

In the study by Wanasika *et al.* (2010: 236), respondents expressed 'a clear desire for leaders to be action oriented and decisive in implementing programs for change and economic development'. It seems that Africans see the need for change. The purpose of the change, its target (the content of change) and how the change is implemented will determine its success. The point is: the change trajectory may be different in Africa given its economic, social and cultural context. Organizational change models which do not take this into account are not likely to be good theories in this context. As Kurt Lewin put it: 'there is nothing so practical as a good theory' (quoted in Burnes 2004: 998).

The African culture is an internal variable that change strategists and agents should bear in mind as they implement change. It may constrain or facilitate their ability to drive certain changes in organizations. It may also constrain their choice of the pace of change, how change will be communicated, the leadership style, and how success will be evaluated.

Summary

African economies are developing economies. Capital markets are relatively underdeveloped. African governments have a pervasive impact on the environment of business. These economies have shown steady growth rates for a decade. This has attracted FDI to Africa. The emergence and growth of the middle class has contributed to the attractiveness of the environment.

In spite of economic growth, Africa continues to have some challenges. Poverty levels remain high. There is also a dearth of talent (skilled labour) to spur further growth.

The African cultural context is also different from that of the US or other Western contexts. For example, Ubuntu is characteristic of Africa. Western nations have a more instrumentalist view of the human person. The kind of leader who can be effective in leading change in Africa is likely to be different from the outstanding leader in Western contexts.

Change models developed in the West may not be applicable (at least wholly) to Africa. For example, there may be differences in leadership, ways of communicating change, effectively overcoming resistance to change and winning commitment to change, etc. Even the drivers of change (and thus what managers should watch out for) may be different in each context. We argue that the economic context and the values and beliefs of Africans influence organizational change leadership in the continent.

While an organizational change model for Africa may not be completely different, nuances dictated by the African context make it imperative for change strategists and agents to adopt models that facilitate effective change leadership in Africa.

Notes

1 Lions on the move: the progress and potential of African economies (2010:7). McKinsey Global Institute.
2 Ibid p.1.
3 IMF: World Bank Financial Surveys. Regional Economic Outlook. Sub-Saharan Africa (October 2012: 1).
4 Lions on the move: the progress and potential of African economies (2010: 9). McKinsey Global Institute.
5 Ibid p.3.
6 Ibid p.2.
7 Ibid p.12.
8 Doing Business 2013 Fact Sheet: Sub-Saharan Africa. International Finance Corporation & The World Bank. www.doingbusiness.org
9 Lions on the move: the progress and potential of African economies (2010: 11). McKinsey Global Institute.
10 Ibid p.16.
11 African Economic Outlook 2010, AfDB.

2

THE DRIVERS OF CHANGE

Introduction

In the last chapter, we introduced the change model which will be developed in this book and described the economic and cultural context of Africa. The model is underpinned by Kurt Lewin's change theory. It is a model of planned organizational change which is open to the environment. It enables change strategists to listen to changes in the environment (internal and external) as they make decisions regarding change. It is a dynamic model of change; it is continuously evaluated against current reality. We presented a theoretical framework and analysed organizational change in the African context.

In this chapter, we discuss the change drivers. By drivers we mean: 'whatever gave birth to the desire or need for change in the organization' (Whelan-Berry and Somerville 2010). The chapter is structured in this manner: first we present a theoretical framework. We show from the organizational change literature that change drivers may be at the micro, meso or macro levels. Next, the drivers of change in emerging economies are analysed. We close the chapter with a discussion of what it takes to see the need for change.

Theoretical Framework: Drivers of Change

African economies are undergoing profound changes. From telecommunications to banking and food and beverage, the story is the same. Organizations in Africa are facing some of the most transformational environmental changes in their recent history. In this chapter, we examine the drivers of change and the fundamental choice that change strategists must make.

According to Pettigrew (1988), the answer to the question 'why change?' is derived from an analysis of the inner and outer context of the organization.

The inner context is made up of the structures, culture, strategies, procedures and practices of the organization. The outer context is the environment in which the organization operates (the industry and the institutional framework).

The resource based view and the industry based view have been proposed as explanations of firm success or failure. Strategic change is said to be driven by factors inside the firm (an organization's stock of resources, capabilities) or by industry characteristics (Peng *et al.* 2008). The former is represented by the Resource Based View and the latter by the Industry Based View. Peng *et al.* (2008) argue for a third perspective: the institution based view. The need for change may be driven by factors at either of these levels or a combination of them.

We can therefore distinguish three levels of change drivers: factors in the inner context of the organization (the micro level); factors in the outer context (industry based and institution based views) which operate at the meso or macro levels respectively. The need or desire for organizational change may be a result of factors in these levels.

Micro Level Drivers of Change

The Resource Based View (RBV) examines the 'link between a firm's internal characteristics and performance' (Barney 1991: 101). To derive competitive advantage organizations analyse their internal capabilities (physical, human and organizational). Change may be driven by a desire to acquire new capabilities or strengthen existing ones. According to the RBV, 'firms work from the inside out' (Dixon and Day 2010: 277). The need for change is driven by internal factors.

Organizations may proactively seek changes in their internal arrangements in order to align their structures, processes, and systems with the environment. Change may be driven by the perceived need to build resources – procedures, culture, systems – which will improve the competitive position of the organization and enable it to increase its effectiveness and efficiency. One indication of a need for change may be poor financial performance.

It is difficult for incumbents to see the need for change without outside influences. This may be due to inertia. Managers may feel that if it is not broken don't try to fix it. It may take a new chief executive officer or other significant person(s) to perceive the need for change.

The need for change may also arise from increased levels of organizational complexity due to movement along the Organizational Life Cycle (OLC) (Greiner 1972, 1998). As the organization moves from the birth to the growth stage, the entrepreneur finds it difficult to manage the new demands on his or her skills and time. The control and command style which worked in the past is no longer tenable. There may be a need to devolve more responsibility. Dixon and Day (2010) found in their study of Yukos in Russia that the eventual demise of the organization was due in part to a control and command style by the CEO.

When he was arrested, his trusted buddies could not keep the company afloat. Hatum and Pettigrew (2010: 270) also found that the life cycle of family firms and the role of the founder were among the factors that influenced adaptation of these firms.

Meso Level Drivers of Change

Organizational change may be driven by changes in industry conditions (Peng *et al.* 2008). Porter (1980) identified five forces which affect industry profitability: intensity of rivalry, new entrants, large number of buyers and suppliers and the threat of substitutes. Changes in any or a combination of these forces affect the attractiveness of the industry and the competitive position of firms in the industry.

A new entrant in the industry with innovative technology or a dynamic go-to-market model is likely to affect profit levels of incumbents in the industry. The latter may decide to initiate change in their organizations in order to retain or even snatch market share from other industry players.

Macro Level Drivers of Change

According to Suhomlinova (2006: 1538), the open system view of organizations proposed by Scott (1988) has dominated organizational studies for over 30 years. Organizations operate within an environment – a larger macroeconomic and socio-political environment. They engage in exchanges with the environment. They obtain resources (such as raw materials and capital) from the environment and provide some outputs (goods and services). This exchange is vital for the survival of the organization. Through these exchanges, environments shape organizations and organizations also shape the environment (Scott 1992).

Peng *et al.* (2008: 920) argued for an Institution Based View (IBV) of international business. Institutions provide the laws, regulations and norms which 'provide the context of competition'. They determine the framework within which organizations operate. They can limit the choices available to firms (North 1990, cited in Child and Tsai 2005: 97). For example, the Central Bank controls commercial banks through its rules and directives. By increasing the minimum capital base of commercial banks, the central bank effectively drives change in the industry.

The study by Child and Tsai (2005: 97) suggests that institutions drive change not only by the promulgation of laws and rules but by the enforcement of these laws: 'institutions potentially dominate other organizations through the enforcement of laws, rules and norms that constitute both formal and informal constraints'. This is especially true in emerging economies. For example, environmental protection laws constitute the context within which firms in a country may operate. But the enforcement of government regulations may differ from one country to another. For example, Child and Tsai (2005) found that Chinese Environmental Protection Officers were more flexible in the implementation of Environment Protection laws that their Taiwanese counterparts. Managers of a chemical plant in China may not feel constrained by these laws but should they want to open a plant in Taiwan, they will have to adapt to the Taiwanese environment.

Peng *et al*. (2008: 921) argue that institutions in developed economies differ significantly from those in emerging economies. In the latter, institutions not only create the conditions but they 'directly determine what arrows a firm has in its quiver as it struggles to formulate and implement strategy and to create competitive advantage' (Ingram and Silverman 2002, quoted in Peng *et al*. 2008: 923). According to these authors, 'a hallmark of emerging economies is that they tend to have more fundamental and comprehensive changes introduced to the formal and informal rules of the game' (Peng *et al*. 2008: 924). These rules change and frequently too.

Organizational survival depends on the 'fit' between an organization and its environment (Suhomlinova, 2006). This is perhaps more so in an emerging economy context. Dixon and Day (2010) in their study of the rise and fall of Yukos in Russia suggest that the demise of Yukos was due to the disconnect between the internal transformation of the organization and the changes in the external institutional context. In 2003 Yukos was a leading oil firm in Russia. Three years later, it was declared bankrupt. Dixon and Day (2010) concluded that, in unstable emerging economies, firms must adapt to the changing external institutional environment if they are to survive.

Summary

Drivers of change may be internal to the organization (operating at the micro level) or they may be external (at the meso or macro levels). At the micro level, change drivers include the presence of a new CEO and movement along the OLC. At the meso level, new entrants into the industry and changes in intensity of competition may lead to a need for change. Change drivers may be the same in emerging and developed countries at both the micro and meso levels. At the macro level, however, there are important differences. This is because institutions in both contexts are very different. For one thing, changes in the laws, regulations and their enforcement tend to be more frequent in emerging economies. According to Peng *et al*. (2008) these changes may be fundamental and comprehensive. A major driver of change in this context may be changes in the institutional context.

Drivers of Change in the African Context

In the last section we discussed the literature on the forces for change in the micro, meso and macro environment. We argued that the forces for change in emerging economies are likely to be strongest at the macro level (the institutional environment). The changes driven by institutions are not only profound, they are also frequent. In the following sections, we examine the drivers of change in the African context. We close the chapter with a discussion of the critical success factors for seeing the need for change. First, we clarify relevant concepts to our discussion of change drivers: first order and second order changes.

First and Second Order Changes

Meyer *et al.* (1990) made the distinction between first and second order changes. First order changes are those organizational changes that do not cause any major upheavals. They occur within stable systems which remain unchanged (Meyer *et al.* 1990). Second order changes on the other hand are shifts or discontinuities. This kind of change 'transforms fundamental properties or states of the system' (Meyer *et al.* 1990: 94). They often threaten the existence of firms. An example: in July 2004 the Central Bank of Nigeria announced its decision to increase the minimum capital requirement of commercial banks from 2 billion to 25 billion Naira. The banks were given until 31 December that year to comply with the new directive.

This single pronouncement led to the transformation of the banking industry in Nigeria. From 85 banks in 2004, the number of banks was reduced to 25 by January of the following year. The change spurred mergers and acquisitions, changes in Board membership, processes and ICT infrastructure. Most of the surviving banks implemented profound changes in mission, strategy, structures and even culture. In most cases, the new entities had little resemblance to the banks that existed before 31 December 2004. This was a second order change driven by the regulatory environment. The change was discontinuous and it challenged the banks' strategies, competencies, etc.

Unlike second order changes, first order changes are not transformational. The need for change may be so mild that it is ignored for a long period of time. Changes in consumer taste, for example, may not be easily perceived. In the 1980s and early-1990s, Leventis and Kingsway Stores were thriving department stores in Nigeria. They met the needs of the middle to upper class in the major cities of the country. Many adults today recall going to Kingsway Stores to see Father Christmas or simply ride on the escalator.

By the beginning of the 2000s, consumer taste had changed. As the economy recovered from the post Structural Adjustment Programme and a middle class began to emerge, people became more affluent. They were also more exposed to new and better products through frequent trips abroad, the internet, etc. The result was a gradual change in taste. Consumers no longer wanted basic commodities. Product quality and brand name became important. Kingsway and Leventis did not see the need for change. New entrants such as Park & Shop opened stores and effectively drove Kingsway and Leventis Stores out of the market. Today, Ebeano supermarket is a big player in this segment of the industry in Lagos.

First order changes in the environment are not abrupt or sudden changes. They do not bring about discontinuities in the market. Organizations therefore, tend to adapt to first order changes in the environment in an incremental fashion (Meyer *et al.* 1990). These changes act very much like water in the crevices of a rock. While not as abrupt as a pickaxe, they can destroy the rock with time.

Both first and second order changes may be driven by micro, meso or macro forces for change. Second order changes within the firm may be due to movements along the OLC, CEO succession, and the introduction of new technology which obsoletes current technologies. First order changes within the firm are minor shifts often driven by internal forces.

Drivers of Change

Several forces in the environment and in organizations drive changes in organizations in Africa. In this section, we discuss the drivers of change in both the inner and outer context of organizations. The context for this discussion is Africa, with particular reference to Nigeria, Kenya and South Africa.

Micro Level Change Drivers

In the last section we showed that change is often driven by environmental factors. However, there are some forces for change that are internal to an organization. In this section, we discuss some of these change drivers.

The Organizational Life Cycle as a Driver of Change

An important driver of change in organizations is the transition from one stage of the organizational life cycle to another. The organizational life cycle is made up of four stages: birth, growth, maturity and decline. As the organization moves from one stage of the OLC to another, it faces new challenges (Greiner 1998). These challenges have to be overcome if the organization is to survive. These changes may render the organization's established processes of self maintenance ineffective and this may lead to the demise of the organization (Kaufman 1975).

At the birth stage, the challenge is the development of the product or service and finding a niche in the market. Very often, the founder/CEO runs the organization through informal channels. The level of complexity is low and reporting lines tend to be blurred. It is difficult to distinguish between the founder and the organization as their relationship is nearly isomorphic (Heneman and Tansky 2002).

As the organization moves from the birth stage to the growth stage, it faces the challenge of increasing complexity. The lack of clear responsibilities, systems and processes, which perhaps made for quick decision making and an entrepreneurial spirit during the birth stage, may lead to inefficiencies. The owner-manager can no longer lead the organization alone; he or she must delegate. A need for change arises. The purpose of change at the growth stage is the creation of a professionally managed organization with systems, structures and procedures.

As the organization matures, there is a need to rejuvenate it if it is to remain successful. Maturity presents new challenges. Growth has slowed and decline may begin if the organization is not renewed. Change is needed to revitalize and begin a new OLC. Typically, a lot of focus at this stage is on innovation (new products/services, new markets) and cost reduction.

Many organizations in Africa are small businesses. Not many have been able to make the move (successfully) from small to mid-sized businesses. If an organization is to grow and move along the OLC, it must be able to adapt. The failure of many small businesses to transit to medium and large enterprises may be due to non-recognition of the need for change as the organization moves from the birth to the growth stage.

Yomi Badejo-Okusanya, the owner-manager of CMC Connect, perceived the need for change. The increased complexity of running the business (everyone reported to him) led him to feel he had to do something. Finally, he read a book which brought everything home and gave him clarity. He crafted a vision of the organization and went on to implement the change.

CEO Succession

A new CEO typically initiates changes. Research on the taking charge process by John Gabarro of Harvard Business School shows that though the new managers took charge in different ways, a pattern emerged. Gabarro (1987) identified five stages in the taking charge process: taking hold, immersion, reshaping, consolidation and refinement. The taking hold stage lasted some three to six months. During this time, the new manager introduced a number of organizational changes, mainly in systems and personnel. Insiders, those who had five or more years of experience in the new company's industry, introduced more changes than the outsiders. The next round of organizational change activity was during the reshaping stage (between the 12th and 18th months). The organizational change activity here was focused on changing how the company operates. New systems were also introduced.

Finally, between the 24th and 30th months a few changes were again introduced. These changes were more profound as the manager had learnt enough about the company and the environment. During the immersion and consolidation stages, few changes were introduced. The managers spent the time assessing the impact of changes introduced in the previous change and taking corrective actions.

As the saying goes, a new broom sweeps clean. A new CEO usually brings a fresh perspective. Even if the new CEO is an insider, he or she typically initiates changes.

This is understandable. He or she probably had a number of things he or she wanted to change but could not push through from his or her position. His or her appointment as CEO gives him or her the opportunity to implement these changes.

A new CEO typically takes charge with a clear mandate from the Board to deliver specific results within a specified time frame. Dora Akunyili was given a mandate by President Olusegun Obasanjo to turn around the National Agency for Food and Drug Administration and Control (NAFDAC) and eradicate fake and adulterated drugs and food from Nigeria. She was, in a sense, appointed as a change agent. Col. Tunde Reis was appointed Executive Chairman of the Federal Housing Authority with a clear mandate to turn it around. These leaders took their mandate seriously and implemented changes in their organizations within a short time.

Sometimes people invest in specific companies in order to turn them around. When Wale Tinubu and his team took over Unipetrol plc in 2001, they immediately initiated a major transformation in the organization. Today, few people in Nigeria remember Unipetrol. Wale Tinubu transformed the largely bureaucratic Unipetrol into a performance-driven Oando plc – a company quoted on both the Lagos and Johannesburg Stock Exchanges.

'Me too'

Another driver of change is the 'me too' phenomenon. Some organizations introduce changes for the simple reason that their competitors or other significant players have done or are doing so. Some years ago, the Management of Cadbury Nigeria plc decided to restructure its operations to focus on its core business and also improve coordination among departments in the company. The change resulted in the laying off of about 300 members of staff. The change was peaceful in spite of the fact that there was an in-house union and the National Union of Food and Beverage Workers was very strong.

Within a week, a few human resource directors called the human resource director of Cadbury Nigeria plc for assistance on how they could restructure their businesses. When he asked them why they needed a restructuring, the responses were vague. It became obvious that the reason was they felt if Cadbury had laid off people, they had better do the same. The action by a respected company sent shivers through the system that change was necessary.

Outdated processes or technology, and inefficiencies in the supply chain are other drivers of change which are internal to the organization. For example, the driver for change may simply be the need to implement a new Enterprise Resource Planning (ERP) system.

So far, we have discussed micro level factors. However, a configuration of micro, meso and macro factors may drive change in an organization. When Dora Akunyili took charge of NAFDAC in 2001, President Olusegun Obasanjo had felt the need for change. In fact, she was chosen by the President to turn around the agency and protect the lives of Nigerians. The need for change was compelling. Dora found that the agency lacked modern laboratories and other resources. The employees lacked the skills to perform their jobs and the culture was bureaucratic and corrupt. Even the strategy of litigation was not yielding the desired results. The drivers of change in NAFDAC were multifarious.

Meso Level Drivers of Organizational Change

In the preceding section, we examined the micro level drivers of organizational change. In the African context, the drivers include a new CEO, movements along the OLC and the 'me too' phenomenon. In this section, we discuss the meso environment, specifically the industry, as a driver of organizational change.

Industry is an important aspect of the environment. The macroeconomic environment, government regulation etc. affect all the firms in the environment. Industry dynamics impact especially the firms in the industry. Porter (1979) identified five competitive forces that determine what he called the 'profit potential in an industry'. They are: the threat of new entrants, the bargaining power of suppliers and buyers, threat of new substitutes and rivalry among existing firms. The differing ability of firms to deal with the challenges posed by the competitive forces may account for success and failure (Porter 1979: 3).

A major change in one or a combination of these forces brings about a change in the structure of the industry and puts pressure on incumbents to change or become marginal. To survive, each company must 'find a position in the industry where the company can best defend itself against these competitive forces or can influence them in its favour' (Porter 1979: 4). For example, when the barriers to entry into the telecommunications industry in Nigeria were lowered in 2000, four firms entered the industry. Within months, competition had intensified. NITEL, which until then had a monopoly of telephone services in Nigeria, was caught napping. It could not defend itself against the new entrants; since then it has been a marginal player in the industry.

According to Porter (1979: 17), 'firms are mutually dependent'. The actions of one firm in the industry may create a need for repositioning by other firms in the same industry. Rivalry among a few firms may not be intense. The entrance of a new firm that has a reputation for aggressive behaviour is likely to lead to reactions from incumbent firms and lead to intense competition in the industry. Before 2008, the Nigerian brewery industry was made up of two major national players (Nigerian Breweries plc and Guinness Nigeria plc) and several regional breweries. The industry had experienced a revolution in the 1980s when the importation of an essential raw material was banned. The recent entry of SAB Miller into the Nigerian brewery industry is likely to bring about stiff competition as the big three jostle for position in the industry.

The entrance of multinational corporations (MNCs) into emerging markets often leads to a shakeup of the industry. MTN, a company headquartered in

South Africa, was one of the first telecommunications firms to enter the Nigerian market. MTN very quickly established itself as the market leader. NITEL, a government owned establishment and the incumbent could not compete with MTN, Econet and GLO. When the fundamentals of a business change, the business must itself change or at best remain marginal.

In her article on 'How Industries Change', Anita McGahan (2004) argues that an industry changes when its core assets (knowledge, brand, patents, etc.) and/or core activities face threats of obsolescence. The introduction of new technology could lead to a radical change trajectory in an industry, i.e., both assets and core activities are threatened with obsolescence. Where core activities such as the relationship with suppliers and buyers are threatened, but core assets (brands, knowledge, etc.) are not threatened, the industry is following an intermediating change trajectory. Where only the industry's assets are threatened, the industry is on a creative change trajectory. In the progressive change trajectory, the industry faces no threats of obsolescence. For firms in industries on radical change trajectories, everything is changing and each firm must transform in order to survive.

Changes in an industry typically drive change in the firms in that industry but may not affect all firms in the same way. However, they may threaten core assets and/or activities in the industry and, ultimately, industry profitability. To survive, firms must analyse the industry, recognize the trajectory and where the industry is on that trajectory. Even firms in a progressive industry trajectory must continuously adapt to changes in the competitive forces.

The entrance of a MNC into an emerging market may threaten both core assets and activities of the industry and place the industry on a radical change trajectory; or it may threaten core assets but not core activities (creative change trajectory). The bottom line for local firms in the emerging markets is that the entrance of a MNC is often a threat to their existence. The MNC often enters the market with brand(s), knowledge, technology and patents. Local firms are often unable to compete on a radical change trajectory. However, if the MNC lacks core activities such as relationships with suppliers and buyers, key relationships with government officials and the ability to execute, local firms find a space where affiliation or partnership with the MNC can be mutually beneficial. The local firms' knowledge of the environment and their ability to execute in this environment becomes their key asset.

Mike Macharia, the CEO of Seven Seas Technologies, Kenya, recognized that more foreign firms were entering the African market. He was particularly concerned about those entering the ICT industry. Mike was convinced that these new entrants had technology and huge resources. They probably lacked the capacity to execute in the local environment. To remain competitive, SST developed its execution skills.[1] He hoped that with SST's knowledge of the industry and the market and its capacity to get things done in Africa, the organization would continue to compete favourably with MNCs and might partner with one with the right assets (brand and technology).

The introduction of substitute products or services also poses a big challenge and drives change in organizations. When Perm Relaxers replaced Jerry Curls in the early 1980s, at least one company did not recognize the shift. It continued to push the sales of Jerry Curl kits and activators until it went under.

Pure water sachets which are sold at five Naira a sachet (about one-sixth of the price of a soda) in Nigeria are a major threat to the soft drinks industry. Companies are beginning to realize that the range of substitutes to their products is very wide. Companies in the fast moving consumer goods business experienced a drop in sales as people reallocated their incomes to fund their new life style with the introduction of mobile telephones. Between 2001 and 2003 the GSM companies saw their revenues balloon beyond even their own expectations. In July 2004, with the public offers by Guaranty Trust Bank and Zenith International Bank, customers' expenditure on air time dropped sharply. One company in the telecommunications sector lost about 50 per cent of its revenues that month alone. Thus, changes in the competitive forces in an industry create conditions for change. Only those firms that adapt to these changes survive.

A new entrant in the industry with say a new technology may begin a different industry life cycle, slowly build up the business and making obsolete the incumbents' offers. This is especially true of small upstarts that grow imperceptibly, slowly gnawing at the market share and profits of existing firms in the industry. The introduction of integrated banking software has changed the competitive landscape of banking in Kenya. The big banks, including Equity Bank, were early adopters of the new technology. This has enabled them to serve their customers better and faster. The new technology has also provided them with real time information for management control purposes. Early adoption of technology may be one of the factors that have accounted for the widening gap between the Tier I banks and the other two tiers.

Changes in customer preferences create new opportunities and threats for organizations. As we saw earlier, Leventis and Kingsway Stores in Nigeria did not anticipate nor react to the changes in life style of their customers. As the middle to upper class became more exposed to new products, their demand for better quality products increased. Petroleum jelly and dusting powder, for example, were no longer attractive options. Moreover, these could be purchased at lower prices in the open market. Park & Shop understood the change in life style and opened supermarkets where it sold products that met the need of the growing middle class.

In the foregoing, we have discussed the major drivers of change at the meso level (the industry). These drivers have different effects on organizations and the kind of change (1st or 2nd order) which they will implement. Sometimes, it takes a constellation of factors at different levels to bring about second order changes. But some drivers have such a huge impact on the organization that they can, singlehandedly, lead to changes in the organizational mission, structure, culture, etc.

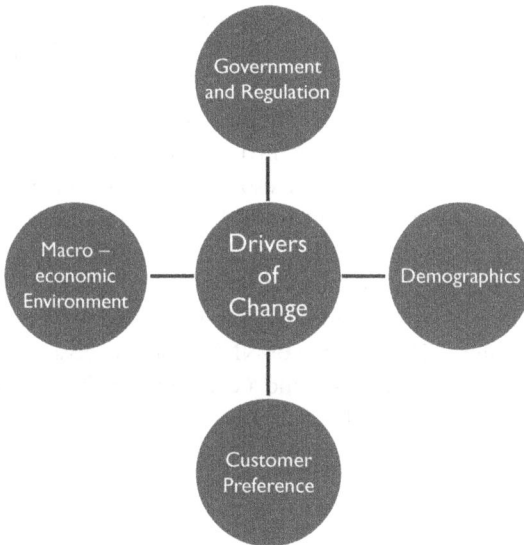

FIGURE 2.1 Macro level change drivers

Macro Level Drivers of Organizational Change

The need for change may be a result of micro, meso or macro level forces. The macro drivers include: the macroeconomic environment, changes in government regulation and its enforcement, and changes in customer preferences (Figure 2.1). As the macro environment changes, a mismatch occurs between the firm's strategy, structure, culture and the requirements of the environment. Organizational change is a response to the need for congruence between a firm and its environment. We now discuss the macro change drivers in African economies.

The Size and Pervasive Influence of Government

Government plays a big role in African economies. The reason may be historical. After independence, many African countries saw the need to kickstart the industrialization of their economies. While private initiative was encouraged in many cases, government owned not only the infrastructure but also factories and other businesses. For example, the Nigerian government owned companies in oil, cement, fertilizer, iron and steel production, etc. In Kenya the story is the same; Safaricom and even Kenya Wines were owned by government. Recently, government is privatizing many of these institutions but still remains a very significant player in the economy.

Given the large size of government in African economies, government budget has a huge impact on economic activity in the region. Utomi (1998) reports that Nigerian firms typically wait for the announcement of the Federal Government

Budget each year before making their plans for the year. Delays in the release of the budget (for as long as two months in some cases) meant that most businesses are paralyzed for several months.

Government's participation in economic activity through its quasi-government agencies also has an impact on firms in these sectors. In a number of cases, government is not only a regulator but also a participant – a competitor – in the industry. In Nigeria, the Nigerian National Petroleum Corporation (NNPC) is the regulator of the oil industry. It is also a joint venture partner in oil exploration; it owns and runs the only refineries in Nigeria and it has a network of petrol stations. One of NNPC's subsidiaries determines the prices of petroleum products sold in the country. The activities of NNPC have a pervasive effect on firms in the industry. NNPC is a regulator and a competitor in both the upstream and downstream sectors of the oil industry in Nigeria.

Macroeconomic Environment

According to Utomi (1998), inflation and exchange rate policies are the macroeconomic factors most critical to choices regarding resource allocation in an emerging economy like Nigeria. Macroeconomic shifts are an important driver of change in emerging economies. Changes in interest rates and in inflation have a huge impact on purchasing power. In 2010, inflation was 10.52 per cent in Sub-Saharan Africa. This presented major challenges to companies especially those producing fast moving consumer goods. As more people became poor (poverty levels are as high as 60 per cent in some African countries), they sought cheap substitutes for goods they previously purchased or did without them altogether. Promasidor was one of the first companies to respond to the harsh macroeconomic environment by selling in mini packs (enough for one use). Today, milk, beverages, detergents etc. are sold in small sachets.

Changes in Government Regulation

Government regulation is perhaps the most important driver of change in African economies. This is because of frequent and profound changes in government policies. These cause a mismatch between the external and internal environment of the firm. To survive and thrive, the firm must adapt to its environment as major shifts in the institutional context may threaten the firm's business model.

Government, through its regulations, defines the laws, sanctions and rules governing economic activity. These laws establish what is legally acceptable in the environment. To be considered legitimate, organizations must conform to these rules and laws. The challenge of government regulation in Africa is not the existence of laws and sanctions (every country has them). Rather, it is the frequency with which these rules are changed. Some of these policy changes have led to the transformation of whole industries. In the Nigerian economic landscape changes in government regulation have been common, and they have been abrupt. They have caused upheavals in several industries. A few examples in Nigeria will illustrate the point.

Until 2003, when Mrs Okonjo-Iweala became the Finance Minister, tariff schedules in Nigeria were reviewed annually. Goods banned one year could have the ban lifted the next year. No information was given as to when the ban would be lifted. Little long term planning was done given the unstable environment of business. Many business leaders waited for the government budget before drawing up their annual budgets.

Deregulation has had a huge impact on the African economy. Its impact has been most pronounced in the financial services and telecommunications sectors. Companies that operated in these highly regulated environments (often characterized by limited competition and inefficiencies) suddenly had to adapt to the dramatic changes in order to survive.

Before the deregulation of the banking industry in Nigeria, there were few banks. Customer service was generally poor: a bank transaction such as a cash withdrawal took hours; it took days to get a bank draft, and banking halls were dull, if not drab.

The deregulation of the financial services sector in 1987 brought stiff competition to the industry. The number of banks grew from 40 in 1986 to 89 in 1998. The new generation banks, as the new entrants were called, changed the rules of the game. Guaranty Trust Bank, for example, redefined service in the industry: customers could cash their cheques, obtain bank drafts, etc. within minutes. The new banks soon began to take some market share from the older banks. The latter had to adapt to the dramatic changes to survive. In 1995, United Bank for Africa (one of the old banks) embarked on a transformational change. Its closest rival, First Bank, followed suit.

The industry enjoyed some relative peace until July 2005 when the Central Bank announced that the minimum paid up capital for banks in Nigeria had been raised from 2 billion to 25 billion Naira. The directive was to take effect on 31 December that year. Banks that could not achieve this level of capitalization were advised to merge with or be acquired by others, or have their licenses revoked. This regulation had far reaching implications on the Nigerian economy in general and the banking industry in particular. The intensity of competition increased but stronger banks emerged. In January 2006, the Central Bank revoked the licences of 14 banks that were unable to meet the minimum capitalization requirement. By the end of that year, the number of banks had reduced from 87 to 25.

The Central Bank introduced universal banking in 2000. Banks were allowed to engage in activities previously reserved for issuing houses, fund management companies, insurance companies, etc. Several banks became universal banks with a capital firm, an issuing house, and an insurance company. The issuing houses and insurance firms suddenly found themselves competing with very strong banks with large branch networks.

The impact of these directives on the banking industry was huge. With increased capital available, most of the banks have introduced new technology. They have also opened branches in other countries especially along the west coast of Africa. A few opened subsidiaries in East Africa. Some of these banks are now able to fund big ticket transactions in the oil industry and the telecommunications sector.

In 2010, universal banking was revoked by the Central Bank. Banks were required to divest their non-commercial banking interests. Once again, the regulator was driving change in the industry.

The impact of deregulation on the financial services in Kenya mirrored that of Nigeria. The minimum capital base was significantly increased, universal banking was introduced and legislation which forced banks to lend to particular sectors was introduced.

The deregulation of the telecommunications industry was a major driver of change in the industry in Africa. It brought fierce competition which led to the development of innovative products and services. In 2008, there were as many as 260 million mobile telephone subscribers in Africa[2]; over 25 per cent of the population.

From the above, it is clear that government regulation has a huge impact on the environment of business and is a major driver of change in organizations. Changes in the pharmaceutical industry in Nigeria suggest that the leadership of a regulatory agency can be a major driver of change in the African context, a topic we turn to in the next section.

Enforcement of Regulation – the Role of Leadership

Utomi (1998) argued that government and its officials have a pervasive influence on the environment of business in emerging economies. Because these economies have weak institutions, laws are often not enforced. However, the right leadership in a government institution can be an important driver of change in the industry the agency was established to regulate. Recent changes in the Nigerian pharmaceutical industry can be attributed to the enforcement of regulation by the National Food and Drug Agency (NAFDAC) under the leadership of Dora Akunyili.

When Dora Akunyili became Director General of the Agency in 2001, the pharmaceutical companies had been losing market share to importers of fake and adulterated drugs for years. A number of foreign owned pharmaceutical firms closed shop; the future of the industry was bleak. Dora focused on the enforcement of the law and the education of stakeholders. Factories, bakeries, drug markets, etc. which did not comply with the standards were shut down. For less severe offences, sanctions and fines were imposed.

Her single-minded focus on safeguarding the health of Nigerians soon produced results. Within a few years, pharmaceutical companies that had been on the brink of bankruptcy became profitable. More importantly, the quantity of fake and substandard drugs in the market was significantly reduced. Within a few years, the industry had changed.

In summary, government is a major driver of change in African economies. Government policies and policy somersaults (Utomi, 1998) have often introduced shocks into the environment. These policy changes are frequent, and are abrupt. They have caused major upheavals in several industries. Changes in government policies lead to a mismatch between the external and internal environment of the firm; they sometimes threaten an organization's business model. If the firm does not adapt to these external shifts, death may be inevitable. Table 2.1 shows some meso and macro change drivers and their likely impact on the organization.

The drivers of any one organizational change initiative may be varied. While the need for change may be internal, some macro or meso forces may also be at work. An example: the management and staff of Equity Building Society knew there was need for profound changes in the organization in 1994. The balance sheet and the profit and loss statements showed that the organization was in financial distress. The Central Bank of Kenya decided to give the owners an opportunity to turn the Society around.

A configuration of factors was driving change in Equity Building Society. The first was the business model. Equity took deposits from customers and gave some of them mortgage loans. These loans were not used to build or buy houses. Customers wanted loans to finance their small businesses, send their children to school, etc. The lack of skills and the poor service culture of the organization were other drivers of the poor performance of Equity. While the need for change was driven by the organization's poor performance and the need to institute good corporate governance, it was the Central Bank of Kenya that forced the organization to change.

TABLE 2.1 The Impact of Meso and Macro Change Drivers on Organizations in Emerging

External change driver	Likely impact on the organization	Type of change
Changes in government regulation	Profound impact	2nd order change
Changes in the enforcement of regulation	Moderate impact	1st order change
Changes in industry dynamics	Moderate to high impact	1st or 2nd order change
Changes in consumer tastes and preferences	Low to moderate impact	1st or 2nd order change
Changes in the macroeconomic environment	Low to moderate impact	1st order change

We asked managers who were attending a strategy programme at the Strathmore Business School, Nairobi and the Lagos Business School what was driving change in their organizations. The results for both groups were similar: changes in customer preferences, competition and government regulation were the major drivers. The macroeconomic environment was also a significant driver especially inflation and exchange rate.

Meyer and Botha (2011: 11) in their work on organizational development and transformation in South Africa asserted: 'the major contemporary environmental forces [driving change] are technology, globalisation, the legal environment, economic, socio-economic and socio-cultural factors'. They went on to say that: 'two important challenges from the legislative environment in South Africa are the Employment Equity Act and the Skills Development Act' (Meyer and Botha 2011: 12).

Before the end of Apartheid in 1994, most South African businesses were focused on the local market. They could not operate in other markets because of the sanctions by the international community. The end of apartheid exposed these firms to increased competition from new entrants from other markets. South African firms began to internationalize. Thus, competition brought profound changes to South African firms.

A major impetus for change was the Employment Equity Act of 1998. Organizations are implementing diversity initiatives aimed at ensuring adequate representation of blacks and coloured not only in the organizations but in their management cadre.

In summary: the drivers of organizational change in the African context include the institutions (government regulation, norms and their enforcement), the intensity of competition in the industry (especially new entrants into the industry by foreign firms) as well as factors internal to the organization such as low efficiency shown in a decline in profitability. This is expected in emerging economies where changes in government regulation are frequent and often demand transformational changes (second order change).

The ability to anticipate the need for change (whether driven by micro, meso or macro forces) and adaptation may provide an organization with at least a first mover advantage. For example, GTBank and Zenith Bank built up their capital base to over 25 billion Naira before the Central Bank of Nigeria introduced a new regulation requiring all banks to have a minimum capital base of 25 billion Naira. However, the drivers of change may not be obvious, that is, not all managers may perceive the need for change. It sometimes takes a shock to get the organization to see that change is necessary. In the next section, we discuss what it takes to see, even anticipate, the need for change.

Seeing the Need for Change

The need for change ultimately results from a performance gap (Zaltman and Duncan 1977). A performance gap occurs when expectations are not met or new events occur that create a tension, a misalignment between the current state and a preferred state. The performance gap is driven by forces in the micro, meso or macro environment or a combination of these forces.

Let us look at some examples. Equity Ltd Kenya had been serving the common folk (nwananchi) for decades as a mortgage institution. In 1994, it became a micro finance institution. Equity grew with its customers. By 2004, a number of Equity's customers had grown and were now mid-sized companies. The products and services offered by Equity no longer met all their needs. These customers wanted foreign exchange and corporate banking services. Equity could not provide these because it was licensed as a micro finance institution. There was in effect, a performance gap. Equity was running the risk of losing customers it had served for over 10 years.

One of the challenges of another company, a consulting firm, was that new entrants into the industry were providing the same services and successfully taking market share. The firm also had internal issues; its tax, financial advisory and management consulting arms worked in silos. Profits began to dip and projections had to be adjusted downward.

In the two cases mentioned above, changes in customer needs, new entrants and lack of internal cooperation created a performance gap. In the case of Equity the performance gap did not show in the bottom line (profits were growing in double digits). It arose from the gap between the services Equity offered and the new needs of some of its most loyal customers. These two organizations saw the need for change and decided to initiate change.

Pettigrew *et al.* (2001: 699), referring to work done by Pettigrew and Whipp (1991) on seeing the need for change, stated that: 'The relative slowness of the sensing and adaptation process of firms, and their failure to recognize that the bases of competition may have changed in their sector, can be a key factor explaining their loss of competitive performance'.

The ability of an organization to perceive shifts in its competitive environment and act on them will depend on the ability of its members to overcome personal (cognitive and emotional) as well as political pressures resisting change. It will also depend on their ability to monitor the environment, both internal and external. According to Weick (1979), managers construct, rearrange, single out, and demolish many objective features of their surroundings. The picture they work on may be a reality that is 'selectively perceived, rearranged cognitively, and negotiated interpersonally' (Weick 1979: 164). Thus, they may not see a performance gap.

For instance, United Bank for Africa (UBA) in 1994 did not recognize the impact of the deregulation of the industry on the bank. A former Deputy Governor of the Central Bank predicted, at the time, the collapse of the big old banks. Yet, the management of the largest and oldest four banks did not see the need for change. Management's instinct was probably dulled by years of good financial results. The leaders of the new generation banks (banks established after the deregulation of the sector) were perceived by the old timers as young people who did not understand banking. After all, customers queued (sometimes for hours) to be served. It took new owners and a new chairman to get UBA to see the need for change.

It is important to make a distinction between the objective and the subjective environment. Even though the objective environment exists independently of our perception of it, we see the world through our lenses. The picture of the environment that organizational members have is often coloured by their interests, experiences, attitudes, etc.

Managers sometimes rationalize the signals in the environment that change is needed. A major upheaval in the meso or macro environment may be necessary to jolt them out of their comfort zones and to convince them of the need for change. While the outer environment may make change an imperative, it is the felt need for change that triggers change. Changes in the micro, meso or macro environment must be perceived by the right people if organizational transformation is to take place.

As the impact of the radical changes in the institutional environment begins to be felt in the organization, managers who had enacted their environments soon perceive the objective environment as profits nose-dive and competitors struggle to adapt their organizations to the changing circumstances. If profit projections for the year are not met, the company is likely to take active steps to address the shortfall.

Firms take concrete steps to secure their future in the face of threats and opportunities in environment. However, not all decision makers have discernment nor do they all have the same ability to read the environment and understand the challenges it presents. The ability to scan the environment is an essential ingredient for success in the African context which seems prone to frequent shocks. Given the resilience of the African economies, it is likely that more foreign firms will be attracted to the continent. It is therefore likely that major shake-ups of industries will occur. African economies present both opportunities and challenges.

These environmental challenges and opportunities will force organizations to re-assess their strengths and weaknesses, where they are and where they should be going. It is the gap if any, between where the organization is and where it should be headed, that creates the need for change. Changes in the internal and/or external environment do not automatically lead to a need for change. The impact of these changes must be felt and assessed. Organizational members will ask themselves if the environmental changes are transient. They will want to know how important these changes are. A cold, objective analysis of the situation is required.

Why People do not See the Need for Change

It is sometimes difficult for people within the company to see the need for change because of the emotional attachment they may have to the status quo: the current products, processes and systems. The product manager and marketing manager of an organization realized that their flagship product was draining organizational resources. After much repackaging and investment in advertising had produced little result they recommended that the product be eliminated. The CEO, however, refused to kill the product. He was emotionally attached to it; it was the first product he was put in charge of when he joined the organization as a management trainee!

Another reason why managers do not see the need for change is that they develop routines which glue them to their comfort zones. Routines make life easier as we do not have to think before carrying out the activity. But routines may also make us less likely to see the need for change. Participants of change management programmes admitted to taking the same route home and sitting on the same chair and position in their living room and dining room. Many also sit on the same pew in church!

Routines make life easier; we can carry out many activities without reflection and conscious choice. We are too lazy to go through the thought process each time we want to carry out an action. Our past choices seem good enough. Thus, looking at things differently is uncommon even at a personal level. Many of us have always seen our living room from a particular angle. Perhaps we have had the experience of visiting friends and being told by the little child not to sit on daddy's chair! The problem with routines is that they habituate us to the forces of inertia and make it difficult for us to see the need for change.

It is the perception of a performance gap, of a need for change, that leads to a decision to change. Changes in the micro, meso or macro environment will not lead an organization to initiate change unless and until these changes are perceived and a need for change is felt by some organizational members. In the next section, we discuss the critical success factors for perceiving the need for change.

Critical Success Factors at this Stage

In a developing country context, the ability to read the external environment cannot be overemphasized. A good understanding of the macroeconomic environment, the socio-political environment and industry dynamics are critical for success in anticipating and implementing change. Changes in government and in government officials have an impact on the environment of business. Good environmental scanning gave EMZOR Pharmaceuticals an edge in the market for generics in Nigeria. When the late Professor Ransome-Kuti, the Minister of Health at the time, introduced the essential drug list, many pharmaceutical companies were caught napping. They could no longer sell branded products at a premium; all drugs on the list were declared essential and no company was allowed to sell a branded product. The Professor had made his stand known long before he was made the Health Minister. Environmental scanning once he was named Minister would have enabled the other players to anticipate the change.

Good environmental scanning enabled companies like Promasidor in Nigeria to excel in a very short time in a very competitive market. The statistics showed clearly that purchasing power was reducing. Many daily-paid workers could not afford to buy beverages in tins or large packs. Promasidor was the first company in the fast moving consuming goods industry to introduce milk in small sachets – the quantity needed for one use. Even though the company was a late entrant into the market, it re-defined the industry. Today, many products (including detergents and beverages) are available in small sachets.

If organizations are to see the need for change they must re-think their strategic planning and review processes. Good strategy departments help organizations understand the environment. However, for many companies, the strategic planning process is not different from the budgeting process. Strategy sessions are reduced to a discussion of the coming year's budget. Each business or department makes a presentation to the top team. Questions are asked, agreements are reached and everyone goes home.

Some organizations find it worthwhile to invite a consultant from outside who does not have an emotional attachment to the status quo to help the organization analyse the environment and its likely impact on the organization. The consultant's role is to stimulate the group to think about changes in the environment and the impact these changes could have. However, the 2- to 3-day format does not allow much time for reflection. Managers are often more concerned about getting approval for their budget. As one manager put it: 'Sometimes these retreats are about filling-in an excel spread sheet'. Few, if any, new ideas come from the strategy retreats.

The senior and middle managers of a mid-sized engineering firm held a 2-day strategy retreat in January each year. The Finance Director presented the results of the previous year and reviewed performance against set goals. A discussion on why goals were not met often took half a day. The rest of the strategy retreat was spent on discussing budget presentations by the heads of the business units. A guest then gave a motivational speech.

On the advice of a consultant, the Managing Director decided to change the format of the retreat. He began with a presentation in which he outlined the agenda for the weekend. He invited the managers to ask the following questions:

- Why are we here? What did we do well last year? Where did we not do so well? Why?
- Did we make the right decisions regarding our vision, values and strategy? If not, which decisions were wrong?
- Are there opportunities in the environment – the country, market, competition, government regulation, etc.? Which? Are there any threats to our business? Which?
- Where do we want to go? Which strategy will get us there?

TABLE 2.2 Some of the Big Issues

What technological, demographic or social/cultural and regulatory changes are likely to occur in the environment in the next few years?
What opportunities or challenges will they create for the industry in the near future?
How are these changes likely to affect our business?
What should we do today to prepare for tomorrow?
What are competitors doing?
What are their likely reactions to our moves?
What are our customers saying about our offer?
Do our people have the energy, the passion, to win?

• Looking at our people, the operating environment, the way we do things, the resources we have, what do we have that can help us get to where we want to go? What must we get?

The Managing Director was pleasantly surprised by the amount of energy in the room as he spoke. The managers were apparently fed up of the dull speeches and the tweaking of budgets at the previous retreats. Now at last the Managing Director was willing to address the key issues (Table 2.2).

If strategy retreats are to be effective, enough time should be given to reflection on the big issues. The discussion at strategy retreats should be about the big questions. It may not be possible to find answers to these questions at the retreat, but the right conversations would have begun.

Let us look at how Equity Bank, Kenya, developed its strategy map. In 2004, the Management of Equity saw the need to metamorphose into a bank. The institution had been in existence for ten years, first as a mortgage institution and later as a micro finance institution. The strategy process began with an examination of the mission and values of the firm and the articulation of a new mission and values. Senior and middle level managers participated in the process. Next the key success factors for the mission were identified. By the end of 2004, seven critical success factors had been identified. The articulation of the mission and values and the critical success factors took almost one year. During the year, consultants facilitated a dialogue among senior and middle level managers. Decisions were made at several meetings and a strategy map emerged. In 2005, Equity obtained a licence to operate as a bank. Since then, its strategy sessions are focused on how well the mission is being realized and an examination of the key success factors.

In turbulent environments such as in African economies, strategic reviews should be frequent. The weekend at Ogere or Peninsula Resort in Nigeria – Nirvasha or Mombasa in Kenya – may be insufficient. More frequent reviews should be planned. This should enable organizations to use information obtained from the environmental scan to make strategic decisions. For example, at the end of 2008 and the beginning of 2009, the Apapa Port in Lagos was congested.

Interest rates increased significantly. The Managing Director of an organization that imports and distributes cosmetics called a meeting to discuss how the organization should react to these changes. The business model of the company was under threat. Some strategic decisions had to be taken, and quickly too.

Getting the right information on the table is important if the right strategies are to be adopted. Sales people and customer-facing personnel usually get at least a whiff of changing times in the industry. Every organizational member, including those in the lower rungs of the organizational ladder, should be encouraged to share ideas on how the organization can stay nimble. A culture that encourages openness, in which people at all levels can ask questions, can contribute to discussions about the future, is critical for seeing the need for change.

Research suggests that power distance is very high in most African countries (House *et al.* 2004). While all the five Sub-Saharan countries had a very low value for power distance, the practice was very significant. In Nigeria for example, the value of power distance was about 2.7 while the practice was 5.8. Subordinates are expected to obey their bosses without question. 'The management team in some companies (especially in owner-managed companies) parrot the CEO's beliefs as they think they owe their job and all the perks to the CEO. Contradicting him or showing him his blind spots may be dangerous for one's future career and security' (Ovadje 2002: 57).

Many people find it difficult to express a contrary view or opinion to an elderly person or the boss. This is considered rebelliousness in many organizations. People therefore weigh their opinions to be certain that they align with the boss. Not surprisingly, subordinates do not find it easy to question the strategy put forward by a boss.

The Globe Study (House *et al.* 2004) also suggests that Sub-Saharan African countries have little value for assertiveness in organizations; this cultural dimension had the second lowest score. In Nigeria and South Africa (black sample), assertiveness in practice had a higher score than the value of assertiveness in these cultures. The findings of the Globe Study also suggest that the future orientation of organizations in Sub-Saharan Africa is very low. More attention seems to be focused in practice on resolving current crisis. What do the findings of these studies mean for managing in the turbulent environment of Africa?

CEOs of African organizations should recognize that 'The unity of the firm does not depend on everyone thinking the same way, nor should diversity of opinion be considered a sign of disunity or disloyalty' (Fontrodona 2002: 77). Instead they should create 'a climate of dialogue in which opinions are expressed freely' Fontrodona (2002: 77).

To create this climate of dialogue, the CEO must go out of his or her way to encourage candour. The risk, to subordinates, of speaking the truth should be reduced. How management deals with the bearer of bad news encourages or discourages conversations among different levels of the organization. External signs of power distance could be removed to encourage frank discussions.

An example of an avant-guard organization in this respect is GTBank plc. After the bank acquired a banking licence in 1990, the management set out to build a team of professionals who would provide exceptional customer service to customers. From the beginning, everyone (from the Managing Director to the receptionists and drivers) was addressed by his or her first name. There are no private parking spaces; there is only one dining room. The MD and senior management spent a day at the front desk (as paying or receiving cashiers). Team work very quickly developed and barriers were broken. Officers at lower rungs of the ladder found it easy to question their bosses, make suggestions on how customers could be better served, etc. In spite of their rapid growth, they have maintained their customer service culture.

Equity Bank, Kenya, has developed a customer-focused organization in line with its mission. It has institutionalized a feedback mechanism that enables it to listen to customers and act on information from the field. Through regular customer surveys, listening to customers in the branches, etc. the Bank captures information from the customers. Customer complaints are followed up with visits to listen more closely and address the issues. The branch manager's office is located near the entrance to the branch and the door is always left open. Any customer can see the branch manager about anything. One branch manager commented that he sees an average of 50 customers each day.

During the branch meetings, members of staff share their experience, challenges, etc. A lot of time is spent analysing feedback from customers. During the performance planning and review meetings, branch managers share their experiences. The bank also has a Director in charge of Customer Service.

Today, Equity Bank is the most innovative bank in Kenya. It has the largest number of customers (over 4.5 million). It has entered into strategic alliances with several organizations to provide a wide variety of products to its teeming customer base. It is the fastest growing bank in Kenya.

The leaders of these organizations realized that wisdom does not sit at the top of the organization. Rather, it can be found at all rungs of the ladder. They have been able to tap the collective wisdom of their people and make better decisions.

Andrew Grove, in the book *Only the Paranoid Survive* (Grove 1996), suggests that top management should cultivate the fear of losing in all employees. All stakeholders have precisely that, a stake in the business. Company growth and survival is in the employee's interests.

The CEO must also see his or her role as a strategic one. Instead of looking down and micromanaging the organization, a CEO that reflects, that analyses the environment developing different scenarios, their likely impact, and the organization's response, will not be caught napping when shocks occur.

Anticipating the future has its risks; sometimes the future does not materialize or it takes time to do so. One company that operates in both the upstream and downstream sectors of the oil industry anticipated the deregulation of the downstream sector in the early 2000s. It set up systems, changed its structure and began to work as though the environment had been deregulated. But deregulation did not happen for many years.

According to du Toit (2003: 14), 'enterprises in developing countries continue to be surprised by undesirable changes in the environment and it appears that the advancement in managing intelligence is as yet largely unknown to these countries'. These organizations are slow to sense the need for change (Pettigrew *et al.* 2001). Du Toit (2003) found in his study of South African organizations that, even though the CEOs of the organizations he studied considered having a competitive intelligence unit important, only a quarter of the organizations had such a unit. Less than half of the organizations carried out formal environmental scanning.

It seems that managers are aware of at least some of the external drivers of change in their organizations but continue to be focused on internal issues. Few formal scanning systems exist. It is no wonder, therefore, that environmental changes take them by surprise.

In Table 2.3, we provide answers to two questions on the minds of many senior managers: what can organizations do to see the need for change? How can they monitor the drivers of change and successfully anticipate change?

Monitoring the Change Drivers

Organizations should monitor the environment and develop the capacity to anticipate change. Government regulation is a major driver of change in a developing

TABLE 2.3 Seeing the Need for Change

Change driver	Monitoring and seeing the need for change
Changes in and enforcement of government regulation	• Active in industry groups to influence regulation • Build networks in government • Analysis of government plans, budgets, MDGs, etc.
Changes in industry dynamics	• Active in trade groups • Attendance at trade fairs • Scan for new technologies, possible new entrants into the industry
Changes in customer taste and preferences	• Customer surveys • Encourage open dialogue within the organization • Regular visits to clients • Market research
Changes in the macroeconomic environment	• Track macroeconomic statistics • Discuss implications of changes
Company performance	• Monthly performance reports • Understanding of financial information and its implications by all organizational members

country environment. The legal environment may constrain the actions of firms. To anticipate what government (legislators and the executive) are likely to do in the future, organizations must be close to them. CEOs and strategy departments need to be more in tune with government plans, budgets, etc. at both the national and provincial or state levels. The impact of possible changes in legislation can be analysed and a decision made to change the organization or begin to prepare it for change.

To influence legislation, an organization may not want to speak with a lone voice. Membership of an industry group or a larger group such as the Nigerian Economic Summit Group can be very effective in this regard. Child and Tsai (2005: 117) found that MNCs in China often established networks through which they tried to influence the institutions which impacted their operations. By lending their expertise to these institutions, MNCs participated in institutional development.

Monitoring industry dynamics can be difficult. Membership of industry groups and attendance of trade fairs are important as they are useful ways organizations can employ to track technology changes, new entrants to the industry, etc. Some competitive intelligence may also be necessary. Du Toit (2003) found that common sources of competitor intelligence used by firms include: newspapers, annual reports and trade shows. Distributors and retailers often have competitor intelligence and can make it available to all suppliers. There are ethical considerations here and organizations will do well to ensure that employees are ethical in carrying out their jobs.

Organizations that give a lot of importance to customer feedback and monitor customer satisfaction tend to win in the market. Through market research, customer surveys and other ways of listening to customers, they are able to see the future. Where an organization sells all its products through distributors, it is perhaps even more important to keep a tap on the final consumers.

It is difficult to be successful in business in developing countries without an understanding of the macroeconomic environment. The outlook for exchange rates, interest rates, and inflation is a very important piece of information that managers require for decision making. Will the currency be devalued? What is the outlook for commodity prices? Answers to these questions feed into the strategy retreats and help managers make better informed decisions.

To survive in today's challenging environment, organizations must change or die. They have to develop antennae to sense the need for change so they can anticipate it and carry out change initiatives before they have to. Strategy departments, strategy retreats, fostering dialogue within the organization about the key issues, as well as customer surveys, are some mechanisms organizations have put in place to stay abreast of what is going to happen in the environment – external and also internal. Once the need for change has been felt, a decision has to be taken to change, or to do nothing.

The Decision to Change

Once the performance gap has been recognized and the need for change felt, the choice to be made is whether or not to initiate change. Companies that do not consciously make this decision in effect accept the current situation, that is, to do nothing. If a decision is taken to initiate change in the organization, a vision for the change must then be articulated. This is the subject of the next chapter.

Summary

In this chapter, we discussed the environmental and internal drivers of change. We argued that change results from a performance gap. This gap must be perceived by the right people if change is to happen.

The need for change may not be obvious. Managers may be emotionally tied to the status quo. A culture that does not encourage candour and questioning is also an obstacle to seeing the need for change. We discussed some key success factors for seeing the need for change. When the need for change is recognized, a decision may be taken to initiate change.

In the next chapter, we examine the next choice in the model; the choice of vision for the change.

Notes

1 Ovadje, F. (2011). *Seven Seas Technologies* (B). Lagos Business School.
2 African Telecommunication/ICT Indicators 2008.

3
THE CHANGE VISION

Introduction

In the last chapter we saw that the need for change arises from internal and/or external forces. Changes in the environment once perceived are evaluated to assess their likely impact on the organization. This involves an understanding of where the organization is and the threats and opportunities in the internal and external environment. Finally a performance gap is identified. A decision is taken to do nothing or to initiate change in the organization. In this chapter, we argue that the strategic decision to initiate change in the organization should be followed by the articulation of a vision for the change. The vision is very important as it determines the future direction of the organization and is the basis and springboard for all other decisions around the change.

The Importance of Organizational Vision

A distinction is made between the organizational mission (the organization's purpose or reason for being) and the vision – a statement of how the organization would like to look at some time in the future. The importance of such a picture of the future for successful organizational change has been emphasized in the change literature.

Getting the vision right is one of the eight steps to successful change proposed by Kotter and Cohen (2002). According to Jick and Peiperl (2003: 91) 'common sense tells us that a change must be "seen", its direction in some way charted before anything happens'. For Cummings and Worley (2005), crafting a vision is a critical step in organizational change. This is because the organizational vision enhances the chances of organizational success (Foster and Akdere 2007: 107).

The latter argue that 'having a strong organizational vision is a sound strategy for increasing competitiveness in uncertain business environments'.

In the leadership literature, inspiring others with a vision is a characteristic of transformational and charismatic leadership. Transformational leaders inspire followers by articulating a compelling vision of the future (Peterson *et al.* 2009: 352). In fact, inspirational motivation is one of the dimensions of transformational leadership.

Charismatic leaders also inspire followers with a strong vision. They are 'extraordinarily gifted people who gain the respect, pride, trust and confidence of followers by transmitting a strong sense of vision and mission' (Gardner and Avolio 1998, cited in Walumbwa and Lawler 2003: 1085).

Visioning is one of the behaviours of transformational and charismatic leaders. According to Van Knippenberg and Sitkin (2013: 46), 'visionary leadership is the verbal communication of an image of a future for a collective with the intention to persuade others to contribute to the realization of that future'. They argue that visions imply change; visions suggest pursuing a future that is different from today (Van Knippenberg and Sitkin 2013: 47). Walumbwa and Lawler (2003) found that transformational leadership had a positive impact on organizational commitment. Hwang *et al.* (2005) found in their study of visions and charisma in Singapore, New Zealand and India that vision was related to performance.

What is a Vision?

A vision is a vivid description of the future state of the organization, business unit, department, etc. It articulates what the organization will look like in the future when the change is actualized. It establishes the direction of the change. Without a vision the organization has no clear destination and will most probably drift. It is especially important in turbulent environments for an organization to have a clear destination. The vision is simply a vivid description of the destination; of the desired future state, the end result; what the company or unit will look like once the performance gap has been closed. It is a statement of aspiration; of what we want to be.

Consider this. If you asked a number of people to go with you from Nairobi to Nirvasha on foot, you would have to explain to them why they should go, and why on foot and not by car. Naturally, your would-be companions would want to know the purpose of the trip in order to determine whether the effort is worthwhile or not. It will certainly help if you described the beauty of Longonot, Hell's Gate, Nirvasha Lake, etc. With this beautiful destination in mind, they are likely to sign up for the long trek. It is the same with change initiatives. Because change requires people to get out of their comfort zones and begin a long often tedious journey, a description of the destination helps people get going.

A vivid description of the destination makes the change journey easier. An African proverb says: it is easy to climb the mountain when the person one loves is at the top of the mountain. Change often involves climbing a mountain, walking seemingly impossible distances. Change agents must let people know what the top of the mountain looks like; they should describe the view from the top, explaining why the arduous journey is worthwhile. People want to reach the future with their mind's eye before setting out for it. A vision takes the people to the future before they get there.

Levels of Vision

Visions give coherence to change actions. Change may require a new organizational vision. A transformational or radical change often requires a new organizational vision. Radical change brings about fundamental changes in how the organization works. An example of a radical change is the integration of two firms as a result of a merger or acquisition. A new culture may have to be introduced, new reporting relationships developed, systems and processes integrated, etc. The new organizational vision describes what the organization will look like when the two firms have been successfully integrated. The new vision gives coherence to the various changes being introduced. In the absence of an overarching vision, change initiatives may be viewed as add-ons to existing systems and are not likely to succeed.

Every change, whether radical or not, requires a vision. Some change initiatives do not make obsolete existing systems, processes, reporting relationships, etc. Rather they are aimed at improving existing systems in order to actualize the organizational vision. These changes therefore do not require a new vision for the whole organization. Instead, a vision for that change, in the department or unit where change is to be implemented, is all that is required.

Those changes that do not require a new organizational vision have their visions embedded in the organizational vision. Thus the vision of a paperless office, of the HR department after the installation of Oracle, etc. must be clear to the people who have to realize these visions and should be embedded in the organizational vision.

No matter the scope of the change, a vision (a description of the future state) is necessary to get people on board. The organizational vision may not change, but the vision of a part of the organization may have to change.

Characteristics of a Good Vision

According to Levin (2000: 92) 'there ... is considerable agreement about the key attributes of an effective vision. It should be future oriented, compelling, bold, aspiring, and inspiring, yet believable and achievable'. Visions tell a story of the future; of what tomorrow will look like. Visions create a tension between the

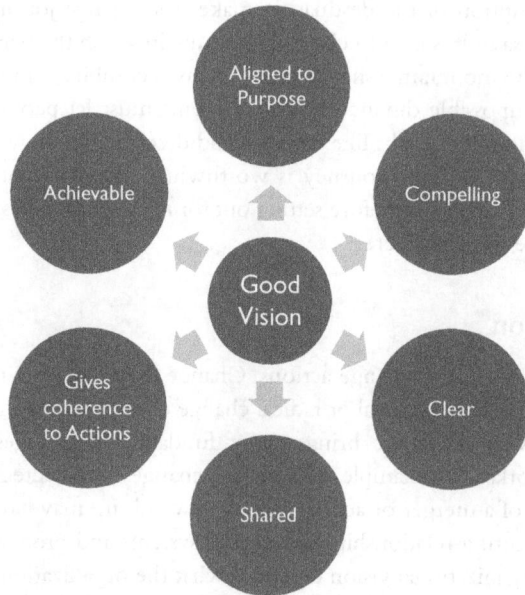

FIGURE 3.1 Characteristics of good visions

present and the future state. They are therefore an effective means of fighting organizational inertia, attachment to routines, etc.

Change is often uncomfortable, even threatening. To effect change, the forces for change must overcome those resistant to change. In this dialectic, visions are very useful. A vision of a better future is important for winning the battle of change. Without a clear vision of where the organization is going, people very easily fall back into their old routines. See Figure 3.1 for the characteristics of good visions.

A Good Vision is Compelling

According to Hwang *et al.* (2005: 963), 'a compelling vision gives clarity and direction to followers and thus focuses followers' effort toward goal attainment'. A vision should have a motivational pull; it must be challenging and inspiring. Some authors have argued that in implementing change, feelings are more important than reason. The problem with feelings is that they are transient. The vision should touch people on the heart as well as the head. When people see a purpose that is worth sacrificing for, they are more likely to work speedily towards achieving it.

If the vision is to be compelling, it must incorporate the interests of key stakeholders. If the change programme threatens entrenched interest groups the level of resistance from these groups could derail the transformation completely. It is thus necessary to get the commitment of at least the key interest groups. The new vision must be comprehensive if it is to be compelling. Visions inspire and motivate by connecting and aligning people intellectually and emotionally to the organization. Such visions increase the prospects of a successful transformation (Nutt and Backoff 1997).

A Vision Should be Clear

The picture of the destination should not be blurred or fuzzy. Rather it should be clear, vivid and easy to remember. When Professor Dora Akunyili took charge of the National Food and Drug Administration and Control Agency (NAFDAC), the agency was moribund. Nigeria was rated as one of the countries with the highest incidence of fake and counterfeit drugs. Neighbouring countries did not allow drugs from Nigeria into their domains. The agency's staff were demoralized; legislation was lacking or inadequate.

Within weeks of taking charge, Dora asked the managers to organize a retreat to articulate a mission and vision for the agency and map out strategies for transforming the agency. According to Dora, 'the Management of NAFDAC has resolved that counterfeit medicines must be brought to the barest minimum in the shortest possible time. Our team believes that we are called to a mission to eradicate this evil and to achieve this, we have a clear vision, set goal and strategies'.[1]

The transformation of NAFDAC is perhaps one of the most successful and impactful transformations of a public institution in Nigeria. A key success factor was Dora's conviction that she and her staff were called to actualize a mission and vision. Her single-minded focus on 'safeguarding the health of Nigerians' paid off. The vision was crystal clear and all her actions were directed at realizing the vision.

A Good Vision is Aligned with the Core Purpose of the Organization

Whether the vision is for the whole organization or a part of it, it should contribute to the realization of the core purpose of the organization. Let me give an example. The Medical Director of a hospital had crafted a vision of improved patient care in the hospital. The parameters were clear: improvement in the time to correct diagnosis, improvements in hygiene and the quality of food, in time taken to see a doctor, etc. He said he wanted to improve patient care because patients wanted better care. But why should the hospital improve care? The answer was, to retain and even increase market share and profits. Why was an increase in market share and profits desirable? To buy better equipment, etc. For what purpose? To improve quality of healthcare? Why is this desirable? The Medical Director responded: 'Because this is why we exist. Our mission is to provide good health care services to our patients while living our values of respect, empathy and service'. Answers to these questions led the Medical Director to the core purpose and values of the organization. They then asked: 'When healthcare has improved what will the hospital look like?' They drew up a number of parameters, and a vivid description of the end state began to emerge. As Hwang *et al.* (2005: 963) put it: 'not any future state will rally followers to a leader's cause but rather a specific future state that is personally meaningful to followers'.

The Vision Gives Coherence to Change Actions or Initiatives

Sometimes change is so broad based and complex that change recipients ask why so many changes are taking place. They see the structure, the culture, the sales channel, etc. changing and can hardly make sense of these changes. They may resist the change because they do not see the connections.

The picture of where the organization is going (the vision) is what connects what may seem to be disparate change initiatives. People can see that the various change initiatives are all geared to the actualization of the vision.

An Effective Vision must be Achievable, Doable

Some visions have an emotional appeal but if change recipients believe that the vision is not achievable, it remains just a good idea; change does not happen. Visions are dreams. Change agents must ask themselves how the organization will actualize the dream; how competitors will react to the change; what resources the company will be able to attract to make the big jump from say number eight in industry ranking to number one in 3 years. If an 'also-ran' wants to become number one, they must give their followers a road map of how they will get there; how they intend to change the rules of the game. It should be possible to translate the vision into action steps. Change recipients want to see that the organization can become what it wants to be – that the new order is possible.

Consider the following example of an organizational vision: Yomi Badejo-Okusanya, Managing Director of CMC Connect, was on vacation when he read the book that he later commented changed his life, or, at least, his business. He immediately set out to analyse the situation in the company, and crafted a vision for CMC Connect: 'the best public relations firm in the west coast of Africa'.[2] He moved the offices to 'The Bridge House' because as he said: 'Our image must reflect who we are and what we do…. We act as a bridge. We take people from obscurity to fame, hatred to love; and from misconception to reality.'[3]

Pictures of bridges from all over the world were to be used to decorate the offices. A new logo was launched. It was inscribed in lapel pins, cuff links, etc. Yomi used every opportunity to communicate the vision. In spite of this, there were mixed reactions from employees. Some doubted whether the vision could be realized while others were convinced the vision would be a reality. Comments from two employees reflect the typical reactions to the vision:

> I think we should first lead in Nigeria before going out to the rest of Africa. There are PR companies that are well respected in Nigeria. They will not just sit there and wait for CMC to take over the market. The question is: 'What are you doing to make CMC Connect the company to be emulated, the company good PR guys out there want to work for, the company clients want to work with?'

Another employee commented: 'I trust that the MD will take us where we think we should be. The vision should be realized within the next two years.'

The company had a theme song; a popular song in the 1980s which in the managing director's (MD's) opinion captured how he felt about the company. Once a month all members of staff worked out to the rhythm of the song. A few employees also expressed mixed reactions to the theme song:

> The theme song is simply disco; it does not motivate anyone. It provides entertainment for people. The MD likes it and wants us to take it seriously.
>
> It is a nice song. We all know it. Once you hear it, you remember your target. It is the CMC song.
>
> To be frank, it really motivates me. 'Ain't no stopping us now' reminds us to start doing something.
>
> I don't know the words of the song. I don't know if it is motivational or not. I don't really like music. My MD has a vision. There are challenges. He believes that by singing that song, the vision will get into our head and nothing will stop us.[4]

The CMC story highlights the importance of a realistic vision. If some employees believe that the vision is not realizable, that management is building castles in the air, they are not likely to put the effort required to actualize the vision. The vision must meet the reality check; it must be believable and achievable.

It is not enough to have the resources needed to actualize the vision. It is also necessary to turn visions into goals and strategies. Berson *et al.* (2001: 67) found that transformational leaders crafted visions that were optimistic and instilled faith in a better future in followers. But they also tied these exciting visions to goals and objectives. The objectives outline how the organization will pursue its desired future and define key markers for gauging progress towards it (Levin 2000: 95).

An Effective Vision is Shared

A vision must be well communicated if it is to influence the actions of change recipients. Yomi of CMC Connect communicated his new vision at meetings, through the Bridge House, the new logo, etc. However, the vision was not shared. Employees were aware of the vision but it did not mean much to them and the vision was not actualized. Communication is necessary but not sufficient for a good vision.

Foster and Akdere (2007) cite a case study by Margolis and Hansen (2003) in which the latter concluded that employees held one of three images about their organization: the expected future, the ideal future and the feared future. The vision evoked different images in employees' minds. Thus, there was no shared vision. In the absence of a shared vision, it is easy to work at cross purposes.

Senge (2006: 193) showed that a shared vision is a powerful force for change. A vision is truly shared when organizational members have a similar picture of what the organization wants to create and are committed to it, that is, they care about it. When a vision is shared, a lot of creative energy is produced; energy which makes for the realization of the dream. Senge (2006: 193) asserts that, 'few, if any, forces in human affairs are as powerful as shared vision'.

Foster and Akdere (2007) argue that involving employees in the process of crafting the vision should help ensure that the vision is shared. The vision should not be the personal vision of the CEO or head of department. Involving change recipients in the definition of the vision creates a common image in their minds and facilitates commitment to the vision.

Crafting the Vision

Crafting the vision and setting the strategic direction is the primary responsibility of the chief executive officer or managing director. The CEO must not only believe in the vision, he or she must own it. Owning the vision however does not mean that the CEO should craft the vision with little or no participation from the troops.

There are several approaches to crafting the vision. The vision may be developed by the MD/CEO or head of unit alone, with his or her team or with employees at different rungs of the organizational ladder. Managers at different levels of the organization may be involved in the process or a bottom up approach may be preferred. No matter the approach, the ultimate responsibility for realizing the vision lies with the person at the top. If the vision is crafted by the MD alone or the senior management, the big challenge is that of communicating the vision and getting buy-in. Where, on the other hand, the visioning process involves some or all of the organizational members, the process is more time consuming but the vision is more likely to be shared. Let us look at a few examples.

The Managing Director of CMC Connect crafted the vision on his own and communicated it to the senior management, the board and all employees. He used every opportunity to communicate the vision (even monthly work-out sessions). At the time, the company was making the transition from an entrepreneurial to a mid-sized professionally run firm.

Dora Akunyili, the Director General of NAFDAC involved all managers and the members of the governing council of the agency in the visioning exercise. An off-site retreat was organized with the help of consultants. The purpose of the retreat was to review the existing mission statement and craft a new mission, vision and strategies for the agency. Dora deliberately asked a few managers to organize the retreat and invite consultants to facilitate. Even though she did not agree with some of the choices they made she went along with them in order to win their commitment. She wanted the governing council members and the management to jointly come up with a picture of the future. She knew that fighting the powerful drug barons who imported and distributed adulterated and fake drugs was going to be a herculean task. It was important that the management had the same mission and vision. The vision was to be the fulcrum that would hold together all the changes to be introduced.

The new Chairman of the Federal Housing Authority (FHA) followed the same approach when he assumed office. FHA, like a number of government agencies, was in dire need of change. The Federal Government had hired a consulting firm to carry out a diagnostic review of the organization. The new chairman was given a mandate to implement change in the agency.

The Chairman asked the consultants to facilitate a retreat for the organization with the purpose of defining the institution's Mission, Vision and Core Values as well as strategies to actualize the mandate. Selected members of staff and management participated in the week-long retreat.

He used the opportunity of a full week at an offsite location to get to know the members of staff and management who attended the retreat, to assess them, identify change champions, and to communicate his expectations and his style.

Equity Bank, Kenya, followed a similar approach but involved all members of staff in crafting the vision. In 2004, senior management decided to articulate the bank's mission and vision in preparation for its transformation from a micro finance institution to a bank. Consultants were hired to facilitate the process. All members of staff were involved in the process which lasted several months. By 2005, everyone within Equity knew the mission and vision of the bank and their role in actualizing the vision.

Which approach is best? It depends on a number of factors. A culture of openness usually facilitates participation in the visioning process. In such organizational cultures, people expect to participate in crafting the new vision. Getting buy-in is usually easier if enough people are involved in the visioning process.

Participation by staff and management has a number of advantages. The chairman of FHA, for example, used the retreat for visioning, training and as an informal assessment tool. Since he was new to the organization, the retreat provided an opportunity for him to get to know the people better.

Lack of knowledge of an organization may suggest the use of a more participative visioning process. Dora Akunyili left the university to head NAFDAC. She was an outsider. Involving management and even staff members may have been necessary since she had little or no knowledge of the organization. Yomi Badejo-Okusanya, on the other hand, was the founder/managing director of CMC Connect. He knew where he wanted to go and he knew the organization. One can understand why he would craft the vision and spend time communicating it while Dora got the people involved in the process.

Organizational Visions in Africa

We have reviewed the change literature, highlighted the characteristics of a good vision, and discussed how visions may be crafted. An important question remains: what kind of leadership is required for effectiveness in Africa? Are there any peculiarities dictated by the environment regarding visions and vision effectiveness?

The GLOBE Study of different cultures uses six global leadership dimensions to differentiate cultures in terms of the content of their culturally endorsed implicit leadership theory profiles (House *et al.* 2004: 670). Implicit leadership theories are the beliefs individuals have about the behaviours, attributes and personality characteristics of leaders that will lead to outstanding performance. These beliefs held by followers influence their acceptance of a leader. Dorfman *et al.* (in House *et al.* 2004) argue that these leadership beliefs are shared by individuals within a culture (they are culturally endorsed) and can be used to distinguish different cultures. They found that Charismatic/Value-based leadership was strongly endorsed by all cultures as contributing to outstanding performance.

Dorfman *et al.* (in House *et al.* 2004) recognize that Charismatic/Value-based leadership is similar to transformational leadership. Charismatic/Value-based leaders are visionary and self-sacrificing, they inspire, have integrity, are decisive and performance oriented. People in all cultures expect leaders to inspire them with a vision and to sacrifice for the actualization of that vision.

In the GLOBE Study, Sub-Saharan Africa had the highest score compared to other cultures in humane oriented leadership. According to Wanasika *et al.* (2011) the humane oriented leader is supportive, considerate, compassionate and generous. They assert that this cultural characteristic is a distinguishing factor for Sub-Saharan Africa. Thus, Africans expect leaders to inspire them with a vision, to be compassionate and supportive towards them. This has implications for visioning and for vision communication.

One of the characteristics of a good vision is that it is shared. Sharing a vision in the African context will involve turning the vision from an impersonal vision to one that can motivate or inspire. Africans are concerned about the impact of the realization of the vision on people. This is because Africans are their brothers' keepers. A future in which a few of the employees have a role but a large number are declared redundant may not be a future that employees in Africa want to realize. Consideration and empathy are very important attributes of the people. They do not have an instrumental view of the human person. Thus getting rid of people simply to improve the bottom line is difficult to sell. Employees want to be sure that both the company and the people are successful.

An example: Uche Attoh, who was director of HR in three multinational companies in Nigeria and led the integration of at least two companies, commented: '[Employees] are interested in what happens thereafter. They want to be sure you are sympathetic with the people. If you are too harsh they scream: "Do you want to kill him?" You must stop somewhere and let bygones be bygones even if an employee has a case to answer. If you are not careful, the policeman who is investigating the case will ask you why you are pursuing the matter so vigorously.'

Communicating the vision in the African context presents peculiar challenges. Given the large number of uneducated people on the factory floor and the lowest rungs of the organizational ladder, ensuring the vision is well communicated and shared by all employees can be a great challenge. Follower concerns may vary across organizational levels and the vision may mean different things to them. Communicating the vision to a knowledge workforce is very different from communicating it to factory workers.

In communicating the vision, several factors should be borne in mind especially by change strategists who are not members of the local community. First, the strategist must be culturally sensitive. Some organizations are a melting point of cultures. In communicating change to organizational members from such diverse backgrounds, some knowledge of diversity management is important. For example, there are over 250 ethnic groups in Nigeria, each with its cultural norms and values. What is accepted in one culture may not be accepted in another. In communicating vision, change strategists and implementers must be aware of these differences. They must be sensitive to the nuances of different cultures. Old men on the shop floor must be treated with the same respect accorded other groups. In northern Nigeria, a woman does not shake hands with a man. Thus the way the vision is communicated will vary depending on the dominant culture.

The strategists must also be aware of changing demographics and their impact on the organization. In Kenya, young graduates who are entering the job market for the first time are very articulate and confident; they want to apply their own rules and to participate in decision making. To sell a vision to them, one would need to understand their frame of reference (which is very different from that of older Kenyans). The generational differences are likely to have an impact on how the message is received and thus on whether or not the vision is shared.

Language is very important for effective communication. Generally speaking, people in urban areas such as Lagos, Nairobi and Johannesburg have a greater command of English language than those in rural areas or small towns. In the latter, the language of communication is pidgin English, Swahili, or other local languages.

For example, Erogbogbo was sent from Lagos to Aba (in eastern Nigeria) with the mandate of improving manufacturing practices in the Aba factory and ultimately improving product quality. He had achieved impressive results in the main factory in Lagos.

When he took charge of the Aba factory, he introduced a suggestion box and an incentive system to encourage new ideas from the factory workers. He also installed a public address system and regularly communicated to all the staff. A few weeks went by and there were no suggestions. It seemed that nothing had changed. One day, one of the factory workers who had become close to the factory manager told him he could not understand what Erogbogbo said during his weekly meetings. Erogbogbo asked more questions and found that most of the workers on the factory floor understood Igbo (the local language) and pidgin English. They did not understand Erogbogbo but pretended they did.

Erogbogbo found an interpreter who translated what he said into Igbo and pidgin. The situation began to change. A casual worker made a suggestion which saved the company a huge sum of money. Within a short period of time, about 60 per cent of the staff were involved in the change process.

Change strategists and implementers should communicate the benefits of the change to all stakeholders. Change recipients want to know how the change will impact their own and/or others' living standard positively. Communicating the benefits to employees and other stakeholders reduces the level of resistance. The deputy vice chancellor of a Nigerian university initiated change to reduce the number of days it took a new student to register and get a room in one of the university hostels. The process took about two weeks and he wanted it reduced to two days. Software was developed which not only cleared the new students but allocated them halls of residence. The list of residents was then displayed in each hall.

The lodging officers in the halls tore down the lists. Students could not find their names. Security personnel were sent to the halls to guard the lists. One day, the deputy vice chancellor heard that the lodging officers planned to burn down the computer room. He decided to have a meeting with them and communicate the vision and how they fitted into the picture. At the end of his presentation, one of the lodging officers slapped himself on the head and said: 'Sir, why didn't you tell us this earlier?' As soon as they saw a place for themselves in the new scheme of things, they supported the vision and helped realize it.

The alignment of the vision with strategies and day-to-day actions is critical for vision implementation. People have had bad experiences with change. Many are disillusioned or even cynical about the possibility of change. Nigerians, for example, have heard of Vision 2000, which became Vision 2010 and is now Vision 2020. They really do not expect these national visions to be realized. If they are to share the organizational vision, it must be doable; they must see the actions to be taken to ensure success and the commitment of the change strategists.

Finally if the vision is to be shared it must be communicated at every opportunity. Yomi Badejo-Okusanya of CMC Connect did this incredibly well.

To communicate the new vision, a new logo was launched. It was inscribed on several items. The company moved its offices to a highbrow area. The new office had a swimming pool and tennis court. A theme song was adopted and all employees and managers worked out once a month to the rhythm of the theme song. The managing director used notice boards and every meeting as an opportunity to share the vision. T-shirts and face caps with the logo and vision were distributed to members of staff. According to one manager 'the MD goes on and on about it'.[5] In no time, all employees knew the vision.

Vision Implementation

Not all visions are actualized. A number of enablers help vision implementation. They include good communication and vision alignment.

In their review of the literature of effective organizational visions, Foster and Akdere (2007: 107) found a 'consensus among researchers that effective communication is vital to vision implementation. If the vision is to be implemented by employees at all levels of the organization, it must be shared. The vision must evoke the same meaning to employees such that they need not guess at the meaning of the vision and what actions will be required to actualize the vision. Choices have to be made about how the vision will be communicated, who will communicate to the different levels of staff, who will communicate the need for change and the new vision to influential people such as union leaders.'

Foster and Akdere (2007: 107) also found that another enabler of vision implementation is alignment: 'clarifying what the vision means in regard to each individual position within the organization, and making sure that the resources to execute the vision are in place'. The communication of the vision should be tailored to the needs of the people at the different positions in the organization. What the vision means for senior managers in terms of the actions required of them may be different from the implications of the vision for salesmen. Communicating the vision will involve not only painting a picture of the future but also highlighting what this means for the different positions within the organization.

Summary

A vision is a description of a desirable future state. Visions are important for successful organizational change. All change, whether radical or not, whether of an organization or only a part of it, require a vision.

Effective visions are compelling – they provide clarity and direction and galvanize followers. Compelling visions connect followers intellectually and emotionally and focus their efforts on the direction set by the vision. Effective visions are also aligned with the core purpose of the organization – the reason the organization exists. They thus enable the attainment of the organizational mission.

Good visions also provide coherence to change actions. They connect the various change initiatives and give them meaning. Change recipients can see how small actions fit into the picture of the future. We also saw that an important characteristic of good visions is that they be achievable. If change recipients do not believe the vision can be actualized they are not likely to commit to it. Change agents must ensure that resources are available for the change, new skills and competencies can be obtained, etc. Visions remain dreams if employees do not believe they are realistic.

We saw in this chapter that followers often have different images about the future. A good vision is well communicated such that one image of the desired future emerges and becomes prevalent, even universal. Involving employees in crafting the vision is one way to get a common understanding of the vision.

There are two approaches to crafting the vision – a top-down approach or involvement of all levels. We saw that outsiders tend to involve others in crafting a new vision. They hardly know the organization and need input from organizational members. Culture (organizational and societal) may also influence the choice of approach. If employees have expectations of participation it may be wise to ensure they are involved in the process of crafting the vision.

Visions are important in the African cultural context. Humane leadership style and the Charismatic/Value based leadership styles were culturally endorsed by followers as effective leadership styles in Africa. These leaders inspire with a vision, are compassionate and considerate. In sharing the vision, these leaders communicate the benefits of the vision to all.

To ensure the vision is shared, attention should be paid to the level of education of the change recipient, generational differences, ability to speak the lingua franca of the country, etc. Finally, the enablers of vision implementation in this context are communication and vision alignment.

The vision is the starting off point for change. All other choices in the change plan derive from the vision. A strong vision is a necessary but not a sufficient condition for change. Managers need to articulate a vision with a corresponding strategic plan and have the ability to manage the change called for by such plans (Zaccaro and Banks 2004: 368).

Notes

1 Akunyili D. (2004). *Public Sector Performance – The Case of NAFDAC*, p.13.
2 *CMC Connect: The Challenge of Realizing the Company Vision*. Lagos Business School Case.
3 Ibid, p.1.
4 Ibid. p.9.
5 *CMC Connect* Case, p.11.

4

THE CHANGE TARGET – WHAT TO CHANGE

Introduction

Change strategists and agents have to make several choices in leading change in their organizations. Once a decision has been made to initiate change, the next decision to be made is the choice of the change vision. In the last chapter, we argued that a vision is necessary for successful change. The vision describes the destination or end state. People want to see the future before setting out towards it. However, the vision remains a dream, an aspiration unless specific actions are taken to actualize it. One of these actions is the choice of change targets – what to change.

Change leaders must find an answer to the question: what must be changed to get the organization or unit to the desired future state? One reason why change initiatives fail to achieve the desired outcomes is the fact that the vision is not translated into specific targets.

In the last chapter, we saw that Yomi Badejo-Okusanya communicated the new vision of CMC Connect to all employees. Yet, he was frustrated by the slow pace of change. He wondered if employees saw the vision as 'building castles in the air'.

The challenge was that the employees did not see a connection between the vision and their day-to-day activities. One of them commented: 'All employees know the company's vision; the MD goes on and on about it. He communicates the vision at every opportunity. But I don't see it. Okay, you want us to be the best in West Africa, to be the best in this, to be the best in that. But the other day, I said I needed money to buy credit for my phone so that I can make business calls and that was a problem. Everything doesn't fit together.'

While an organizational structure had been defined, roles and reporting lines were not very clear. The resources to actualize the vision were not available at the time. There was also a need to make changes to a number of systems – the performance management system, the reward system, etc. Change did not begin to happen until management started to work on specific change targets.

Identifying Change Targets

The importance of change targets in successful change has been highlighted in the change literature. It is seen as one of the important considerations for effective organizational change. According to Armenakis and Bedeian (1999: 293), change content or targets are the substance of the change. In their review of change literature in the preceding ten year period, they found that the targets investigated by researchers were: new strategies, organizational structures and performance-incentive systems. Self *et al.* (2007: 212) also identified the target variables in the change literature: changes in structure, human resource practices, technology, total quality management, social issues and the physical setting.

Porras and Silvers (1991: 52) presented a model of planned change in which they argue that change interventions alter key organizational target variables and lead to individual and organizational outcomes. The target variables are: organizing arrangements (strategies, structures, formal reward systems, etc.); social factors (culture, management style, etc.); technology (equipment, workflow design, etc.) and physical setting (ambience, space configuration, interior design, etc.).

Every change initiative has a target or content – what has to be changed to realize the vision for the change. Changes in the target variables should result in improved organizational performance (Self *et al.* 2007: 212). Several targets have been identified in the change literature. Burke (2002) argues that if the change is transformational, change targets are more fundamental. For example, a new mission, strategy and culture may be required in a radical change such as integration following a merger. Thus, the nature of the change influences the choice of targets for the change. Radical changes may require not only changes in the mission and strategy but also the organizational vision. The bottom line is that changes in the chosen target(s) should realize the vision and provide the expected outcomes.

Let us now turn our attention to how Alpha plc[1] crafted an organizational change vision and identified change targets. The new managing director of Alpha plc took over a company that was doing well. Stock market analysts classified the company as a blue chip company in the fast-moving consuming goods industry. Less than a year after he took charge, the macroeconomic environment changed. The Naira was devalued by more than 300 per cent. Because the economy was heavily import-dependent prices skyrocketed. The commercial banks became even more short-term oriented, making long-term funds increasingly unavailable. The purchasing power of consumers was reduced.

Like many other companies in the country, Alpha plc felt the impact of the macroeconomic environment. Even though sales grew compared to the previous year, they were only at 85 per cent of the budget projections. Profits began to fall. During his first months in office, the new managing director focused on one change target: improving internal operations. Quality teams were introduced and significant reductions in costs were achieved. However, the managing director felt that something more fundamental had to be done to improve the long-term prospects of the business. The top management team spent a few months rethinking the business. If the company were to begin again what kind of structure would it have? Which processes and systems would be needed? The documentation process, for example, needed an overhaul as computers merely trailed the paper work. They also asked themselves if the company had the right people and if these people were in the right jobs. Together with the top team, the managing director crafted a vision for the company with a four-year time frame.

To make the vision a reality, the top management agreed on a number of change targets with senior managers. It was decided that the company focus on its core competence and outsource non-core activities. Transportation and canteen services, housing maintenance and legal services were to be outsourced. Inefficient processes were identified. New equipment, a new structure of relationships and an upgrading of management capabilities were required if the vision was to become a reality (Figure 4.1).

The Alpha case illustrates the need to identify change targets once a vision has been crafted. Without specific action steps to implement the change in the targets, the vision will not be realized.

Consider the change targets identified by Dora Akunyili and her Team at NAFDAC (Figure 4.2). As we saw in the last chapter, a new mission and vision

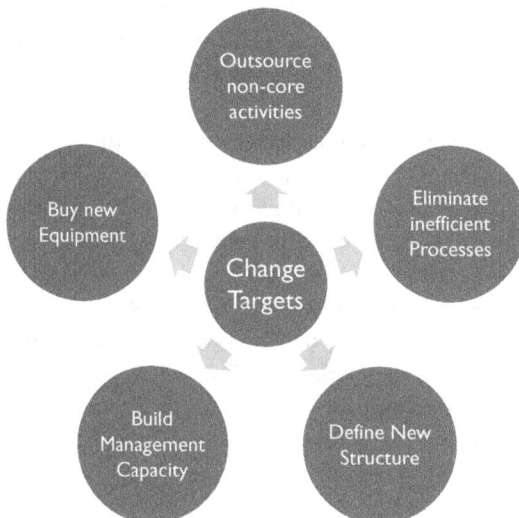

FIGURE 4.1 Change targets in Alpha plc

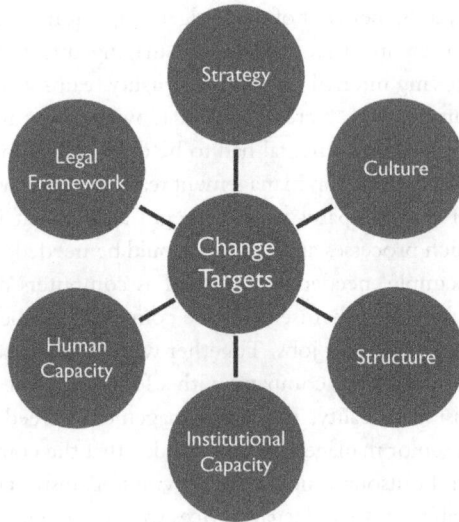

FIGURE 4.2 The change targets at NAFDAC

for the agency were defined and agreed on at a corporate retreat. In order to realize the vision, Dora and her team focused on a number of change targets.

The organizational structure of the agency was changed. The Inspectorate Directorate was split in two: Establishment and Port Inspection. An Enforcement Directorate was created. The latter was to work with the Federal Task Force on Fake and Counterfeit Drugs to ensure no unwholesome drugs were produced or sold in Nigeria. Dora Akunyili recommended with the approval of the Minister of Health that the Director of Enforcement be appointed the Chairman of the National Task Force. Thus, all enforcement in the country was supervised by NAFDAC and potential conflicts with the Federal Task Force were avoided.

Another change target was the legal framework of the agency. The management saw the need to invest the power to hire and fire in the Council (the equivalent of a board of directors). Hitherto, the Civil Service Commission took all decisions regarding hiring, discipline and firing. There was also a need to review upward the penalties for offences by producers and marketers of fake and adulterated products. A proposal was sent to the National Assembly and was enacted into law. The law provided the necessary framework to enable NAFDAC to 'safeguard the health of the Nation'. It also made it possible for the agency to generate 70 per cent of its annual revenues from its activities.

Dora Akunyili and her team also focused on building human and institutional capacity. Members of staff were sent on training programmes at home and abroad. Laboratories with up-to-date analytical equipment, refrigerators, generators, etc. were built in different parts of the country.

Perhaps the most important target of the change programme was the organizational culture. During the first few years, NAFDAC's management focused on the fight against corruption within the agency. Members of staff who were found guilty of corrupt activities were fired. An incentive system was also introduced. Any member of staff who caught or provided information leading to the apprehension of a fake drug manufacturer or distributor was sent on a course abroad and received a very attractive travel allowance.

To sum up so far: Dora and her team identified change targets which could bring about change in the moribund agency and actualize the new vision. The new legal framework made it possible for the agency to make money from sanctions. It also gave the Council the power to fire members of staff without recourse to the Civil Service Commission. The new organization structure was aligned with the new strategy of reducing litigation and enforcing standards. The Enforcement Director was appointed the Chairman of the Task Force, a position which gave him the legal powers to shut down the premises of offenders. The state-of-the-art laboratories made it possible for the agency to carry out tests on drugs and food products. The key change targets were the culture, the legal framework, the structure, and institutional and human capacity. By focusing on these targets, Dora and her team effectively changed the agency and actualized the change vision.

Achieving Alignment of Change Targets with the Vision

According to Porras and Silvers (1991: 55), the change vision shapes the change targets and give them coherence and direction. The Equity Bank case highlights the importance of alignment between the company mission, the vision for the change and the change targets. This alignment energizes employees as they see a connection between the mission, the vision and the day-to-day actions in the organization. As Kretzschmar put it: 'As a result of this high alignment employees and managers had a frame of reference for their high level of empowerment. Being an employee at Equity Bank very fast became a kind of status symbol. Equity Bank attracts the most talented people in the country to join the bank as employees and to work at Equity Bank's mission and vision.'[2]

How did Equity achieve alignment? Equity Bank's mission has not changed over the years. Before Equity (which was a micro finance institution) became a bank in 2006, management led the organization in the definition of the vision for the bank. The key success factors for the realization of the vision were identified and management focused its attention and action on these factors (Table 4.1). By working on these change targets (the seven critical success factors), management was confident that the vision would be actualized.

The transformation involved changes to the following: culture, technology, customer value proposition, governance, quality of asset portfolio, operations, and strategic expansion. For each critical success factor, activities to be carried out

TABLE 4.1 Equity Bank's Critical Success Factors for the Mission and Vision

An organizational culture that values people, enhances performance and supports the business
Market led, innovative and customer focused
Quality effective and efficient operations
Growing a high-quality asset portfolio
Robust, efficient and effective systems and processes
Value maximization to stakeholders
Execution of strategically planned expansion
Customer experience and brand protection

were identified and measurable goals were set. By working on these change targets, management was confident that the vision would be realized, and it was.

To summarize thus far. The cases discussed above highlight the importance of the choice of change targets for the success of a change initiative. The change target focuses action on the actualization of the vision. While the vision tells us *who* we want to be, the target answers the question *what* do we have to do to get to the desired destination?

Obviously, the change target will depend on the vision and the organizational context. Likely targets of change are: the business model, the organizational structure, technology, processes, systems, and organizational culture. Even the physical layout of the office or factory may need to change to actualize the vision. In the next section, we discuss some common change targets in the developing country context.

Some Change Targets in the African Context

In the first chapter of this book, we presented some data which shows that African economies are growing. Many African nations are implementing reforms. These reforms have made these countries attractive for foreign direct investments. We argued that, if Africa's growth is to be sustained, organizations in Africa must take advantage of the improved environment and overcome the challenges of operating in these markets. One such challenge is the shortage of a skilled workforce (Kamoche 2011: 1).

Building Human Capacity

The multinationals, as well as the large companies, are able to offer a better employee value proposition and attract skilled people to their organizations. Many local firms lack the wherewithal to compete favourably with the multinationals. The problem is compounded by the fact that the limited talent pool tends to command a premium and to move from one organization to another. A number of firms have initiated change in order to develop requisite skills and competencies.

Both GTBank in Nigeria and Equity Bank in Kenya have instituted new employee development programmes. The former has a 4-month induction programme. In addition to building technical skills, new recruits are taught the values and culture of the Bank. At the end of the period, new recruits must pass an examination to qualify to work in GTBank. Those who fail are immediately offered employment by competitors. The bank has not employed an expatriate since its inception.

Seven Seas Technologies in Kenya and Computer Warehouse Group in Nigeria also build talent for their companies and for the industry. Computer Warehouse Group has an academy where new recruits are trained. The firm keeps about 25 per cent of the new recruits, another 25 per cent go to their customers and the rest are taken up by the industry. They consciously develop talent for the industry and thus increase the pool of talent available in the country.

Changing Organizational Structure

African countries have privatized state-owned enterprises and implemented other reforms. These have made their economies more stable and attractive for investment. The influx of Chinese firms as well as other multinationals has increased the level of competition in many industries. Many organizations (both private and public) have implemented turnaround strategies. Some of the targets of these changes were the organizational structure and the culture.

Dora Akunyili and her team turned around NAFDAC. One target of the change was the structure. She created the Enforcement Directorate which was responsible for enforcing regulation on food, drug and other products. She split the inspectorate division into two: establishment and port inspection. This made for focus and greater efficiency.

Changing Organizational Culture

House *et al.* (2004: 244) defined culture as the 'assumptions, values and practices developed over time that influence the nature of interrelationships within the community. These assumptions help determine desirable and undesirable behaviour among the members and sustain the community.' A number of change initiatives in the African environment involved substantial change in these organizations. In many of these turnarounds, the organizational culture was a target of change. Many of the culture changes were driven by mergers and acquisitions, changes in the business model, etc. In all of these changes, there was a need to realize a new vision.

According to Schein (2010: 293), changing culture through turnaround involves: 'defining new values and goals through teaching, coaching, changing the structure and process where necessary, consistently paying attention to rewarding evidence of learning the new ways, creating new slogans, stories, myths and rituals, and in other ways coercing people into adopting new behaviours'. This is what Dora Akunyili and her team did at NAFDAC.

President Obasanjo called Dora Akunyili in 2001 and asked her to take charge of NAFDAC and turn it around. Corruption, bureaucracy and a nonchalant attitude to work were the norm at NAFDAC at the time. Dora and her team were convinced that the prevailing culture was an obstacle to the realization of the vision. They therefore took active steps to rid the agency of corruption and to change the attitude of the staff. New values and norms were defined and employees were encouraged to imbibe them; those who did not were fired.

She introduced incentives to encourage members of staff to report cases of fake or adulterated drugs and products. Those who reported these cases not only witnessed the destruction of the fake products, but also they were sent on training programmes abroad and paid attractive travel allowances. There were sanctions for failing to report cases and for accepting bribes. A disciplinary committee met every month for two years to discuss cases of corruption. Those who were found guilty were fired. A lot of time and money was spent on building the capacity of employees so they could carry out their functions. In five years, the culture had changed.

Equity Bank Kenya went through a major change in 1994. The change driver, James Mwangi, wanted to instil a customer service culture in the organization. James and a consultant conducted training programmes to build the new values into the organization. Deviant behavior was sanctioned. James Mwangi, who later became the managing director of Equity Bank said: 'I champion the DNA of the bank. I cascade the vision. My role is to live the mission and vision; to set the example, to the best of my ability. I never do anything even subconsciously that goes against the mission and vision. Our mission and vision have remained the same over the years. What we have done is give it a wider geographical space, scale it up, use words that reflect the changing times. The spirit has not changed. We built the culture over time. I pushed it till it acquired a life of its own. I never in my actions or behaviour contradict the culture.'[3] Today, Equity Bank is one of the most profitable banks in Kenya.

Tushman and O'Reilly (1997: 100) asserted that 'the values and norms that drive behaviour are among the most critical factors in determining long-term strategic success'. A new strategy may require certain behaviours and not others. If the values and norms are not shared the culture does not exist, and the strategy will not be successful. Therefore, '[t]o manage organizational culture effectively managers must be clear in their minds about the type of culture and the specific norms and values that will help the organization reach its strategic goals: next they must decide how to promote the needed norms and to diminish the importance of those that may hinder the attainment of critical tasks'[4] (see Table 4.2).

One of the challenges of leadership is the creation of a culture that supports and realizes the change vision. An innovation strategy may require new norms and values. Tushman and O'Reilly (1997) found that innovative companies had

TABLE 4.2 Developing the Norms and Values of a New Culture

What are our core values?
What values will ensure realization of the business strategy?
How do we ensure that these values are truly shared?
How do we ensure that they are applied?
How do we pass the values on to new entrants?
What happens when the values are violated?
What should be done to ensure we live the values?
How do we build the appropriate culture in our units?
Which practices, systems etc. go against the culture and send wrong signals?

---

norms and values that promoted both creativity and implementation. The norms that promote innovation are support for risk-taking and tolerance of mistakes. Obviously, if there is a low tolerance of mistakes, little innovation is likely to occur as people become risk averse. The innovative companies had a culture that, among other things, encouraged experimentation, fast decision making and openness, and tolerated mistakes.

The mergers in the banking industry in Nigeria threw up many cultural challenges. No two organizations have exactly the same way of doing things. In bringing together four banks, a clash of cultures is inevitable. A major challenge for the management of the new entity is the destruction of aspects of the old culture and the creation of a new culture that will deliver business objectives and create a healthy work environment. This involves unlearning old ways and learning new ones. The new culture acts as glue; it brings together people from different legacy companies.

Change is ultimately about people. It requires people to think and to do things differently. The change in behaviour is expected to result in improved individual performance and this should lead to improved organizational performance (Burke 2002). A change in attitude is often required for successful organizational change; people drive the processes, systems, technology, strategy and even the vision.

So far we have argued that the recognition of a performance gap and the felt need for change lead to a decision to change or to accept the status quo. If a decision to change is taken, a vision of the future is then crafted. Next, the change targets are identified. Change targets are those aspects of the organization that must be changed if the vision is to be realized. In the next section, we make a distinction between primary and secondary targets of change.

Primary and Secondary Change Targets

Let us begin with an example. Data Technologies (name disguised) began operations in Lagos. Some years later, it opened branches in Abuja, Port Harcourt and Warri. The marketing department, which was in Lagos, sourced projects for all the branches. The branches were responsible for the implementation of projects and reported to the head of the engineering department in Lagos.

A few years later, the general manager felt there was a need to grow the company's revenues more aggressively and create opportunities for people to grow within the organization. He had benefited from such growth. He now headed a subsidiary within a group and wanted to create business units which could later become subsidiaries of Data Technologies. He decided to create subsidiaries in the different towns. Even though many of Data Technologies' customers all over the country had their headquarters in Lagos, he felt that Data Technologies could develop the markets outside Lagos. He decided to restructure the organization. He was convinced that if the managers developed the local markets the company could optimize the technology it had deployed and create growth opportunities for the staff.

The HR Manager of Data Technologies was very concerned about this change. Who would the branch managers (now business unit managers) report to? The Head of Marketing? Engineering? The General Manager? The branches were run by engineers whose experience was limited to installation and mainte-nance of systems. Some of them had never been involved in marketing or busi-ness development. Will they make the transition to business managers? Should she attract people from outside the organization to run the branches when the whole idea was to create opportunities for staff? Perhaps some training and coach-ing would help. She knew one engineer who was looking forward to becoming a business unit manager but who could not manage people.

The question of rewards was also on her mind. How will the business manag-ers be rewarded? The head of the Lagos office will get a large majority of the accounts simply because he is based in Lagos. How would performance be com-pared across branches? Who would evaluate the performance of the business unit managers?

This short case highlights a number of issues. The decision to change the structure had implications for other systems. Thus, while the structure was the primary target of the change, some secondary targets were necessary to reinforce the change in the primary target. Some of the secondary targets in this case were: the performance management and reward systems. In choosing change targets, strategists must ask themselves if the main or primary targets are enough to bring about the desired changes, or if the primary targets should be supported with the secondary targets.

The secondary targets must be aligned with the primary target. The decision to implement a matrix structure opens up new decision points: selection of busi-ness unit managers, identification of development needs, planning and execution of development plans, re-design of the performance and reward system.

A decision to devolve power down the organizational ladder raises the issue of control and incentives. Empowerment involves moving not only power, infor-mation and knowledge but also rewards. Therefore, a decision to re-allocate decision rights (primary target) would have to be supported by secondary targets (reward structure, control systems).

A few words about choosing change targets: managers may find some frameworks useful in choosing appropriate change targets. For example, Galbraith's (1995: 12) Star Model is a useful framework for understanding the need for alignment between strategy and other organizing elements. According to Galbraith (1995), strategy should be aligned with structure, people, processes and rewards. A change in strategy will necessitate a change in structure (roles, reporting relationships and what he calls decision making power). It may also require a change in processes and other people practices. The new strategy may have implications for employee skills and competencies. The organization may have to develop talent to ensure they have the right competencies. Finally, the reward system can be used to align employee and organizational goals.

In the next section, we present what we consider the key success factors for choosing appropriate change targets.

Key Success Factors

The ability to identify what needs to change is critical for the success of the change effort. If the right targets are not selected and acted upon, the vision will not be realized.

We saw earlier in this chapter that the target of the change at Alpha plc was the structure. In the harsh macroeconomic environment at the time, management felt that by focusing on its core competence it would actualize its vision of becoming the best manufacturing firm in the country. On a closer look, however, one wonders if management did not miss a more important target of change. At the time, Alpha's receivables and inventories were at an all-time high and interest rates were very high. The build-up of inventory and receivables was due to a sales competition. Salesmen were pushing goods to distributors and collecting their bonuses and awards while the company's cash position deteriorated until it became a major challenge. The management of receivables should have been identified as one of the change targets.

Each target should have a time frame. Very often, an immediate overhaul is impossible. It is important therefore to have the primary targets divided up into short-, medium- and long-term targets all of which will make the vision a reality. Change agents should bear in mind the need for quick wins. Thus in choosing targets some easy but significant targets should be planned for early in the change programme. This helps gather momentum for the change. Equity Bank identified change targets (the critical success factors) and then for each target, activities to be carried out were agreed, measures for each of the activities were set and finally timelines for delivery were determined.

Who should identify the change targets? There are many approaches. The senior management team and/or the change agents may spearhead the process for not only agreeing the vision but also the change targets. In Alpha plc, the change targets were identified at the management retreat and subsequent meetings which were attended by middle and senior-level managers.

However, management may not have all the answers. Input from people at other levels of the organization may be desirable. The whole organization can be challenged to contribute to the future. An example: the new CEO of an organization wanted to initiate change in the ailing institution. With the aid of consultants, a business model was agreed. The organization would serve micro, small and medium-sized enterprises. The proportion of equity to loans was agreed.

The entire team was divided into small groups and given specific assignments: they were to examine the present situation, identify what would get in the way of the vision, and make proposals on moving ahead. Part of their task was to study other successful institutions that had implemented change of this nature (whether in the same industry or not). Several teams visited successful companies and interviewed managers in these companies.

Finally, the teams came together and agreed on the change targets. They agreed that the organization would be structured around the market segments. The structure would also be flattened (from 12 levels to 7 or 8 levels). Processes would to be automated, control systems developed and, finally, ways to attract funds into the institution for onward lending and/or investment were agreed.

Summary

For change to happen, it is not enough to have a clear vision. Choice of change targets is critical. This will depend on the nature of the change. Radical changes may require a change in targets such as strategy, culture and organizational structure.

All targets must be aligned with the vision and contribute to its realization. The change vision gives coherence to the change targets. A vision of a paperless office without a target of automating processes is not likely to be realized. The alignment of vision and change targets communicates to change recipients that the vision is achievable and can help galvanize energies towards the realization of the vision.

We argued that one of the challenges of sustained growth in Africa is the shortage of skilled workforce. Some organizations in Africa develop a talent pool for their own needs and for the industry. After a rigorous selection exercise, these organizations hire candidates and take them through several months of training to equip them with the skills and attitudes required for performance.

We made a distinction between primary and secondary targets. While the primary targets of change may be the organizational structure, secondary targets such as performance management and reward systems may be needed to support the change in the primary target and ensure the vision is realized.

Change strategists and implementers should ensure that the appropriate change targets are chosen and acted upon. Choice of the wrong targets may lead the organization into a lull – nothing happens and the change vision is not realized. Change recipients may become disillusioned.

Finally, target should have timeframes. In deciding on timelines, change strategists and implementers should look out for potential quick wins in the short term which will communicate to organizational members that change is actually happening. In the next chapter, we discuss the choice of success measures.

Notes

1 The company name has been disguised.
2 Ketzschmar, F., quoted in MicroSave 2007, p.6.
3 *The Transformation of Equity Bank*, p.8.
4 Tushman and O'Reilly (1997), p.101.

5

SUCCESS MEASURES

Introduction

The change model presented in this book is a decision-making model. We have argued that change strategists and agents have to take a number of decisions around change. These decisions should be coherent among themselves; they should all lead to the actualization of the change vision. In this chapter, we discuss the choice of success measures. During the planning stage, change actors should agree on the measures of performance – the indicators that the desired future is being realized.

The chapter is structured thus: first we explain why measures of organizational change success are important. Next we highlight, both from the literature and practice, the typical measures of success used to evaluate the impact of change initiatives. Before we discuss success measures in the African context, we highlight some of the key success factors in determining good evaluation criteria for organizational change.

The Importance of Measures of Organizational Change Success

The purpose of planned change is to shift an organization from an initial state to a different end state in order to achieve one or more objectives (Hempel and Martinsons 2009: 461). Change initiatives are undertaken, in spite of the costs and huge challenges, to achieve a number of objectives or outcomes. However, past research suggests that most change initiatives lack measurement criteria. Skinner (2004) noted that plans for the implementation of change initiatives did not include an explicit assessment of either the implementation or the impact of the initiative on the organization. Hempel and Martinsons (2009) also found in their study that formal evaluation criteria for judging the success or otherwise of change initiatives were not developed. Without clear performance metrics it is difficult to evaluate the success of change.

The restructuring exercise by Alpha plc referred to earlier in this book was carried out with clinical accuracy and attention to detail. Employees who lost their jobs as a result of the exercise received redundancy letters together with cheques covering their emoluments the same day they were told their jobs were no longer needed. Despite the fact that Alpha had two in-house unions, the restructuring exercise was peaceful.

At the end of the exercise, the Human Resource Director was asked if the change had been successful. His answer was vague: people are now busy and there is no loitering; he had not given much thought to the evaluation of the outcomes of the restructuring exercise. People had been let go, new structures were in place but because the primary objective of the change was not clear, it could not be measured.

If measures of success are not agreed *ab initio* and responsibility for monitoring results assigned, an evaluation of the change is difficult. The measures of success are the template against which the success of the change initiative is evaluated during and at the end of implementation. In the absence of measures of success there may be no concrete evidence that change has occurred.

The management of NAFDAC did not specify the criteria for evaluating the success of the change initiative in the agency at the beginning of the change. Results were not slow in coming but there was no objective information to show that the agency had changed and was succeeding in safeguarding the lives of Nigerians. It was generally believed that the agency had changed but no one knew by how much. About five years after the change initiative began, the management commissioned a study to assess the impact of the change. The results of the study provided baseline data and made it possible to track specific measures over time. Any sceptics, in the face of data showing that the agency was indeed realizing its vision, would have had to admit that change had taken place at NAFDAC.

Many researchers have pointed out the need for evaluation of change initiatives for successful change (Doyle *et al.* 2000). However, change initiatives are not often evaluated formally (Skinner 2004). Instead, informal evaluations are carried out by people using different criteria and coming to disparate, and sometimes conflicting, conclusions.

In the absence of success measures and formal measurement of outcomes, individuals at all levels make their own assessments and construct their own reality (Skinner 2004: 15). These evaluations tend to reflect personal viewpoints and perspectives; they are not often shared. The challenge is that future actions may be taken based on 'personal perception and subjective evaluations that result from relatively narrow perspectives' (Skinner 2004: 16). Thus, followers may not be working towards the achievement of the same outcomes.

Measures of success enable change implementers to do a number of things. The performance metrics keep followers on the same page. Everyone in the organization knows the desired outcome or destination. The milestones and indicators give a clear indication as to whether or not the vision is being realized. The success measures also make it possible for managers and employees to focus attention and resources on what counts. Without landmarks and performance indicators it is difficult to know how the organization is doing, how close it is to the desired destination.

Clarity regarding outcome measures makes it easier for change strategists to focus on what counts for the vision. As soon as Ken Olori took charge of the moribund government agency, he worked with the staff in crafting a new vision for the agency. The vision was to be actualized through a change in the business model, changes in the organizational culture, structure and processes. He set up transformational teams who worked with the Project Steering Committee. The first task of the teams was to come up with performance indicators, milestones and timelines.

They agreed on an overarching goal for the next four years and a goal for each year. Clarity regarding what needed to be achieved and at what time helped Ken Olori attract the resources he needed and overcome the huge political and motivational challenges he faced. Without the key performance indicators, it would have been difficult to remain focused on the change initiative – let alone achieve anything.

Thus, success measures provide evidence of progress or lack of it and facilitate action taking. They also make it possible for a change strategist to gauge his or her contribution. In the case of NAFDAC, the study of the impact of the changes provided baseline data for assessing future performance of the agency.

What to Measure

The measures of organizational change success may be at the organizational or individual level (Hempel and Martinsons 2009: 462) since change initiatives may be undertaken to actualize a new vision for the whole organization or a part of it. Success measures may be measures of change outcomes (organizational and individual outcomes), the change implementation process and the change inputs.

Outcome Measures

Change is introduced in order to achieve certain objectives or outcomes. Typical outcome measures include: revenues, profits, cash flow, market share, return on equity, production efficiency rates, customer satisfaction indices, and number of repeat customers. For NAFDAC, measures of success include: percentage reduction in the incidence of fake drugs, reduction in the number of deaths due to consumption of fake or adulterated products, number of products which bear the NAFDAC registration number and best-before dates.

The vision of the change initiative may vary from one change initiative to another and across organizations. Measures of success will therefore vary widely. An acquisition may have been made for strategic reasons. Thus, financial measures may not be the principal evaluation criterion. If a telecommunications firm acquired another in a particular country mainly to enable it to build the network across the continent, the criteria for evaluating the success of the acquisition would be more strategic than financial.

For Equity Bank, success is not measured primarily in terms of profitability. Its mission and vision are centred on the economic and social empowerment of the *mwananchi*, the common folk. For the bank, therefore, success has many faces: growth in number of customers, volume of customer deposits and gross loans, in addition to growth in profits, total assets and shareholder funds. Success to Equity Bank means that more of the common folk have access to financial services; more of them can obtain loans to grow their small businesses; success means meeting the aspirations of the *mwananchi*.

An important consideration in determining the measures of success is the stakeholder perspective. A question change strategists and agents should ask themselves is: how will key stakeholders measure the success of the change initiative? One change management team identified five important stakeholders: customers, employees, investors, government, and creditors and other suppliers. The team defined performance metrics for each of these stakeholders.

The company had accumulated losses of millions of Naira. The team recognized that investors would measure the success of the turnaround in terms of return to profitability and return on investment. Creditors and suppliers were likely to focus on the financial capability of the organization. A success measure for these two groups would be an improvement in the cash flow.

The government was particularly interested in safety due to several mishaps in the industry in recent times. The regulator was thus likely to measure a successful turnaround with the level of safety in the operations. Finally, customers would be interested in increased levels of satisfaction. The management believed that customer satisfaction would be driven by employee satisfaction. The agreed metrics included an improvement in overall customer satisfaction rating of a specific percentage over the previous year and an improvement in employee satisfaction – this in spite of planned layoffs. Table 5.1 shows the performance indicators which were agreed as the measures of success of the turnaround.

Success may also be assessed at the level of the individual. According to Armenakis and Bedeian (1999: 304), 'attention to "bottom-line" criteria alone is insufficient for assessing successful change'. They argue that affective and behavioural measures should be included in the list of desired outcomes of the change initiative. One reason for the failure of change initiatives is the lack of attention to the impact of change on people. Tracking measures such as employee commitment or loyalty should help change agents reduce the risk of unexpected negative outcomes of the change initiative or the process. By choosing success measures at

TABLE 5.1 Success Measures using a Stakeholder Perspective

Customer satisfaction indices
Increase of X% in overall customer satisfaction over previous year
Employee satisfaction rating
Improvement in overall employee satisfaction of Y% over previous year in spite of intended layoffs
Government
Safety – zero tolerance
Creditors and other suppliers
Improvement in the cash flow
Investors
Return to profitability
Return on investment of Z%

---

the individual level, change strategists want to ensure that change agents do not negatively impact these factors as they implement change in the organization.

Even though the senior management of Alpha plc did not set out performance criteria to measure the success of the change initiative, they evaluated the impact of the restructuring exercise a week after implementation. An instrument designed to measure reactions to the change was administered to employees at all levels of the organizational structure. Employees were asked why the restructuring was done, and whether the process was fair and well managed. Results of the study shaped subsequent communication and interventions.

Measures of Change Inputs and the Implementation Process

In order to bring about change, the implementers of change usually sensitize employees about the new vision, communicate the change plan, organize training programmes, etc. They plan a number of interventions aimed at effecting the change. Change implementers can measure the inputs into the change process such as the timeliness and quality of these interventions. One reason why some organizations measure change inputs is that the inputs contribute to the quality of the change outcomes. If awareness sessions are delayed, communication of the vision is poor and training on new skills and competencies is not done, resistance to change may be so stiff that it overwhelms the change. By measuring inputs into the change process, the organization ensures that change implementers are working according to the change plan.

Poor change management has consequences for the business and the people: low morale, low productivity, higher employee turnover intention, etc. All these lower the rate of adoption of the new systems or processes which the change was designed to facilitate. Therefore, as people go through various stages of change, it is important to measure their reactions. How many employees are actively resisting the change? How many are not only resisting the change but have developed a followership? How many are reflecting on whether or not to commit to the change? How many are apathetic towards the change? As Armenakis and Bedeian (1999: 304) in their review of research on outcome variables stated: 'The actions required to implement a desired change may evoke unintended responses like denial and resistance, and further result in employees experiencing feelings of stress and cynicism, as well as reduced organizational commitment. Both research and practical experience suggest that such responses can serve as complementary criteria or markers for tracking the likelihood of employees enacting behaviors necessary for achieving desired changes.'

It is also important to measure the rate of adoption of the new system. For example, an organization was automating its processes and introducing Oracle software. Some sensitization and training sessions were scheduled. It was considered important to track the speed of adoption of Oracle (i.e., the number of people using the new system), proficiency in the use of the product, etc. These were included in the measures of implementation success. During the implementation, the change agents tracked how many people had changed their behaviour and were fully engaged with the system and how many were still taking baby steps or simply refusing to change.

Having success measures *ab initio* facilitates the evaluation and refinement of the change and ultimately contributes to the success of the change. Change should not result in a demoralized workforce. At least, if it does, this should be spotted early enough and some interventions carried out to bring morale levels back up. The understanding gained from these measures should 'alert change agents to the need for modifying selected implementation procedures necessary for the adoption and institutionalization of change' (Armenakis and Bedeian 1999: 308).

Key Success Factors

The first requirement for good measures of success is that they be consistent with the vision. The measures of success simply specify the change destination in measurable terms. Outcome measures should be linked to the change vision.

In establishing success measures, how the information will be obtained, the timelines and the cost of obtaining the information for tracking purposes should be considered. Otherwise, tracking is not possible and information is not available for decision making.

The appropriate technology can make management information available in a timely manner. For example, after Equity Bank launched a new banking software, performance information became available real time. The information architecture supported the needs of the change team. Management had access to information no matter where they happened to be. Each branch manager could track the indices of performance of his branch and of other branches. Information technology made it possible for both change agents and recipients to track their performance. Immediate recognition for exceptional performance became possible.

Different organizational levels may require different measures. This makes it possible for change recipients to see the connection between their objectives and the overall goals of the change programme. Measures should be cascaded from the corporate level to the business, then to the departments, teams and finally to team members.

Ideally, the performance metrics should be SMART, that is, Specific, Measurable, Achievable, Relevant and Time bound. It may not be possible to measure improvements in all the relevant performance indicators. However, some approximate measures should be established. Qualitative measures may be used where quantitative measures are not possible or do not make much sense.

Responsibility for providing the measures, for supplying the information and for tracking should be assigned. The people to whom these tasks are assigned should be held accountable (the provision of this information in a timely manner may be part of their performance objectives).

Finally, change agents should bear in mind the purpose of the change and the desired outcomes (the success measures) as they take decisions regarding the pace of change, leadership style and winning commitment.

Success Measures in the African Context

As in other environments, performance metrics are not usually identified before the change is implemented. It is therefore difficult to demonstrate that changes are leading to bottom line results. Mutual agreement regarding the need for change and how success will be measured is important for successful change initiatives. To win commitment to change, it is important to track and show as the organization changes.

Success measures in the African context are usually not purely financial measures such as return on investment, profitability and growth in market share. Several interest groups may have a stake in the change. It is advisable to look at social and community issues.

Because the literacy level is low (especially for employees on the lowest rung of the organizational ladder), displaying performance metrics on dashboards on the factory floor or in offices enables tracking and can motivate performance. All employees can track the measures and take corrective action. This transparent system is much appreciated; employees can see what their efforts have contributed to during the period.

It is pertinent to note the difficulty of obtaining reliable data which can serve as the baseline for success measures in the African context. Few databases exist and many of them do not have the same information. Most of the data on Africa which is available are estimates. It is important for change actors therefore to examine the underlying assumptions of these estimates. For example, it is often difficult to obtain data on the relative market share of firms in an industry. If one of the measures of success is improvement in market share, the change agents are likely to encounter difficulties in obtaining reliable data.

While reliable market information may be available from some market research firms in the continent, the cost of the information may be prohibitive for small and mid-sized firms. Change strategists and agents will do well to consider the cost–benefit ratio of obtaining the measures. A survey like the one carried out by NAFDAC to measure the impact of its activities costs money. On the other hand, it is difficult to establish some performance measures without knowledge of the market.

Summary

In this chapter, we argued that change evaluation is not often done. Where it is done, it is often informal using different performance metrics and coming to disparate conclusions. This may be one reason why change initiatives fail.

Performance metrics are a necessary template against which to measure organizational change success. They provide evidence that change has or has not occurred. They enable change agents and recipients to focus energy and resources on what counts for success. Clarity regarding the desired outcomes makes it easier to obtain resources for change from senior management.

The measures of success will depend on the purpose of the change and the desired outcomes. Measures of success can be established at the organizational or the individual level. At the organizational level, performance measures may be financial or strategic. The stakeholder perspective may be adopted in determining measures of organizational change success.

At the individual level, measures of success may include behavioural and attitudinal measures. Employee commitment, resistance to change and stress levels are examples of success measures at the individual level. To reduce the risk of negative outcomes, it is important to track the impact of the change on the people.

In addition to measures of change outcomes, measures of change inputs and implementation should be agreed. For example, the adoption rate and level of proficiency in the use of the new process are performance metrics which provide change strategists and implementers with information for decision making.

In choosing measures of success, the costs of obtaining the required information in a timely manner should be considered. In the African context, obtaining reliable data is difficult. Change agents need to examine the underlying assumptions and make choices regarding which data sources to use.

Finally, measures in the African context are not purely financial. Social measures (such as those used by Equity Bank) are important for successful organizational change.

In the next chapter, we discuss another choice opportunity: the pace and sequence of change.

6

PACE AND SEQUENCE OF CHANGE

Introduction

Change strategists and agents make several strategic decisions as they plan for organizational change. Having decided on the vision for the change and the targets and success measures, they make decisions regarding the pace of the change and its sequence. Pettigrew *et al.* (2001: 704) argue that the more difficult questions in change research are related to where to begin a change initiative (sequence of the change) and what pace of change is appropriate in different settings. Choosing the appropriate pace and sequence of organizational change is difficult in practice.

In this chapter, we discuss the choices regarding pace and sequence of change. First we examine why these choices are important. Then we review research on pace and sequence. Finally, we look at African examples.

Pace and sequence are important decisions in the management of change. Gravenhorst *et al.* (2003: 84) found in their study that resistance to change was related to the way the change process was managed. Both pace and sequence are dimensions of the change process. They are important determinants of change outcomes (Amis *et al.* 2004). The pace of change is the speed and comprehensiveness with which change is introduced while sequence has to do with the order in which key elements (the targets) are changed (Liguori 2012: 507). How fast or how slow a change initiative is implemented is important for the success of the change. Many change initiatives fail because they drag on so long that they wear out even their most enthusiastic champions.

The pace of change can affect recipients' emotional reaction to the change. According to Smollan *et al.* (2010: 29), organizational change can be an emotion-charged experience for change recipients. Anxiety or anger can result from change that is too quick, too slow or poorly timed. Emotions are important for successful organizational change. They may be positive or negative. Negative emotions can arise if there is no time for recipients to make sense of the new world that has been communicated to them.

Board members often require CEOs to commit to very specific time scales and milestones for organizational change. CEOs are often evaluated on these criteria. In a turnaround situation, shareholders are especially concerned about time; they want to know when the company will begin to show profits. Change recipients also need a sense of how long the change will take and when change outcomes are expected.

Pace of Change

Pace of organizational change refers to the speed of the change (Liguori 2012: 507): how slowly or how swiftly change is implemented. The speed of change is one of the strategic choices that managers explicitly or implicitly make in planning for change (Kotter and Schlesinger 2008). Although researchers agree that the pacing of organizational change is important, there is no agreement regarding which pace is more likely to lead to successful organizational change. Smollan *et al.* (2010: 46) advised managers to distinguish temporal issues from the content of change (targets). They assert that people may not be resistant to the change targets but to temporal aspects of organizational change such as pace.

Research on the pace of organizational change can be divided into two streams: research that seems to indicate that radical change should be revolutionary – key elements should be changed quickly. The study by Romanelli and Tushman (1994) of minicomputer firms represents this view. The second research stream suggests that change should be carried out more slowly to allow recipients assimilate the change (Amis *et al.* 2004; Liguori 2012).

Romanelli and Tushman (1994) argue that radical change should be implemented quickly throughout the organization. This way, momentum for change is created and change agents can shake up the status quo and get the organization to change. Otherwise, resistance could overwhelm the change initiative.

The study by Smollan *et al.* (2010: 46) suggests that participants at different organizational levels had negative emotional reactions to fast-paced change in their organizations. If the change was sudden and fast-paced, negative emotions multiplied. They argue that this may be because fast paced change requires employees to learn new skills and new ways of working quickly. These negative emotions affect the chances of success of organizational change initiatives.

Amis *et al.* (2004) and Liguori (2012) found in their studies that pace did not matter for organizational change success. Results of the longitudinal study of 30 National Sports Organizations in Canada by Amis *et al.* (2004) suggest that organizations which were successful in introducing change in the 12 years of the study followed different paths: some made many fast-paced changes at the beginning and others did not. Liguori (2012: 530) found that radical change was associated with both a fast and a gradual pace; pace did not seem to influence change outcomes.

Change may be gradual (evolutionary) at first. This gives change recipients time to assimilate the change. As recipients learn and become more familiar with the new ways, the pace may be faster (more revolutionary). Liguori (2012: 531) cited Pettigrew *et al.* (1992) who noted that 'a slower change doesn't ensure change to be more manageable, nor does a faster one guarantee the actual transformation of the organization.' However, Kotter and Schlesinger (2008: 138) noted that change efforts that involve a large number of people, but are implemented quickly, may become stalled.

From the literature of organizational change, it seems that there is no conclusive evidence for a fast or slow pace of change. It may depend on the organizational context or pressures in the external environment. Kotter and Schlesinger (2008) conceptualize the pace of organizational change as a continuum varying from rapid implementation to a slower-paced change process. Change agents and strategists choose the appropriate pace depending on a number of factors. Change which is delayed may not deliver benefits. Change which is rushed may not allow time to adapt, and create initiative fatigue, encouraging decay (Buchanan *et al.* 2005: 202).

Factors to Consider in Choosing an Appropriate Pace of Change

The choice of pace of organizational change will depend on a number of factors: the nature of the change target(s), the organizational readiness for change, resource availability, the pressure for results (temporal perspective of change drivers). In the Alpha case referred to above, the pace was slow during the planning and decision-making stage, but the implementation was fast paced.

An important factor that affects the choice of pace is the content of the change: the change targets. Huy (2001) argued that time and content of change are related because some organizational elements can be changed faster than others. For example, organizational structures can be changed much faster than organizational culture.

Changes in some organizing elements cannot be achieved overnight or by fiat. For example, changes in work processes (reengineering) typically take time. Employees must learn new work habits. Changes in processes often require the collaboration of the people who run these processes. They often have tacit knowledge of processes and equipment. 'Frontline employees, who possess much of the tacit knowledge, have to be convinced to articulate part of their know-how which is then validated and programmed' (Huy 2001: 618). The pace of change is likely to be moderate.

A change in the organizational culture requires changing the beliefs and values of the people. Change recipients have to unlearn old behaviours and learn new ones. It also means a change in attitude. People need time to adapt and adopt new ways. This takes time. If change agents are to challenge the values in use they will need to help people learn. For example, a change agent found that employees were in denial regarding the poor customer service provided by the organization. He filmed service failures and aired the videos. Employees analysed the videos, identified root causes of the failures and proffered solutions to the service failures. While this did not bring about a culture change, it did start the employees on the right path. It takes time to change people's beliefs and fundamental assumptions. Culture change usually takes time and change recipients may have to be involved in the process if it is to succeed. Results can be expected in the medium to long term.

It is argued that a fast pace of change makes it possible for people to move on faster. This is especially so if the change involves layoffs. Uncertainty creates a lot of fear and anxiety which distracts from the change initiative. A long drawn out change effort may also give people time to mount political and other pressures to derail the change initiative.

Another consideration in choosing the pace of change is the organizational readiness for change. The study by Smollan *et al.* (2010) suggests that resistance has a temporal dimension. Employees may be resistant to the timing of the change, and not the change itself. Readiness reflects the extent to which an individual or individuals are cognitively and emotionally inclined to accept, embrace, and adopt a particular plan to purposefully alter the status quo (Holt *et al.* 2007: 235). Readiness can be assessed qualitatively (observation or interviews) or quantitatively through the survey instruments (Holt *et al.* 2007). A fast-paced change may be appropriate if employees are generally ready. If not, a slow paced one may be advisable.

Resource availability will affect how fast the change can be implemented. Change costs money. If the resources to fund the change are not available at the beginning, the change agents may decide on a slow pace of change. Without funding, it is difficult to run the training programmes, buy the new equipment or re-brand the organization. The pace of change will be limited by the availability of resources.

Finally, the temporal perspective of the change strategist also influences the choice of pace of change. If the board or important stakeholders expect results in the short term, it is likely that the pace of change will be fast. If the organizational elements to be changed are however not amenable to fast-paced change, desired outcomes may not be achieved. Thus, change agents may be tempted to choose change targets that can produce some results in the short term even though this compromises medium term results.

The Sequence of Organizational Change

An organization is made up of parts; divisions, departments, geographical regions, etc. A question change agents often ask themselves is whether change should be implemented in the whole organization at once or different parts should undergo change at different times. For example, Equity Bank has branches in different regions in Kenya and in other parts of East Africa. An important question for change strategists and agents in the bank is where the change initiative should begin. A sequel to this question is which elements should be changed first.

The sequence of organizational change refers to the order in which key elements should be changed to achieve the change outcomes (Liguori 2012). Sequence is important for a number of reasons. First, by forcing change agents to think through the events, activities and the ordering, it makes change, especially large scale change, more manageable. If sequencing is well done, there is logic in the order of events and they are timed in such a way that they capture 'windows of opportunity in which an intervention could benefit from better receptivity to change and more bountiful resources' (Huy 2001: 613).

An organizational transformation may involve changing reporting relationships (structure), the organizational culture, systems; opening subsidiaries in other markets; etc. Change agents have to consider whether all these targets can/ should be changed at the same time. In some cases, it may not be possible or even advisable to initiative a change in all the targets across the organization at the same time.

Amis et al. (2004) reviewed two schools of thought on the sequence of organizational change. One school (represented by Beer et al. 1990) argues that peripheral elements should be changed first otherwise the change may be truncated by powerful interests who may lose power or other currency by a change to the key elements. The second school of thought holds that high impact elements should be changed first (Greenwood and Hinings 1988). The latter found in their study that organizations that completed change processes changed high-impact elements first. For Tushman and Romanelli (1994), radical change should be implemented quickly and the key elements changed quickly.

Amis et al. (2004) found support in their study for changing high impact elements first. Whether change was fast-paced or not did not matter. 'What is important is the sequence in which organization elements are altered' (Amis et al. 2004: 35). Successful organizations altered high-impact elements first. They concluded: 'the majority of evidence points toward the need to change more central elements earlier on ... changing who has decision-making authority over some important organization function not only alters an important technical aspect of the operation, but also communicates to all the organization's stakeholders that the transformation process is intended to significantly alter the ways in which the organization operates'. Liguori (2012) found support for the supremacy of sequence over pace of organizational change. Sequence is important. Changing key elements first sends a signal to organizational members and other stakeholders that the change is for real. Changing peripheral elements does not.

An example: a new CEO was appointed to transform an ailing airline. Customer service in this airline was one of the worst in the industry. On lost baggage, on-time performance and other key indices, the airline was doing very badly. The CEO and the top team crafted a new vision for the airline. Some of the change targets were: the culture (build a customer service culture), the organizational structure, and finally develop a new brand (through advertising and new livery). It would not make sense to develop a new brand (spend a lot of money on advertising) while the service culture remained awful.

Where to begin (i.e., which unit, department or division) is an important decision. If the change initiative is started in the wrong place, it may meet with so much resistance as to kill the change effort. Take the example of a consultant who was automating the branches of a large bank in Nigeria. The team agreed with the management of the bank that they should begin with the largest branch where the impact would be most felt. However, after a few weeks during which little progress was made, the consultants were frustrated. The branch manager was overtly resistant to the change. His reaction was understandable.

In the prevailing dispensation, branch managers had a lot of power. People queued to cash their cheques, collect bank drafts and for any other transaction. Those who wanted a fast track went to the branch manager's office to beg him to kindly speed up their request. This particular branch served some of the bank's largest customers so the branch manager had a lot of power. With automation, he would lose this power: customers would be served over the counter and within a few minutes.

However, not all the branch managers in the bank were resistant to change. If the consultant had found a change champion among the other managers, he would have proved that the change was possible and then gone to the largest branch with tangible results. The manager of the largest branch would have been less resistant since it would have been perceived as a lack of competence if his branch could not be automated when another branch had done it successfully. It is advisable to begin the change where it is likely to be successful. The consultant could have done a better job of clarifying the role and relevance of branch managers in the new order.

Change agents should ask themselves which part of the organization is ready for change. It is also important to identify the change champions, especially those people who have influence and who believe in the change. Answers to these and similar questions should help change agents in deciding where to begin.

Thus, the elements which should be changed first will depend on a number of factors. If, for example, the level of commitment to the change is high (especially among influencers and those who have to implement these changes), it may not matter so much which elements are changed first. Resource availability may be a constraint. If the resources are not available when needed, it may be difficult to change everything at once. Sequencing the change may be a matter of necessity.

Sequence and Timing of Organizational Change

According to Huy (2001: 613), 'timing refers to the moment an event happens or is planned to happen in a sequence of related events'. Decisions about timing answer the questions: what should be done at each moment in time? What should be achieved at specific times? Timing is, simply, deciding when to do what (Gersick 1994). Timing is related to sequence: the order in which different parts of the organization should be changed.

Timing of different change initiatives is important. Start and end dates, even if tentative, give people a sense that it will be over some day. Timing also helps create 'a more tolerable and effective change rhythm' Huy (2001: 614). Good timing and sequencing prevent an organization from changing too much too fast.

Having a time frame in mind is important; it makes it possible for change agents to evaluate progress against specific delivery dates (Gersick 1994: 13). For example, a change agent committed herself to getting an Enterprise Resource Programme installed and functional in the human resources department of a company in six months. This formed part of her appraisal for that year. Having a specific time frame helped her focus on the goal and assess progress toward achievement of the goal on a regular basis.

Timing is important for winning commitment to change. Alpha plc carried out a restructuring exercise which resulted in 300 employees losing their jobs. About a year before the exercise, the CEO had been doing what Rosabeth Kanter called 'sowing seeds'. In many of his speeches and other communication, he had been talking to employees about the need for change; the macroeconomic environment was changing and a number of companies had laid off employees. When the restructuring was announced, it did not come as a shock to the employees. The management also timed the exercise so that it was a few weeks after the annual general meeting. They effectively avoided a rowdy general meeting.

Factors that Affect the Choice of Sequence of Change

An organization may not have the resources to alter all its parts at the same time. How fast a change initiative can be implemented will depend on the resources available for the change. An organization wanted to introduce an Enterprise Resource Planning (ERP) system to integrate its customer relationship management, manufacturing resource management, supply chain management, finance resource management, and human resource management. This change would involve streamlining processes, changes in work practices and would require employees to learn new skills. The change would impact every part of the business.

For several reasons, it was decided that the change be introduced slowly and one function at a time. The change agents thought it was important to experiment and learn as they progressed. It was common knowledge that these changes tended to take longer than planned and were not always successful. Another reason was that the amount of investment required (in time and money) was huge. By sequencing rollout it was possible to stagger payment and not cause an upheaval in the whole organization at the same time.

In the absence of sufficient resources, change agents may ask themselves a few additional questions: Where will the change initiative have the required impact? Where will learning be assimilated and easily diffused to other parts of the organization? Answers to these and similar questions will help them decide where to begin. In the case of the ERP system implementation, the change agents decided to begin with the human resource management system. This was thought to be easier, would have an impact on employees in terms of improved HR services and hopefully this would help generate commitment to the change. Besides, the HR Director was a champion of the change.

Another consideration in deciding the change sequence is the availability of change agents. Sometimes, there are many change initiatives being implemented in an organization and the same change agents are involved in several of these initiatives. It may be advisable to bring some initiatives to a close before starting new ones. In one organization, the change agents (typically high-potential managers) were involved in several change initiatives. These initiatives were not coordinated. Employees did not perceive a sequence, an ordering of events within each change initiative and across the initiatives. They were overwhelmed by the sheer number of work requirements, e-mails, and meetings. New change initiatives were launched even when old ones had not been concluded. The result was change fatigue. Many of the laudable change visions were not actualized.

Pace and Sequence in the Africa Context

From the literature referred to in this chapter, it is clear that there is no agreement as to what speed or sequence will bring about successful organizational change. Not much research has been done on the pace and sequence of organizational change in the African context. In most of the organizations we studied (the case studies of which are included in this book), it seems that change agents did not make conscious choices regarding the pace and sequence of the change initiative. However, the case of Alpha plc is an exception.

The senior managers of Alpha plc decided, at a senior management meeting, the pace and timing of the re-structuring they were about to initiate. It was to start two weeks after the annual general meeting. The senior managers (the managing director and other executive directors) wanted to avoid disruption of the annual general meeting by employees who would lose their job during the restructuring.

For over six months, the managing director had been talking about the need for change but there was nothing concrete. The external environment was also changing: a number of firms had downsized. The senior management team decided to implement change during one week. They chose the week to carry out the change and agreed on the tasks and activities to be done that week and assigned responsibility for each task/activity.

The directors of finance and human resources spent the weekend previous to the restructuring exercise in a hotel. They prepared the termination letters and the cheques for those to be asked to leave. On Monday morning, they were in the office as usual. The next day, the human resource director met with the senior staff union to sell the restructuring exercise. At about the same time, a manager from the human resource department met with the junior staff union to do the same thing.

On Wednesday, the managing director had a briefing session on the change initiative with senior managers. The corporate affairs manager prepared a press statement which he sent to the press. An official note was sent to the Nigerian Stock Exchange and the finance director went to the Exchange to provide more information on the need and purpose of the restructuring exercise.

On Thursday the human resource manager met with the executives of the national staff union. The managing director sent a memo to all staff explaining the reasons for the restructuring and the decision to shut down the factory the following week. During the afternoon of Thursday and most of Friday, termination letters were given to those who were affected by the restructuring exercise.

When the company was re-opened after the week of recess, all the directors were on hand to welcome their people back and reassure them that the exercise was over.

The management of Alpha plc made conscious decisions about the pace and sequence of organizational change. The restructuring of Alpha plc was planned, the pace and sequence of activities were agreed and followed and, very importantly, it did not meet with resistance even though 300 employees were let go. The company's share price was also not negatively affected.

Choices regarding the pace and sequence of change may not be affected by context (Western or African). Managers should pay more attention to the temporal dimension of change because it facilitates successful change.

Summary

In this chapter, we discussed the choice of the pace and sequence of organizational change. We saw that pace is the speed of the change; it can be fast or slow. The sequence of change is the ordering of the activities of the change initiative. There are two schools of thought regarding pace and sequence of change. One school posits that change is best implemented quickly and all at once. The other school has found support for the thesis that the pace of change may not be so important for organizational success. What is absolutely important is the sequence of change: how the change targets are ordered.

There is a discussion around which targets should be changed first: the key targets or the peripheral targets. Key targets are those that are likely to have a huge impact on the change outcome. By changing these targets, change strategists and agents communicate to the organization that they are serious about the change and employees are to some extent 'forced' to change.

Resistance has a temporal dimension. Employees may resist not the change content itself but the pace and sequence of the change. Thus, in making decisions regarding the pace and sequence of organizational change, change agents should consider a number of factors: the availability of resources for the change, organizational readiness for change, and the temporal perspective of the CEO or other major stakeholder (the pressure for results).

Changing many elements (change targets) too fast may lead to confusion. Employees want to understand the need for change and to adapt. Change is an emotion-laden experience. Negative emotions, if strong and shared among many, can derail a change initiative.

The choice of pace and sequence of organizational change should be consistent with other choices around the change initiative. For example, a fast-paced change by a new CEO who wants to record successes as soon as possible may not allow enough time to plan for the change, to examine likely reactions to the change, to check resources available for the change. The change meets several hurdles in its early days and it is difficult to get traction and support.

Change agents have to balance the pressures for results with the organizational realities. The latter refer to the organization's readiness for change, its change capacity and the resources available for the change. A good sequence should allow for learning, trust-building and signalling. As the saying goes, 'it is not how fast, but how well'. Amis *et al.* (2004) argue that changing everything at the same time and very quickly may be a recipe for failure.

7

SUPPORTING SYSTEMS AND STRUCTURES

Introduction

In the previous chapters of this book, we discussed several decisions which change strategists and implementers have to make in planning for change. Choices regarding the change vision, the targets of the change initiative, the measures of success, the pace and leadership style have to be made. We argue in this chapter that it is also important to take decisions regarding support systems: those anchors which will facilitate the sustainability of the change over time.

Many change efforts fail to achieve the results they were intended to achieve at the beginning of the initiative. Where these results are achieved, many are not sustained over time; after a few years, the organization is close to where it was before change was implemented.

Buchanan *et al.* (2005), in their review of the literature on sustaining organizational change, state that there is evidence of initiative decay (not sustaining the momentum of the change or not achieving the expected results over a considerable length of time). They refer to the NHS Modernisation Agency (2002: 12) who defined sustainability thus: 'Sustainability is when new ways of working and improved outcomes become the norm. Not only have the process and outcome changed, but the thinking and attitudes behind them are fundamentally altered and the systems surrounding them are transformed in support.' Sustainability brings to mind the third stage of Lewin's change model: refreezing (Lewin 1951; cited in Burnes 2004). New ways have to be frozen to make them irreversible; to prevent people from going back to their old ways.

Why Sustaining Organizational Change is Important

Refreezing the new ways or sustaining the momentum is not always easy. Success measures look good and the organization believes it has changed. Results are, however, not long lasting. Within a very short time the organization slides back to almost pre-change levels.

Change leaders may be carried away by intermediate outcomes which indicate the organization is changing. But the change may not last. One reason why change outcomes may not be sustained is that the organization declares victory too soon. While celebrating quick wins (early successes) is great for winning commitment to the change, it could also stall the change. Change recipients – even change agents – may feel that the organization has changed. Change agents may reduce the momentum and spend more time on their regular assignments (if they were assigned to the change team on a part-time basis). Change recipients, especially resistors of the change, may hijack the change, tell everyone the goals have been achieved and encourage everyone to relax. As Reisner (2002: 52) put it: 'our tremendous success in improving delivery times, which we enthusiastically celebrated, blinded us to the need for strategic change. For a time, we slipped into complacency, ignoring our competition and challenges and declaring ourselves the winner in a race with ourselves.' If one is not careful, an early success may be the beginning of change decay. It is not enough to win the battle. One must win the war and this often takes time.

In some cases, change recipients keep the old ways running alongside the new in spite of the extra work involved. The fear of errors in the new system which may negatively affect their job, or simply lack of trust of the new system prevents them from abandoning the old ways completely. Ultimately, there has been no fundamental change in attitudes or values. Without the appropriate support systems, it is very easy for change recipients to go back to the old ways.

Change anchors force employees to pay attention to what the change requires of them in spite of their other commitments. For example, there may be more than one change initiative being implemented at the same time in the organization. People may be torn between them. As soon as the results of one initiative become visible, change recipients move on to the next thing and not much of the other initiative remains. Support systems make it difficult for them to fall back; at least they are costs to this.

To summarize thus far: sustaining organizational change over time is sometimes desirable. However, change decay happens, change actors declare victory too soon, there is no fundamental change in attitudes and values of change recipients. Employees may suffer from change fatigue. By creating support systems for the change initiative, management communicates its commitment to the change.

Organizational change sustainability is not always desirable. Refreezing new ways may make people less flexible such that they resist even better ways of doing things. The environment is dynamic; employees must learn to be adaptable.

On the other hand, organizations embark on change initiatives in order to achieve some objectives. Change costs a lot of time, money and even emotional energy. Common sense dictates that a change strategist would not initiate change if he or she did not want sustainable results, at least for an appropriate length of time. The central issue may be sustainability for periods appropriate in a given context (Buchanan *et al.* 2005: 191). Change strategists and agents will need to choose support systems which will facilitate the sustainability of the change. In the next section, we discuss these systems.

Organizational Change Anchors

Support systems are change anchors: they facilitate the realization and sustainability of the change. The choice of support systems will depend on the nature of the change and expected outcomes. For example, a culture change will require different support systems than those required for a change such as the automation of cheque writing. If an organization wants to initiate change which will institute a culture of teamwork and interdepartmental collaboration, the support systems may include changes in several systems, policies and even structures. On the other hand, the automation of cheque writing may not require much support beyond training.

However, Kotter (1995) argues that change should be anchored in the organizational culture if it is to be sustained. Changes that are anchored in the culture tend to stick: they become part of the way things are done in the organization.

Performance Management, Reward and Other Human Resource Systems

Human resource systems are very often important anchors of change. A review of the human resource systems for their alignment with the new direction is important if the change is to take root and be sustained. For example, one change team reviewed the performance management systems and organizational policies to find out the behaviours which were appraised and rewarded in the past order. They then determined what would be rewarded in the new dispensation and ensured that these were aligned with the direction of the change. The signal was clear to all organizational members: management was serious about the change.

On the other hand, consider the case of a company in the telecommunications sector. The top management initiated a change whose purpose was to build a more customer-focused organization. However, the rewards of customer-facing employees continued to be based on sales and number of customers served. Some improvements in customer satisfaction ratings were recorded in the first year of the change but after the annual performance appraisal exercise many employees realized that the metrics had not changed and they fell back to the old ways. The results recorded in the first year were not sustained. The customer-service training which had cost so much money did not yield lasting results.

If the customer service experience is to improve in a sustainable way, the performance management system and the reward system must be reviewed to align with the new direction. Employees should be appraised on the values of the new culture. The reward system should also be in harmony with the new direction.

Kerr (1975) argues that it is folly to pay people for a set of behaviours while expecting them to behave otherwise. Incentive systems are very powerful: they signal the kinds of behaviours that are rewarded in an organization. The challenge is how to link the new behaviours to the incentive and promotion systems while avoiding a situation where employees run after the rewards without any fundamental changes in values.

If the change is to be institutionalized, promotion decisions should also be based (at least in part) on whether or not the candidates live the new values. The promotion decision is a very important managerial decision. Employees interpret the decision and try to decipher the criteria for success in the organization. Ambitious employees are likely to model their behaviour on these success criteria.

As long as people who do not clearly live the new values are promoted, the change will not be institutionalized. The general perception will be that management is paying lip service to the change. Kotter (1995: 67) advises that attention be paid to who is promoted, who is hired and how they are developed.

Other human resource systems may be reviewed to ensure their alignment with the change. For example, an organization that is implementing an ERP system which typically involves a review of processes, automation and training of employees, may review job specifications to include knowledge of Enterprise Resource Planning (ERP) systems. In future, this will be taken into account in recruitment and selection decisions. Training on the particular ERP system could be included in the Induction Programme. What is important is to ensure that the change gets into the DNA of the organization: that all human resource systems are consistent with the change.

Share the Gains

Another way of institutionalizing the change is to share the gains: the benefits that accrue from the change. Most change initiatives are driven by effectiveness and efficiency concerns. They demand effort and time. [I]f all the gains from extra ingenuity and effort go to top management or to shareholders (unless these are also employees), people will soon view the situation as unfair, become discouraged, and abandon their efforts (Pfeiffer 2005: 98).

Gains need not be financial. Employees acquire new knowledge and skills during change. These are tangible benefits of the change which change agents can bring to their consciousness. Improved company reputation (if it is a result of the change) rubs off on all employees. The gains for the organization, employees and other stakeholders should be communicated. If employees see that the benefits from the change are being shared, they are likely to feel that the change was worthwhile and commit to the change in the long haul.

In the case of the transformation of NAFDAC, as the agency changed, employees became proud of their membership of the organization. They were knowledgeable and were respected by stakeholders. Most importantly, they felt they were professionals and they made more money doing things the right way. The general public enjoyed better health and NAFDAC employees were also better off. When employees take pride in the new organization, change strategists are assured that the change is to some extent anchored.

Appealing to Higher Order Motives

Instilling meaning and communicating the purpose of the change can be an important anchor of change. It enables employees find a higher motive for performance and for continued membership of the organization. Tayo Adenirokun and James Mwangi did this in their respective organizations. The purpose of the changes at GTBank (including the change to a retail bank) was not simply to make money or to become the number one bank in the industry. The overarching purpose was to build an ethical institution that would be a reference point in and from Nigeria.

James Mwangi built a movement in Equity Bank. Empowering the average citizen or mwananchi became a cause. According to James Mwangi: 'The whole organization is aligned to the cause. It is difficult to fit into Equity without seeking a meaning in your life. The organization is not about money: it is about championing a cause: about being the voice of the voiceless' (Ovadje 2009: 9). Employees who see the connections, who realize that the proposed changes are aimed at realizing the mission, find meaning in their work. This makes it much easier for them to embrace the desired changes and sustain them.

As we saw in the chapter on visioning, the top management of NAFDAC changed the mission of the agency. The overarching purpose became to safeguard the health of Nigerians. This mission gave meaning to the work of employees. The agency was not just regulating food and drugs, or applying sanctions: its purpose was to safeguard the lives of the people. By imbuing the change with this sense of meaning, it was possible for change actors to satisfy not only their extrinsic and intrinsic motives, but also their transcendent or altruistic motives (Perez Lopez 1993).

Organizational Culture as a Support System

According to Kotter (2007), one of the reasons why change initiatives fail is that changes are often not anchored in the organizational culture. Without the anchors, it is difficult to maintain the momentum over time and institutionalize the change. Change recipients easily fall back to their old ways and the change effort is undone.

If change is to be institutionalized the values that underlie the new behaviours must become part of the organization's value system, its culture. That is, the new ways must become part of the taken-for-granted assumptions or norms of the organization. This suggests that, to some extent, every change programme has an element of culture change. While reward systems can be used to reinforce certain behaviours, it is the culture change that ensures that the change is sustained – institutionalized.

In this regard, the role of the top management in defining and building the culture cannot be overemphasized. Harris and Ogbonna (2002: 43) found in their study of ten companies undergoing culture change in the United Kingdom that '[i]nconsistent management actions ... small actions and decisions which were inconsistent with the espoused culture took on symbolic meaning and were quickly disseminated through informal channels of communication'.

The behaviour of senior executives is an important signal to the organization. Senior executives 'must appreciate the fact that they are visible: that whatever they say or do is interpreted by the organization as signalling what counts or does not count. In a change process, managers and employees are looking for cues in the CEO's behaviour to show that he is serious about the change' (Ovadje 2002). As Kotter (2007: 100) put it: 'Nothing undermines change more than behaviour by important individuals that is inconsistent with their words.' He argues that to build the change into the culture, two things are required.

First, top management must personify the new approach; they must walk the talk. Second, change agents should communicate the cause and effect relationships so that change recipients appreciate the causes of improved performance. Employees may not make the right connections between performance improvement and the change. Change strategists and agents will have to demonstrate that changes are yielding the results.

Clear and consistent signals from influential executives are important anchors of change. How did James Mwangi and his team anchor the Equity Bank culture? James led by example: 'I champion the DNA of the bank. I cascade the vision. My role is to live the mission and vision; to set the example, to the best of my ability. I never do anything even subconsciously that goes against the mission and vision ... The spirit has not changed. We built the culture over time. I pushed it till it acquired a life of its own. I never in my actions or behaviour contradict the culture' (Ovadje 2009: 9).

To ensure that new people imbibed the values of the culture, since the organization was growing very fast: the management appointed Culture Ambassadors from among the older members of staff. The latter supplemented the training programmes for new employees by telling anecdotes from the beginnings of Equity: anecdotes which demonstrated the values of the institution and the role these played in the Bank's success.

The behaviour consequences of the new way should be linked to the norms and values of the organization. These should in turn be linked to the performance management and the reward system.

Availability of Resources

Change can be expensive. If consultants are to be hired to facilitate the process, the cost of change may be significant. Even if change agents are chosen from among the staff, their work usually suffers while they are busy implementing change. New processes and systems cost money; training programmes are not free. If resources are not available on time, the pace of change may be negatively affected and the change may stall.

Implementing change requires resources. The absence of resources is often interpreted by change recipients as a sign that management is not serious about the change. Take the case of the change effort at CMC Connect. Employees found it difficult to believe in the vision because they did not have the resources to perform. Though the vision was well communicated, employees did not take active steps to actualize the vision until they saw signs that the managing director was serious about the change.

Change agents should agree on a proposed budget for the change. Communication costs, travel, training and even celebrations are important cost elements. At Seven Seas Technologies, senior managers have a budget to take their team out for dinner. This is part of the effort to improve communication between the senior executives (many of whom are new to the organization) and the employees. The heads of department at GTBank also have a budget for celebrations.

Not only should resources be made available: they should be made available at the right time. This requires good project management and project costing by change agents. It also requires good communication and negotiation skills.

Facilitating Organizational Learning

According to Beitler (2006: 172), 'organizational learning is the organization's capacity to create or acquire new knowledge, and then develop that knowledge for the benefit of the organization'. Organizational learning is an important support for organizational change. New knowledge is often created in organizations undergoing change. However, not many organizations are able to capture this knowledge, develop mechanisms to ensure that new knowledge continues to be created and – most importantly – find ways to transfer and exploit this knowledge.

As people experiment with the change, new knowledge is often created, new skills are acquired and new competencies developed. Knowledge that is created in one part of the organization may be useful to another subsidiary or department. The challenge of change agents is how to capture and transfer this knowledge to other parts of the organization and encourage learning and institutionalization. Sustainable change will come through learning and the application of what one has learnt. Continuous learning is important because, as we have seen, the environment is changing and as Amabile (1997: 42) put it, 'expertise is the foundation for all creative work'.

During change implementation, all change actors may have learnt from the pilot trials and experiments and provided fresh solutions. For example, change agents may have begun to develop an enterprise-wide thinking as a result of their participation in cross-functional project teams. They must now consolidate this learning and provide the context for continuous learning to occur. As change recipients and change agents learn, they develop competencies which make implementation easier and facilitate sustainability of the change.

Some organizations such as GTBank provide employees with learning resources to encourage continuous learning. The bank has a well stocked library with books, journals, videos, and novels. It also has a knowledge management system. According to one senior manager: 'there is no information you require for your job that is not available on the intranet'.[1] One way the organization learns from rare incidents, such as frauds, is to write a case study on the incident including what was done to address the problem and prevent future occurrence. The case is posted on the intranet so employees can read and discuss it. Discussion groups, articles in the company newsletter or the intranet, on and off-the-job training programmes, are but a few ways of encouraging self-directed learning.

Vigeo Limited encourages reading and knowledge-sharing among new employees. The latter are assigned specific reading materials which they discuss in teams. Management trainees are required to read the articles in a monthly management review. Relevant articles are discussed with the team.

Not all knowledge can be codified and disseminated. Some knowledge is tacit: difficult to codify. It is difficult to separate tacit knowledge from the person who has it (Beitler 2006). Therefore, tacit knowledge is best transferred in face-to-face interactions. Take the example of Tade Oyinlola of Ericsson. He wanted to build a crop of talented engineers to replace the expatriates. He realized that the expatriate engineers had tacit knowledge which was difficult to transfer through reading and in classroom discussions. He therefore developed a mechanism for passing on some of this knowledge through a well structured mentoring programme.

Communities of practice is another way of sharing tacit knowledge across an organization. Change agents could encourage their development and foster regular meetings, both virtual and face-to-face.

Change Management Structure

Another support system of organizational change is the change management structure. The responsibilities and deliverables of the change agents, the steering committees and task forces should be clearly stated. The change management structure is often different from the organizational structure. This need not be so. Equity Bank has on its organizational structure a director of change and a director of innovation. The bank drives change through its structure. However, specific change initiatives may require the setting up of a change management structure to oversee the change and report to the management (or a steering committee).

No matter what structure is chosen, it is important that change recipients know who they should go to for specific information and clarifications. The allocation of decision rights between department heads, the change management team, the steering committee and the top management should be clear. Obviously, there will be a lot of learning as they go which will lead to refinements of the structure, responsibilities and decision rights.

If consultants are used, a challenge is to ensure in-house ownership and that knowledge and skills are transferred from the consultants to the in-house team. A collaborative approach in which consultants are involved in design and implementation may be advisable in some cases.

Summary

In spite of the frequent changes in the external environment, sustaining organizational change is often desirable. However, change decay happens. This is sometimes because those who lead the change initiative declare victory too soon and lose traction, or change agents do not persist in driving the change. Support systems are designed to provide anchors on which to rest the organizational changes. They include: human resource systems, sharing the benefits of the change, appealing to higher order motives and the availability of resources for change. Other anchors include: organizational learning, change management structure and, very importantly, the organizational culture. In a sense, all change requires employees to do things differently. To be sustained the new way must be aligned to the organizational culture.

Will a change initiative anchored in the organizational culture survive a change in the CEO of the organization? There is no doubt that support systems increase the likelihood of success of the change initiative. However, if the new CEO does not believe in the change or lacks passion and commitment to it, he or she could over time cause the change initiative to decay. Through his or her decisions, especially those regarding promotion and rewards, he or she can slowly erode the ground already gained.

This is a common challenge especially in the public sector in Africa. Some of these organizations have been transformed by people with competence, passion and commitment. A number of them were managers in the private sector who were appointed by politicians to transform a government agency. The expiry of the term of the politician (a minister or the President) marks the end of the appointment of the change agent. The successor, another political appointee, may lack the commitment and passion for the change. Sustaining the change becomes difficult and change decay may begin.

In conclusion, support systems and structures enable the organization to implement and institutionalize the change. If the support systems are to be effective, they should be aligned with the vision of the change, the change targets and the strategies for winning commitment to the change: the subject of Chapter 9.

Note

1 Ovadje, F. and Ogbechie, R. (2013). GTBank: Doing it right and doing well, p. 8.

8

LEADERSHIP STYLE

Introduction

The choice of leadership style is another strategic choice that change strategists and agents make in planning for organizational change. Leadership style is an aspect of the change process; it answers the question: how will the change initiative be introduced?

Higgs and Rowland (2005: 126), referring to studies by Higgs and Rowland (2001) and Higgs (2003) conclude that there is clear and growing evidence that the role of leaders in the change process does impact significantly on the success of change. Style is important because it has an impact on follower commitment and can influence resistance to change. The success of the change initiative often depends on the commitment of change recipients. The latter are not committed if they consider the leadership style to be inappropriate. Certain styles elicit commitment while others do not. The wrong style could engender such resistance that the change process has to be abandoned.

According to Kotter and Schlesinger (1979, 2008) there is a continuum of change leadership styles (Figure 8.1). At one end of the continuum is the coercive style and, at the other end, the collaborative or participative style. Participatory styles are characterized by the involvement of change recipients in the planning and/or the implementation of the change initiative. Directive leadership styles are coercive styles: the change strategists and/or agents tell the change recipients what they must do. The directive or coercive leadership style is a top-down approach to change with little or no input from change recipients.

The coercive and directive styles are more dictatorial – decisions are taken at higher levels of the organizational structure and communicated to lower levels with little or no involvement of those whose primary role is that of change

| Collaborative | Consultative | Directive | Coercive |

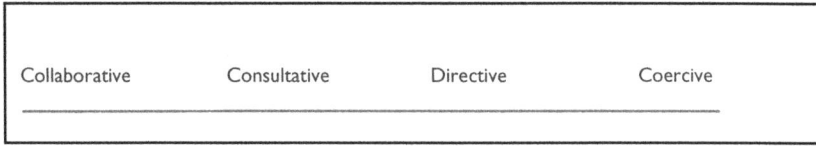

FIGURE 8.1 Continuum of change leadership styles

recipients. The latter are told what they have to do or forced (through rewards and sanctions) to carry out instructions.

Higgs and Rowland (2005) explored, in their study, leadership behaviours that are associated with successful organizational change. They found that shaping (or directive) leadership behaviour was not associated with successful change. Rather it seemed to impair it. Harris and Ogbonna (2002: 42) explored how management actions lead to unintended consequences during culture change. They found that one reason for the failure of culture change initiatives was what they called the Ivory Tower culture change or top-down change. This refers to change that is designed without the participation of people within the organization. They found that where employees were not involved in the development of the culture change plans, these plans were either divorced from the organizational reality or incapable of meaningful implementation.

Thus, Harris and Ogbonna (2002) and Higgs and Rowland (2005) provide evidence that top-down change is not effective: does not lead to successful organizational change. However, Kotter and Schlesinger (2008: 137) posit that in situations where speed is essential and where changes will not be popular regardless of how they are introduced, coercion may be the only option. The coercive and directive styles are likely to bring about compliance or outright resistance. In spite of this, in certain circumstances it may be necessary to use one or other of these styles. Change agents will then have to take steps to manage and overcome the resulting resistance.

Participatory or facilitating leadership style has been found to be more likely to lead to successful organizational change (Higgs and Rowland 2005; Kotter and Schlesinger 2008). Involving employees seems important for successful change. Involvement may be in the change design and/or implementation. This style is likely to lead to commitment as followers are involved in the decisions around the change.

However, the study by Hawkins and Dulewicz (2009) suggests that there is no one appropriate style for every context; the choice of style will depend on a number of contextual factors. Stace and Dunphy (1992: 206) found that successful firms tend to use a situational approach in the choice of change strategies.

To summarize so far: there is a continuum of leadership styles varying from a directive or top-down style to a participatory style. Change strategists and agents must decide how the change initiative will be introduced – styles vary from coercive (little involvement) to full participation. Employees may be involved in the design or planning for the change and/or the implementation stage. For example, in Alpha plc, middle managers were involved in the design of the change but not in the implementation.

Choosing Change Leadership Styles

The choice of leadership style is a very important decision as it can affect the success of the change initiative. Kotter and Schlesinger (2008) argue that where to operate on the continuum depends on four factors: kind and amount of resistance anticipated; the relative power of the change agent; the information needs from recipients, and the stakes involved (Table 8.1).

The choice of style will depend on the kind and level of resistance anticipated. Resistance is often driven by conflict of interests among key stakeholders. If the conflicts are significant, a high level of resistance can be expected. In this case, there may be little basis for collaboration or participation. A directive or coercive strategy may be a more appropriate style. Alternatively, attempts may be made to reduce resistance and encourage collaboration. The change agent could sell the benefits of the change to all stakeholders to win their commitment or at least reduce the level of resistance. By involving people in the planning or implementation of the change, the change agent can forestall resistance (Kotter and Schlesinger 2008: 135). When First Bank of Nigeria plc wanted to lay off some of its staff, the bank offered attractive packages and encouraged employees to leave voluntarily. Some employees took up the offers and left peacefully.

Another consideration in the choice of change leadership style is the relative power of the change strategists/agents vis-à-vis the change recipients. Kotter and Schlesinger (2008) propose that if the initiator of the change is in a weak position compared to the change recipients, a participatory style is more appropriate. For example, when Ken Olori was made Executive Chairman of the public agency, the agency had experienced a churn in its leadership: it had had three executive chairmen in three years.

TABLE 8.1 Choosing Change Leadership Styles

1. Amount and kind of resistance anticipated
2. Relative power of change agents and recipients
3. Information and knowledge required of change recipients
4. Stakes
5. Pressure for performance and time lines
6. Support from top management
7. The target of the change
8. Expectation of change recipients
9. Pace of change

Olori realized that some of the staff were loyal to the ex-chairmen of the agency. Some others had important connections with senior government officials. He was new to the organization. The change programme he wanted to introduce was not likely to be accepted by the large majority of the staff. He invited a select group of staff to a retreat, got a few champions from among them and began the change with these champions.

In choosing change leadership style, change agents should also ask themselves if they need information and knowledge from change recipients. If the support of the latter is necessary and they are an important source of information and knowledge required for the planning and implementation of the change initiative, a participatory style will be more appropriate. Change agents will have to listen to them and involve them in the change otherwise the change will not be successful.

According to Kotter and Schlesinger (2008), if the stakes are high (e.g., there is a crisis or the risk of not achieving the change objectives is high) the appropriate leadership strategy is coercive. The risks of failure may be very high. If the organization is in a crisis, it is easier to understand the need for change. There may be little resistance to a coercive strategy in this situation.

The choice of style will also depend on the pressure for performance and the time frame for results. If the time frame (the period between the initiation of the change and when results are expected) is very short, change agents are often tempted to use a coercive strategy. This may lead to resistance which could overwhelm the change agents and cause unnecessary delays. On the other hand, a participatory style usually takes a longer time even though it may be more effective in the long run. The pace of the change will also influence the choice of style. If the change has to be implemented very quickly across the organization, a participatory style may not be feasible.

Another contextual factor to consider in choosing a change leadership style is the level of commitment of top management to the change initiative. Without unflinching support from the top management, a coercive strategy is unlikely to succeed. Senior managers are likely to shelve the change at the first signs of serious discontent and/or resistance from employees thus leaving change agents without support.

The choice of style may depend on the nature of the change targets. A coercive style may be inappropriate for the implementation of an innovation strategy as it alienates the very people who will develop new products and services. A commanding style is not likely to work in organizations with 'dispersed power structures, such as universities or hospitals' (Huy 2001: 616) or where the change involves building a new culture of say customer service. A participatory style may be more appropriate in these situations.

A change in the organizational culture requires changing the beliefs and values of the people. It is virtually impossible to change deep-seated beliefs by command and coercive techniques. If change agents are to challenge the values in use they will need to help people learn. Culture change usually takes time and change recipients must be involved in the process if it is to succeed. Harris and Ogbonna's (2002) study of ten culture interventions revealed several unintended negative consequences. In most of the organizations they studied, employees seemed to comply with the new cultural demands but their values did not change. They also found that changes which were designed and implemented from the top were not successful.

An important contextual variable to be borne in mind in choosing an appropriate leadership style is the expectation of the people. In some organizations, people expect to be consulted, to participate in key decisions. Participation may be a value of the organizational culture. Change agents in these organizations should be sensitive to these cultural expectations.

Finally, since the commitment of change recipients is very important for the success of the change initiative, change agents are well advised to ensure that they choose leadership styles that will not lead to the demoralization of change recipients. People will not make the transitions, if they are not – at least to some extent – committed to the organization.

So far, we have discussed research results on change styles from the Western context. We now turn our attention to the African context.

Appropriate Change Leadership Styles in the African Context

We have argued that the choice of leadership style is important for successful change. Change leadership ultimately involves transiting people from the current state to a desired state. Change recipients will make the move (follow the leader) if the leader behaves in the way they expect according to their culturally determined implicit leadership theories. This begs the question: what kind of leadership will be acceptable and effective in the African cultural context?

Some considerations are immediately relevant if the change strategists and agents are implementing change in the African cultural context. In Chapter 1 of this book, we highlighted some of the cultural characteristics of Africa. We saw that the African culture is characterized by high power distance, high in-group collectivism and a humane orientation. In these cultures, people defer to authority. Age is to some extent equated with wisdom. According to Jackson (2004: 95), people in high power distance cultures have high dependency needs and expect superiors to act autocratically and benevolently.

Another characteristic of the African culture is high in-group collectivism. Group members are ready to sacrifice personal comforts and ambition for the group (the clan or the extended family). The leader is expected to give up personal ambitions for the sake of the group. In making decisions, he or she is expected to seek the good of the collective and not personal gain. Africans expect their leaders to be benevolent. This is linked to the humane orientation in the African culture.

Africans expect change leaders to be caring and considerate, supportive of followers and concerned about their welfare. Leaders are expected to value the person more than productivity. Change outcomes should therefore be evaluated in terms of outcomes for the person, and for the organization.

Three of the cases included in this book typify the African change leadership style: the Dora Akunyili at NAFDAC, GTBank and Equity Bank cases. The leaders of these organizations implemented change successfully in their organizations. We review these cases in order to glean the leadership style used by these change strategists and agents.

In the first place, all the three leaders (Dora Akunyili, Tayo Adenirokun and James Mwangi) involved employees in the change initiative and the changes were successful. Dora Akunyili was open, transparent, participatory and caring. Within a few months of taking charge of NAFDAC, she asked her team to organize a corporate retreat. Members of the NAFDAC Governing Council were also invited. The management and the council jointly crafted the new mission and vision, and agreed on the immediate goals of the agency.

Tayo (together with co-founder Fola Adeola) had built candour as one of the important values of GTBank. This is a manager on how Tayo encouraged dialogue:

> Candour is a key success factor in this organization. You are not punished for expressing your opinion. You defend your position and no one thinks you are saucy. It is a very open environment so people are not frustrated. People who are frustrated do great damage in a service business. Uncle T [Tayo], like Fola, encourages discourse. You can tell Tayo that you don't agree with him; that you want to be convinced. Everyone talks at the credit committees.

Second, these change leaders reduced power distance: they made themselves accessible to all employees no matter their level. Both Tayo and James were called by their first name in GTBank and Equity Bank respectively. A senior manager at NAFDAC commented on Dora's style:

> [She] is accessible. You can reach her 24 hours a day ... Her accessibility has created room for people to feed her with information. This makes it possible for her to make better decisions.

A GTBank employee commented on Tayo's accessibility and openness:

> He is approachable and in touch with things. Even the lowest cadre of staff can go to him with their problems. The top management encourages openness. Even those who joined and are not so open have become more so. The culture rubs off on them and they become more personable.

> When I joined [GTBank] I had issues with expressing my opinion until I discovered that you can really challenge what your boss says. However, because you are dealing with very intelligent people convincing them is not easy: you have to be prepared and you must be articulate.

James Mwangi emphasized teamwork and became more of a coach and facilitator. James commented on his leadership style: 'We de-emphasize hierarchy. Everyone is addressed by his or her first name. We do not respect positions. We want people to behave as human beings. We look for people who are independent. We have no room for mimicry or sycophancy. We want to sift through our collective knowledge and come up with great solutions.'

A branch manager commented on how he solves problems:

> I am on ground. I take decisions. New issues come up all the time; we deal with very poor people. I throw up issues to the head office. They fine-tune my suggestions, process the information, etc. I talk to James, to Alex. I tell them I am in a fix. I tell them what I have tried and they make suggestions.

Third, these leaders were also performance focused. They pushed for results. A senior manager had this to say about Dora:

> She is very pushy but caring. She appreciates small things and this make people feel really good. Saying 'Thank you' and 'Well done' comes easy to her and this motivates the staff, even the directors. She is compassionate. She recognizes that we all work very hard and many of us very long hours. One manager said he was having some problems with his wife because he was not seeing the family often: they lived outside Abuja. Dora would go to him from time to time and say: 'Hey, you have not seen your family for some time. Do you want to travel?' and she would give him time off to travel and spend time with his family.

Tayo was also very demanding with results. The Monthly Performance Reviews (MPRs) were tough meetings. According to him: 'The MPR can be very brutal ... I don't hate you but if you bring a stupid credit I will ask you if you are dumb.'

Finally, these leaders were humane and supportive of employees. A manager commented on James' leadership style:

> James is a visionary leader. He shares the vision, ensures that the objectives are understood and then allows you run with it. He gives you the resources you need to deliver, and then he demands results. You know he is there for you; you can consult him if you need help. He also consults a lot. He is always looking for new insights so he talks to people a lot.

What can be gleaned from Dora, Tayo and James' styles? They all had participatory styles. They were leaders who listened to the troops, gave them room to perform and encouraged discussion, candour. They were also very people oriented, they cared about their employees. All three leaders seem to combine a strong performance focus with a people orientation. James Mwangi used a dictatorial style in 1994 when the organization was moribund but changed to a more participatory style as the people imbibed the new culture. All three organizations are among the top in their sector.

Dora Akunyili instilled discipline into NAFDAC and the people. She and her team built a new culture. They introduced a movement roster. Employees who were found guilty of bribery and corruption by the disciplinary committee were dismissed. There were no sacred cows: even her brother-in-law was fired. Dora pushed for results while showing care for the people. Staff buses were provided to take people to the office and back home. She showed interest in the people as persons and not as instruments.

GTBank paid the medical bills of staff including the cost of medical evacuation and treatment abroad. Tayo Adenirokun sent get well cards to employees who were ill. In one case, the company found a job for the wife of a deceased employee to enable her to fulfil their dreams for their children.

The story at Equity Bank is the same. For example, at the end of a huge project which involved the installation of new software for the bank, James Mwangi sent a letter to all the project team members thanking them for the sacrifices they had made to get the system up and running in such record time. James also sent a 'Thank you' letter to the spouses of the team members: in appreciation of the sacrifices they had made, he attached a cheque to each letter.

These leaders combined a focus on the job with a focus on people. They were humane; they truly cared about the people but they also cared about the results. They realized that the use of a coercive style for a prolonged period of time could affect the receptiveness to change. A coercive style could demoralize employees, create resistance, and make change implementation difficult if not impossible.

These case studies provide some support for the findings of the GLOBE project in Sub-Saharan Africa. The most effective change leadership styles in the African context may not be a choice between coercive or more participatory strategies. The question may have to change to whether or not the leader is charismatic, team oriented, participatory and humane: four of the GLOBE dimensions of culturally endorsed implicit leadership theories which were found to contribute to outstanding leadership in Africa.

According to the GLOBE study (House *et al.* 2004: 669), people within cultural groups agree in their beliefs about leadership such that there are statistically significant differences among cultures in leadership belief. People within a culture have an image of what makes an outstanding leader (Wanasika *et al.* 2011: 236). According to the latter authors, Africans expect leaders to be forgiving, considerate and supportive of followers' welfare, to develop and maintain good relationships with followers. These assumptions are culturally endorsed; they are shared within a culture and they affect how followers relate with and react to leaders.

Charismatic/value-based leadership, team oriented leadership, participative and humane oriented leadership: the charismatic/value-based leader is inspirational, self-sacrifices and delivers results; the participative leader involves others in decision-making and in implementation; the team oriented leader is collaborative, benevolent and administratively competent; finally, the humane oriented leader is considerate, compassionate and supportive of followers. According to Wanasika *et al.* (2010: 238), there are distinct similarities between the humane orientation and Ubuntu – humaneness. They assert that the humane orientation is a distinct characteristic in Africa. Followers in Africa expect change leaders to be humane.

Finally, how do we reconcile the high power distance which characterizes African culture with the reduction in hierarchy in the cases referred to above? The GLOBE study distinguishes between current practices ('as is') and values (what should be). In this regards, the African sample valued much less power distance than what is practised in Africa today. Africans want to be involved in decision making and in implementation.

Summary

In this chapter, we argued that the choice of leadership style is a strategic choice that change strategists and agents have to make. The wrong choice usually has huge negative consequences for the organization and the change outcomes.

There is a continuum of change leadership styles varying from coercive to more participative styles. We discussed a number of contextual factors which influence the choice of change leadership style; the amount and kind of resistance anticipated, the pace of change, the nature of the change targets, etc.

The African cultural environment is characterized by high power distance, in-group collectivism and a humane orientation. Followers expect leaders to be caring, considerate, to sacrifice for the collective, to take decisions bearing in mind the good of the group.

We then reviewed the case studies included in this book to glean the change leadership styles used by the change agents. We found that all the change agents involved employees. They encouraged dialogue and reduced power distance by going closer to the employees. In two of the three organizations, the managing director was called by his first name. These leaders combined humaneness with a performance orientation.

Change agents will do well to develop a level of flexibility in responding to the context. They should beware of using only one contextual variable in arriving at a decision regarding change leadership style. The context is usually very rich. The ability of change agents to understand the context and choose the appropriate style may determine the success of the change initiative.

9

WINNING COMMITMENT
TO CHANGE

Introduction

The model presented in this book is a decision-making model. We have discussed several decisions around change. In this chapter, we present another decision point: winning commitment to change. This decision is so important that change agents are advised to consider it at every decision point in the model.

The literature on change leadership emphasizes the importance of winning commitment or overcoming resistance to change. In fact, most books on change are primarily focused on overcoming resistance to change. Change often requires employees to invest more time and effort and it is sometimes painful and leads to resistance. It is not surprising therefore that academics have devoted many books to the subject of resistance. Many of us have heard countless times that people do not like change and will resist it as much as they can. This is simply not true. We do not resist all changes. Most people will not resist a promotion, a well furnished large office with a view of the sea or a company car and chauffeur. People tend to accept those changes they perceive to be beneficial and reject the others.

The first step in winning commitment and reducing resistance to change is planning. With a good plan, change actors can anticipate situations, hurdles and sources of resistance. They also feel more confident about what they are trying to achieve when they have a plan. The goal is clear and so is the road map. Getting agreement, enlisting followers, is a much easier task when there is a change plan such as the one described in this book.

Change often requires people to think, do and behave differently; it requires behavioural change. This involves a personal transition. Change recipients are asked to let go of old ways and learn new ones. Winning commitment involves helping them make the transitions. In the next section, we discuss some models of personal transition.

Facilitating Transitions

Garvin (2000), Kotter (1995) and Jick (1991a) presented change models that focus on winning support for change during change implementation. These models are good guides to practitioners in that they highlight the pitfalls in change implementation. Kotter (1995) proposes eight ways to avoid these pitfalls: establish a sense of urgency, form a powerful guiding coalition, create a vision, communicate the vision, empower others to act on the vision, plan for and create short wins, consolidate improvements and institutionalize the change. Jick (1991a) and Garvin (2000) add to their models a critical element: measuring progress.

These models are very useful in practice in implementing organizational change. However, they do not include the process people go through as they let go of the past and learn the new ways. How does behaviour change take place? What do change recipients feel, what needs do they have as the vision is shared and attempts at implementation of the change initiative are made? Answers to these questions should help change agents design or adopt interventions that meet employees at their point of need. The former are thus better able to win the commitment of employees.

Bridges (2003) proposed a framework for understanding personal transitions. According to him, while change is a movement from one state to another, transition is 'psychological; it is a three-phase process that people go through as they internalize and come to terms with the details of the new situation that the change brings about' (Bridges 2003: 3). People go through three phases during change: letting go, the neutral zone and beginning again. For successful change, change agents should help employees go through these stages.

Bridges' (2003) model of personal transitions is reminiscent of Kurt Lewin's change model (Burnes 2004) which involves unfreezing, movement or change, and refreezing. As people go through change, they have to first let go of the past order. As they let go, they enter what Bridges (2003) calls the neutral zone. In this zone, the change is not yet familiar but recipients have let go of the old ways. They have to some extent lost familiar routines and processes and even their 'world and the meaning and identity they got from it' (Bridges 2003: XI). A final transition must be made if behaviour is to change; employees have to begin again. Bridges (2003) draws attention to the psychological processes people go through as organizations implement change.

The utility of this model stems from the fact that it focuses attention on change recipients and the transitions they go through to make change happen. Change recipients are not necessarily passive recipients of change; something happens to them as they go through change.

However, so much happens within change recipients between the neutral phase and beginning again phase that is not captured in the Bridges (2003) model. As a change process unfolds people have an array of thoughts, feelings, perceptions and worries about their role with and consequences of using the innovation

(Hall 2013: 267). Change recipients worry about what they may lose in the new order; they may be concerned about their competence to operate in the new organization or may simply wonder what their role will be in the new order. These worries, concerns and feelings of competence do change as the change implementation progresses from communicating the vision to institutionaliza- tion. The Bridges (2003) model seems to lump a lot (perhaps too much) into one transition (from the neutral to beginning again phase). Change strategists and implementers need models that delineate in a more comprehensive manner the stages through which change recipients go. A nuanced understanding of the stages of personal change and of what is happening to people at each stage has implications for successful organizational change. Change agents are better able to support people through these transitions and win support for change.

To summarize thus far: change often meets resistance; resistance may be so stiff that the change initiative has to be abandoned. Change strategists and implement- ers need a plan for helping employees make the personal transitions that change requires. This transition will involve letting go of the old order and adopting new ways. We emphasized the need for a more comprehensive view of the personal transitions people make as change is implemented in their organization. In the next section, we discuss the Transtheoretical Model of behaviour change which has great utility for understanding these personal transitions.

The Stages of Change

Prochaska *et al.* (1992) proposed the Transtheoretical Model (TTM) in their study of changing problem behaviours. It is a well researched model of behaviour change. Harris and Cole (2007) applied the model to the development of coach- ing skills, and Grant (2010) to the development of leadership skills among manag- ers. According to the TTM, behaviour change involves a movement through five stages: pre-contemplation, contemplation, preparation, action and mainte- nance (Figure 9.1). The five stages are intuitive and can be applied by change agents to understand the thoughts, feelings and perceptions (Hall 2013: 267) of change recipients as they go through change. The level of awareness of the change

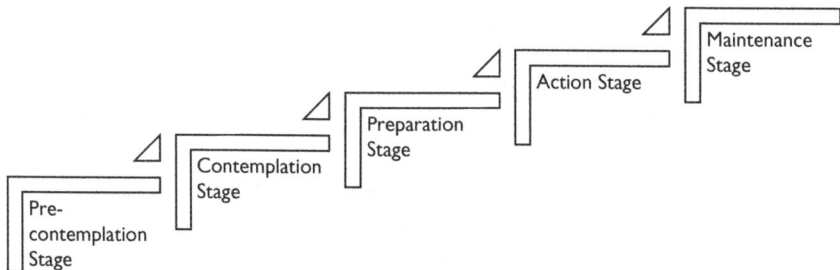

FIGURE 9.1 The stages of change

initiative, involvement in the change and action-taking varies across the five stages. Employees also have different skill levels and feelings of self-efficacy with regard to the change at the first stage compared to later stages.

In the following sub-sections, we explain what happens to change recipients in each of the five stages. After this, we discuss (in the next section) what change implementers can do to support people and facilitate transition from one stage to another.

The Pre-contemplation Stage

At this stage, employees are unaware of the need for change and have no desire for change. In an organization that is doing very well in terms of performance, employees are likely to be at the pre-contemplation stage; they do not see the need for change. The old ways have been institutionalized; have become part of the DNA of the organization. Employees may have become complacent; the organization may be doing so well that there is a general feeling of contentment with the status quo.

On the other hand, the organization may not be doing well but may be stuck in the old model; doing more of the same things that worked in the past and hoping to get the same results. In public enterprises which are not performing, the need for change may not be obvious. When Dora Akunyili took charge of NAFDAC most of the managers and employees did not see any need for change. They seemed content to do things as they had always done them. A big challenge for the change agent at this stage was to get the organization to see the need for change.

The Contemplation Stage

At this second stage, employees are aware of the need for change; they are reflecting on it but are not yet committed to the change. Research by Armenakis *et al.* (1999) on readiness for change suggests that employees assess the need for change. If they see the need, they are likely to move into the preparation stage. During the contemplation stage, change recipients evaluate the pros and cons of the change and make a decision to accept the change or to reject it. Their decision is influenced by a number of factors.

Change recipients assess the appropriateness of the change. Will the change strategy lead to a realization of the vision? Is this what the organization requires, and at this time? If their answers to these questions are in the affirmative, they are likely to move to the next stage.

The change must be perceived to be do-able; collective efforts should bring about the desired change if employees are to move to the preparation stage. At CMC Connect, managers and employees understood the vision but did not think the vision was achievable. If the perception is that management is simply dreaming, employees are not likely to commit to the change.

In assessing do-ability, employees typically gauge top management commitment to the change. If management is not perceived to be committed to the change, employees will not move to the preparation stage. Past experiences with change also play a part in assessing do-ability. If past change efforts were abandoned halfway employees are likely to feel that the proposed change will go the same way as all the others before it. Sometimes, employees do not actively resist the change, but simply appear to support it for a short while. Why commit to a passing phase? It will blow away. As an Igbo proverb says: the tree that resists the wind is uprooted. But the tree that sways with the wind will remain to withstand the next wind. Employees may sway with the wind of change but not change their behaviours.

Finally, change recipients evaluate the impact of the change on themselves, on others and on the organization (Smollan 2006: 147). They want to know what is in it for them. Will they gain power, have more access to resources, earn more, have more time for family? Their concerns may be around how they will be affected. What are the benefits of behaving in the new way? What are the consequences for the business and for the individual? Employees are concerned about losing people with whom they have built a personal relationship. They were probably at the wedding of the employee who is being let go, the funeral of a parent or the naming ceremony of the child. They want to know whether employees and suppliers with whom they have a relationship will be let go.

The CEO of a multinational wanted to shut down one of its factories and import finished goods from another subsidiary abroad. The cost of production at his factory was so high that it was cheaper to import. The directors and staff resisted the proposal so much it had to be abandoned. They feared that many employees would lose their jobs, suppliers would suffer a loss of income and the community would be negatively affected.

Change recipients evaluate the costs of change against the benefits. Change has pros and cons. At the contemplation stage, the costs of change are often more than the benefits, that is, the perceived costs of adopting the new ways are more than the benefits (Grant 2010) while the benefits are likely to outweigh the costs at later stages.

The Preparation Stage

At this stage, some change recipients have weighed the costs and benefits and decided to accept the change (with varying levels of commitment). They begin to take some action; to take baby steps. The costs of the change may still be higher than the benefits at this stage. As they experiment with the change, they may find more hurdles or barriers to the change. The change may appear to be more costly than they expected. For example, competence issues may arise. Employees want to take the baby steps but may not know how. They begin to wonder if they can fit into the new world.

Team leaders are likely to be concerned about how their teams will be affected by the change. How will they behave in the new space? What is the business case for the change? Team leaders need the answers so they can be advocates for the change and coach their teams through the transition.

The number of people using the new system at the preparation stage may be low. If change agents provide the right support at this stage, the recipients get more comfortable with the change; they acquire experience and have more positive sentiments of self-efficacy. The rate of adoption of the change is likely to increase as employees experience feelings of competence. However, if the hurdles are not overcome, if experience is not gained, the perceived costs of change may be much higher than expected leading to a possible relapse. Employees may give up altogether and return to the contemplation stage.

The Action Stage

At this stage, the change is in full throttle. A large majority of the employees are committed to the change and are making it happen. As they experiment with the change, they acquire experience and improved feelings of competence. With improved skills and increased action, the benefits of change become visible. Research suggests that at the action stage, the benefits of change outweigh the costs (Grant 2010). This is not to say that the costs of change are not many. Employees have become accustomed to the new ways. A number of people who were cynics have become converts. The speed of adoption is accelerated as employees learn and grow.

It is important to note here that action does not just happen. Change agents facilitate the transitions. Otherwise, the good ideas remain on paper.

The Maintenance Stage

This is the final stage. The change is in full swing, the adoption rate is high. However, there is need for maintenance. Old ways may be running alongside new ones. For example, after automating the order process in one organization, the change agent found that the manual process was continued alongside the computerized system. It took time to eliminate the manual process even though it was redundant. Employees are making the transition but the new ways have not yet been institutionalized. The challenge for change strategists and agents is to get the change into the DNA of the organization.

In conclusion: the fears, concerns and perceptions of change recipients at each stage of the model are not the same. At the contemplation stage, employees evaluate the do-ability of the change initiative, the change plan, and the commitment of top management. As they move to other stages, concerns about competence and self-efficacy become more important.

It is pertinent to note that all employees do not move from one stage to the other at the same time. While some employees (possibly the champions) are in the action stage, other employees may be in the contemplation stage or the preparation stage. A huge challenge for change agents is to carry along change recipients who are at different stages of change. While addressing the needs of those in, for example, the action stage, change agents cannot forget that some employees are still in earlier stages. We now turn our attention to supporting change recipients to transition from one stage to the next.

Supporting Employees through the Stages of Change

Each stage of change has peculiar characteristics which determine the kind of support employees will need to move from one stage to another. At the pre-contemplation stage, employees do not see the need for change. At the contemplation stage, they begin to reflect on and assess the need. They also evaluate the costs and benefits of the change initiative. The preparation stage is characterized by at least some acceptance of and involvement in the change. As they take action steps, they meet hurdles and encounter other barriers to change. Some may relapse to the contemplation stage when they meet with such difficulties. Finally, the action and maintenance stages are characterized by increased action and the benefits of the change become obvious.

Change readiness and willingness vary across the stages of change (Harris and Cole 2007). Employees at the later stages are likely to be more willing and ready to implement the change than those at earlier stages of change. Research on leadership development suggests that the costs of change are greater at the early stages of change and diminish at later stages. The pros, on the other hand, are higher at a later stage – the action stage.

Grant (2010) found that self-efficacy (confidence in one's ability to change) varied across the stages of change. Self-efficacy grew over time (across stages) as people acquired the required skills and got used to the new ways. At the contemplation stage, for example, the costs of change are high and feelings of self-efficacy are low. Behaviour change may not be desirable.

Supporting the Transition from the Pre-contemplation to the Contemplation Stage

At the pre-contemplation stage, change recipients are not aware of the need for change. To move them to the contemplation stage, change agents must sell the need for change. In making a case for change, they should communicate the facts: the reasons why change is needed. It may be that the organization is losing customers or a new technology has been introduced by a competitor which could make previous technologies obsolete. If the organization is doing well, it may be more difficult for employees to buy in. It may be necessary to let them experience the need. For example, video clips of a customer encounter could be shown to employees to help them see the problem with customer service. The CEO of a firm in the agro-chemical business took employees to see the abandoned warehouse of a competitor. He wanted them to realize that the company could also go under if they did not change.

The new director general of a development agency found great difficulties in getting the senior managers to see the need for change. With the help of consultants, teams were set up to address different aspects of the organization. Each team was asked to visit any business organization they admired to study a particular aspect of the business. These visits helped team members see the need for change and the director general was able to overcome an important hurdle to personal change: the cognitive barrier. This barrier to change (Kim and Mauborgne 2003) is so important that, if it is not overcome, not much change is likely to happen. If people do not see the need for change, they are not likely to take steps to implement the change.

To win the commitment of employees, change agents should sell the benefits of the change (or the reduction in pain that the change will ultimately bring about). A manager in a public utility commented that, from his experience, selling a reduction in pain is more powerful than selling benefits. His challenge was to identify the benefits of the change initiative (which perhaps employees have not experienced) and how it would reduce the pain they were currently experiencing.

The change drivers should acknowledge the costs of the change and help people understand that the benefits will outweigh the costs over time. In some cases, the dangers of not changing should be discussed. Some people will adopt a change only if they have no alternative.

Pathos or emotion is very important in the African context. It is not enough to give reasons why change is an imperative – change agents must also reach the people's hearts. Employees want to know what is changing and how they will be affected. They are interested in the consequences of not changing for the business and for each employee; the benefits and costs of the change to all stakeholders, not just themselves. Employees are concerned about how the change will bring about a better world – for themselves, other employees and the organization. Management should show an understanding of the issues, compassion for the people who have to implement these changes and, above all, they should themselves adopt the changes, that is, they should be ready to walk the talk. Change agents also need an emotional followership. They must engage the minds and hearts of their followers to galvanize support for the change.

The overarching goal of the changes, the purpose of the change, should be shared on all possible occasions. Lawson and Price (2003: 33) argue that if the 'people believe in (the) overall purpose, they will be happy to change their behaviour to serve that purpose – indeed, they will suffer from cognitive dissonance if they don't. But to feel comfortable about change and to carry it out with enthusiasm, people must understand the role of their actions in the unfolding drama of the company's fortunes and believe that it is worthwhile for them to play a part.'

In selling the need for change, attention should be paid to the specific needs of people on various rungs of the organizational ladder. The pains and gains of the change initiative may vary across organizational levels. The nature of the contributions expected of people at various levels also differs. Thus, what is sold to employees on the shop floor may be slightly different from what is sold to their supervisors. Change agents often need the supervisors to coach their team on the new ways. The sales pitch to the supervisors will necessarily be different. In effect, the case for change should be made at the enterprise level, the business, the team and the individual level. People at each level should see how their actions lead to the attainment of the goals at the higher level.

To do this, change agents should influence the conversations in their organizations. Tacking change posters all over the office (even on the walls of the elevator), embossing key messages on face caps and T-shirts, encourages conversations around the change. Managers and employees are involved in many important and urgent tasks daily. The change effort must be on the front burner if the desired results are to be achieved.

To keep the interest alive and provide new topics for conversation, the change message should be changed from time to time. New messages should reflect the shifting focus of the change effort. Whether employees are in the elevator, in front of notice boards, or in the cafeteria the change initiative should be a recurring topic of conversation.

Di Virgilio and Ludema (2009: 78) argue that conversations create energy for action. This involves a number of steps. First, the change agent listens to the constituency she or he wants to influence towards action. She or he tries to understand their interests, concerns, and the 'language' they speak.

Having understood the constituency, the change agent frames the communication in a way that takes into account the needs, language and concerns of the constituency. Next she or he engages the constituency in reframing the change story in a way that makes sense to them and gives meaning to their work. A human resource manager specified: team leaders want to know why the change is necessary, how it will affect their teams and how they will need to behave in the new space. Employees want to know what is changing, how they will be affected, the benefits of behaving in the new way and the consequences of not doing so. The change story should be told in such a way that everyone understands the big picture and how the business, team, or individual fits into the change.

The 'language' in which the change story is told is important. In their study Di Virgilio and Ludema (2009) found that the language of top management was finance while that of IT was technology. It was important to communicate with each constituency in their own language. These conversations create positive emotions about the change. Positive emotions lead to a willingness to cooperate; to take action to implement the change; to dedicate more time, resources, money or other forms of support for the change (Di Virgilio and Ludema 2009).

If communication has been effective, a percentage of the change recipients move to the contemplation stage. Some others, unable to see the need for change, remain at the pre-contemplation stage.

Supporting the Transition from the Contemplation to the Preparation Stage

The contemplation stage is an evaluative stage. Employees reflect on whether or not to commit to the change; they assess the credibility of the change story. The vision, the change plan, and the commitment of top management are evaluated. Change recipients also evaluate the costs and benefits of the change.

Communication is vital if change agents are to win the support of change recipients and get them to commit to the change. This communication should be addressed to employees at both the pre-contemplation and the contemplation stages. Different communication media should be used to ensure the change initiative is in the face of employees. Town hall meetings, video clips, posters on notice boards and on the intranet and frequently asked questions on the intranet are often used to reinforce the change story.

Communication should be two-way; those at the top talking to employees at the bottom and vice versa. It is important for change agents to get feedback from employees to ascertain their reaction to the change message. An enthusiastic applause at the end of a presentation of the change should not be taken as an indication of support for the change. The change strategists and agents must be able to discern when employees say 'yes' and mean 'no' from when their 'yes' is really 'yes'.

Overcoming Barriers to Change

Change recipients have different concerns about change. Some are primarily concerned about the loss of power, clout or influence. Others may be more concerned about whether or not the vision can be achieved; if the roadmap is appropriate and do-able. Some organizational members are worried about how the change will affect people, the pain it will cause them and how much support the organization will provide. Change recipients may also be concerned about whether or not they have the skills to operate in the new world being painted by the change agents. Change agents must show they have taken these concerns into account and explain the actions to be taken to mitigate the impact of any negative forces.

The general manager of the finance department of a large firm decided to automate the cheque writing process. One of his managers spent 4 to 5 hours each day writing cheques. The general manager felt that by freeing his time, the manager could carry out other value-added tasks. After two months, there were hardly any results. The general manager later realized that the manager was resisting the change because he was concerned about his role in the future. After his new role was communicated to him, the manager became supportive of the change.

Grant's (2010) study suggests that self-efficacy is low at the early stage of a change process. This may be one reason why people resist change. Change agents should introduce some training programmes at this stage to build employee knowledge and skill and thus improve their feelings of self-efficacy. Employees will more easily move to the preparation stage if they see the need for change and feel confident that they can carry out the change.

Take the example of an oil company in Kenya that was implementing a Safety, Health and Environment Framework. The change agents realized that employees needed knowledge and skills in health and safety. Workshops were organized to create awareness of the need for the change. They realized that each area of the business had a different risk exposure (e.g., the risks at the depot were different from those at the head office). So they organized targeted training programmes for each area of the business and each job. Employees were also provided with the tools to make the behaviour change: they received safety equipment (such as shoes, fuel-resistant helmets), checklists, safety procedures, etc. Through the training programmes and subsequent coaching by supervisors, the change agents built awareness of the need for safety, and increased the knowledge and skills of the change recipients. The change agents helped recipients overcome the resource barriers to change (Kim and Mauborgne 2003).

At the individual level, change recipients need some resources to make change happen. Tade Oyinlola initiated a competency development programme for young recruits in his department. He wanted to develop local staff and reduce the department's reliance on expatriates. He realized the knowledge gap between the expatriates and the young recruits was considerable. To bridge this gap, Tade and his team prepared the new recruits for knowledge transfer. They developed foundation courses on IT and engineering as well as seminars on interpersonal skills to bring the mentees up to speed. The young men and women also worked in several departments before they were assigned to shadow an expatriate who was given six months to transfer his skills and knowledge.

Resource barriers also exist at the organizational level. In fact, in a developing country environment, resource barriers may be considerable. When Dora took charge of NAFDAC the agency was moribund. It did not have enough income to carry out its functions. The budgetary allocation from the Federal Government was inadequate and the revenue stream from sanctions and registrations was insufficient to turn around the agency. Product registration fees had not been changed in 7 years though the exchange rate had more than quadrupled. Institutional and human capacity had to be built.

To address the resource barriers as well as implement the new strategy, Dora Akunyili proposed a significant change in the laws governing the agency. A new tariff structure was approved which made it possible for it to increase its revenues.

With the additional income, Dora and her team sent members of staff on training programmes, increased salaries and benefits significantly, equipped the laboratories and established functional offices. Thus, with the additional income, the management dealt with resource and motivational barriers to change.

The motivational hurdle is often a big challenge to the successful implementation of change. Change recipients want to know what is in it for them. This is especially so in organizations to which employees have a low moral or affective commitment. In these organizations, employees constantly evaluate the costs and benefits of continuous membership and of performance. Since change often requires extra effort, employees ask why they should make that extra effort. A clear vision would be insufficient to win their commitment to change. The change must have a meaning for the recipients. This meaning may be economic, a feeling of belonging to a successful organization, professional development, etc.

Let us consider what Tade did to facilitate knowledge transfer from expatriates to locals in Ericsson, Nigeria. He realized that it may not be in the interest of the expatriates to mentor the young engineers and literally work themselves out of a job, especially during a global recession. To overcome this motivational barrier, he did a number of things. First, he got the full support of the head of the division. Second, he documented the mentoring programme: number of sessions to be held, content of the sessions, specific feedback times and forms, sign off by both the coach and the young engineer. He also instituted regular feedback from the engineers as to how much they were learning. In effect, he introduced a control system that enabled him ensure coaching was going on. He also ensured that the organization recognized those expatriates who had done a good job of coaching their assignees. This gave the expatriates some visibility within the global organization. Besides, the young recruits had been given some foundational technical courses and had attended training on emotional intelligence and coaching.

Dora Akunyili recognized the importance of motivating the staff if she was to win the battle against fake drugs. She set up a disciplinary committee to investigate cases of bribery and corruption among the staff. Employees who were found guilty were recommended to the board for firing. Any employee who reported a violation by a company or a member of staff was immediately rewarded with a training programme abroad. This was a major incentive for the employees: not only did they improve their skills but they were also paid an attractive daily allowance during the programme.

Finally, the change agent must deal with the political hurdles. Politics is a fact of organizational life. In times of change and uncertainty, organizational politics can become intense. The change initiative may alter the status quo in terms of the distribution of power; vested interests may be challenged and some power bases rendered ineffectual. The political hurdle may be so difficult that the change initiative has to be abandoned.

The change agent must identify the power sources, power brokers, the interests at play and the cliques which may exist. In a highly politicized environment, if people feel they will lose power, clout or position, they could organize an inordinate amount of resistance. Change agents need a critical mass of influential people who believe in the change and are willing to make it happen. According to Kim and Mauborgne (2003: 62), 'once the beliefs and energies of a critical mass of people are engaged, conversion to a new idea will spread like an epidemic, bringing about fundamental change very quickly'.

Assessing the Nature and Causes of Resistance

It is important for change agents to gauge the reactions to change at this contemplative stage and in subsequent stages. Knowledge of how many people are committed to the change and how many are either resisting the change or are apathetic should help change agents develop interventions designed to address resistance.

According to Clawson (2007), there are many possible reactions to change. The full range of reactions varies along a continuum from active resistance to passion for the change (Figure 9.1). Some employees may actively resist the new direction in which the change initiative is trying to take the organization. These active resistors voice their discontent and may even attract a followership. Passive resistance is more covert. Passive resistors do not believe in the new direction but they do not voice their resistance. Instead they slow down implementation, typically by dragging their feet.

Employees who are apathetic do not care one way or the other. They will not actively resist nor support the change. They may view the change with cynicism resulting from prior experience (Self *et al.* 2007: 212). Compliance is a level of support for change. Those who comply will do what is required: they will carry out the instructions. Agreement is a higher level of buy-in to the new vision. Those who agree with the change initiative would like to do what is required of them. Finally, employees with the highest level of support for the change are those who are engaged and are passionate about the change; they believe in the change and will do what is required. They are the change champions; they 'bring lots of energy to their work' Clawson (2007: 3).

If the level of employee support for the change is low, it may be difficult to implement the change initiative successfully. Change agents must ascertain whether or not they have enough change champions (people who are committed to the change and are willing to do what is needed to make it happen). The reality is that some employees will move to the preparation stage while others are in the contemplation or even the pre-contemplation stages. The change agent must develop appropriate strategies for winning the commitment of the latter to the change even as he or she supports those who are moving to the preparation stage to encourage them to make yet another transition: to the action stage.

Active Resistance	Passive Resistance	Apathy	Compliance	Agreement	Engagement

FIGURE 9.2 Reactions to change (Clawson 2007)

Ken Olori was appointed executive chairman of a government agency and given the mandate to transform the agency. He personally selected those members of staff he felt could make the transition to the new culture and invited them to a company retreat. He wanted them to identify the problems facing the agency and articulate an action plan.

During the three-day retreat, the participants analysed the agency and identified the problems. They also came up with some solutions. Each participant was asked to write a one-page submission on what they would do to transform the agency if they were the executive chairman. At the end of the retreat, Olori was certain that a majority of those who attended the retreat were ready to take action to effect the change. He had developed a small group of champions.

To move them from contemplation to some action taking, he arranged 15-minute meetings with everyone who attended the retreat. He discussed the suggestions they had made at the retreat. Suggestions were grouped according to the issues raised and project teams set up around the issues. For example, all those who suggested a review of contracting met with Olori on the same day. He created a project around contracting and appointed a leader for the project. In a very short time, more than 25 transformation projects were up and running. While the rest of the organization remained at the pre-contemplation or contemplation stage, he succeeded in moving some of the retreat participants to the preparation stage.

Sometimes, preconceived notions of resistance prevent change agents from giving people an opportunity to change. In one organization that was automating its processes, the change agent was advised that the older members of staff would resist the change. Many had never used a computer and the new job required some level of proficiency in the use of computers. Some members of the top management team doubted if these 'senior citizens' would adapt and considered terminating their appointment. The change agent, however, insisted on training them and giving them an opportunity. Beyond the computer training programmes, the change agent built the confidence of the employees and in a fun environment they learnt to use the computer. The 'senior citizens' embraced the change and none of them was fired.

Supporting the Transition from the Preparation to the Action Stage

If the training programmes and other interventions in the previous stage have gone well, change recipients enter this stage with higher levels of self-efficacy, skills and knowledge. However, as they take the bigger steps, they encounter new situations, face new challenges and require some support to keep up the tempo and not slide back to the old ways.

Communication at this stage should not be about the need for change only. People want to know what is happening at each stage, what is likely to happen in the future and how it will affect them, their department and the business. Change agents should also communicate the results and celebrate achievements. If the change was started where it is likely to succeed, the change agent will have success stories to share. These success stories give employees the confidence that it can be done; in fact, it has been done.

It is even more important in times of change to show care towards employees. In Equity Bank employees felt supported as they implemented change. When Equity Bank computerized its operations, some managers and their colleagues spent weekends at the office to facilitate a smooth transfer. The managing director, James Mwangi, bought snacks and drinks for the team and stayed with them a few times. It took only four months to install the new system. At the end of the project, James sent a letter of commendation to each member of the project team. He also sent a 'thank you' letter to their spouses with a cheque in appreciation for the sacrifices they had made during the installation of the new system. The letter of appreciation was a great morale booster for the team.

The change agent should consider creating support groups to facilitate knowledge transfer as well as provide support for team members as they go through change. It is pertinent to note that employees enter the stages of change with different levels of knowledge, skill, and self-efficacy. These support groups become avenues for sharing experience, solutions, and also for emotional support. Support groups discuss the challenges and each one talks about what is working and why. They effectively become change agents. Sharing can be done over the intranet. Awards may be given to those employees who shared the most relevant experiences or knowledge. Employees could send their nominations to the change agents.

Further training, coaching and mentoring may also be required to build skill levels and increase self-efficacy. Other barriers to change must be identified and dealt with. One manager was leading the team responsible for automating processes in his division. During implementing, reliable power supply became a problem; the standby generator was not functioning. Employees immediately began to complain. The manager, afraid that employees would go back to the manual system, rented a generator and ensured regular and reliable power supply. The change recipients realized that there was no going back.

Research by Self et al. (2007) suggests that employees are likely to find change justifiable and be less resistant to it if perceived organizational support (POS) is high. Even when the negative impact of the change was high, employees who had high POS found the change justifiable. POS consisted of: recognition of employee performance, assisting employees in solving problems and demonstrating a concern for employee safety, opinion, goals, and values (ibid: 226).

Change agents will do well to ascertain the sources of resistance to the change. They need to find out how many people are at the different stages of change, the level of adoption of the new systems or processes and proficiency levels (where relevant). With this knowledge they can develop appropriate interventions.

If the change is to be successful, the official change agents have to create other agents at all levels of the organization. It is the latter who coach their teams through the transition. During the transformation of Equity Mortgage, team members provided support for each other. They met each day to share experience and strategize. The team became a support group at a time when the institution was considered a village bank and their marketing people were snubbed by other banks.

Supporting the Transition From the Action to the Maintenance Stage

Employees who transit to the action stage have greater awareness of the change initiative, improved skill or competency level and high levels of self-efficacy. The challenge at this stage is that of embedding the change.

Depending on the level of adoption and proficiency, change agents develop support systems so employees persist in using the new ways. Sharing success stories (testimonies) at different fora is a way to winning over other employees to the change. Sometimes, employees are using the new and the old system. For example, in one organization, it took three years to get the employees to abandon the manual system and move to Oracle. Employees were afraid of losing data, of errors in the new system so the two systems ran side by side till the managing director insisted that the organization abandon the manual system.

Change agents should keep communication going. The benefits are much clearer at this stage. It is important to communicate them and to appreciate the efforts of employees who made it possible. Not all change recipients are in the action stage. Some may have remained in earlier stages and have to be won over.

Finally, it takes time to change behaviour, to adopt new systems, processes, etc. It can also be very challenging. Supporting people during change can make a big difference to the success of the change effort.

Resistance can be Good

Even when change barriers have been significantly reduced and a critical mass of people are committed to the change, some employees may continue to resist the change. If the resistance is strong enough, it could derail the change initiative altogether. In these circumstances, it is sometimes necessary to wield the big stick. The CEO of a large, bureaucratic organization wanted to implement drastic change after a very successful first term in office. The change involved business process re-engineering and institutionalizing a new organizational culture. Consultants were called in and training programmes were organized with facilitators from two top business schools.

He found a few champions and many resistors. There were also the 'siddon look' category – those who 'sit down and look' and hope the whole thing will be blown away. The CEO persisted despite advice to the contrary.

After months spent selling the change to employees, resistance continued. He found a very vocal source of resistance was coming from a senior manager with over thirty year's tenure in the organization. The CEO decided to confront the resistance. He called a meeting of the change agents, the consultants and the top team. Those with issues with the programme were encouraged to articulate their objections. The senior manager (a member of the senior management team) made several objections. The consultants responded with slide after slide showing that his concerns had indeed been considered. Resistance continued and the senior manager continued to voice his disapproval of the new direction.

One day, the CEO invited the senior manager to lunch. He told him point blank that he had heard his views but the change would continue with or without him. He went on to give him an ultimatum; "If you are not in with us, you will have to leave." Sometimes, it comes down to this: if you are not in, you have to go.

But resistance is not always negative. In fact, it can be good. Those who resist change tell us something about the change, how it will affect them and/or how it will affect the organization. According to Waddell and Sohal (1998: 545), 'resistance plays a crucial role in drawing attention to aspects of change that may be inappropriate, not well thought through, or perhaps plain wrong'. Change agents require an open mind to listen to the naysayers with the intention of learning more about the barriers to change: both subjective and objective.

So far, our attention has been focused on winning the commitment of employees to the change. The impact of change, however, goes beyond employees and even the organization. A number of groups and institutions have a stake in the organization. Change agents should consider identifying key stakeholders of the change and winning their commitment. This topic is the subject of the next section.

Summary

In this section, we discussed how change agents can facilitate behaviour change through appropriate interventions at the different stages of change. We highlighted the characteristics of each stage of change and discussed the actions change agents could take to get employees committed to the change. We recognized that all change recipients do not make the transitions at the same time. Strategies to win commitment will therefore have to be varied so as to address the needs of employees at different stages of change.

This book is about planned change. If change is to be successful, the destination and the blueprint should be clear. The change agent must recognize the importance of power brokers and form coalitions to drive the change. People should also be energized and learning and growth encouraged. Change strategists and agents must meet the expectations of change recipients and overcome the barriers to change.

Winning Stakeholder Commitment

Stakeholders have a potentially large impact on the organization's reputation and performance. Media reports, negative evaluations by regulators, strikes by unions, demonstrations by advocacy groups may adversely affect an organization.

Negative comments by employees in the community can also have a negative effect on the company's brands.

Change agents may not have the time and resources to personally contact all constituencies who have some stake in the organization. Besides, stakeholders are not of equal importance. The challenge is to identify key publics whose support is critical for the change and who can influence other constituencies and/or persons.

Post et al. (2002: 8) define an organization's stakeholders as 'individuals and constituencies that contribute, either voluntarily or involuntarily, to its wealth-creating capacity and activities, and who are therefore its potential beneficiaries and/or risk bearers'. They argue that the relationship with stakeholders affects the organization's ability to create wealth. To be successful, change agents must be cognizant of the goals, interests and concerns of stakeholders and manage the relationships appropriately. The first step is that of 'understand[ing] a firm's entire set of stakeholder relationships' (Post et al. 2002) and identifying the key stakeholders, their interests and concerns.

Dora Akunyili of NAFDAC identified a broad spectrum of stakeholders with whom she engaged in the transformation of the agency. She developed a good working relationship with the President of the Federal Republic of Nigeria (he hired her for the job), the Minister of Health, the NAFDAC Council and her senior management team. The Council members attended the retreat where the mission, vision, values and strategy of the agency were agreed. She met with the President from time to time to provide him feedback on what she was doing and to seek his support for specific activities.

She organized stakeholders' fora: an avenue for listening to the concerns, suggestions, and interests of stakeholders. At one such forum, some stakeholders complained about the NAFDAC registration guidelines. The management reviewed the guidelines and developed operating procedures for the agency. One result of these meetings was that, in one year, the number of product registrations was more than half of that of the previous seven years.

Dora and her team canvassed the support of several government agencies in the war against fake and adulterated products in Nigeria. They made advocacy visits which led to collaborative agreements with the Inspector General of Police, Nigerian Customs, Nigerian Ports Authority, Nigerian Drug Law Enforcement Agency, to mention a few. The DG and her team shared with these bodies the vision of NAFDAC, the need to cleanse the country of fake drugs and the role the stakeholders could play in the war. The support of these bodies was critical to the successful transformation of NAFDAC. See Figure 9.3 for NAFDAC's stakeholders

NAFDAC's management also organized workshops for pharmaceutical companies, pharmacists, manufacturers, etc. Dora went on to canvass the support of the Press in the war against fake drugs. Her partnership with the Press gave NAFDAC a lot of media coverage which enabled Dora and her team to educate the public on the dangers of fake drugs. One of the results of this partnership was that the public became the main source of information on fake drugs.

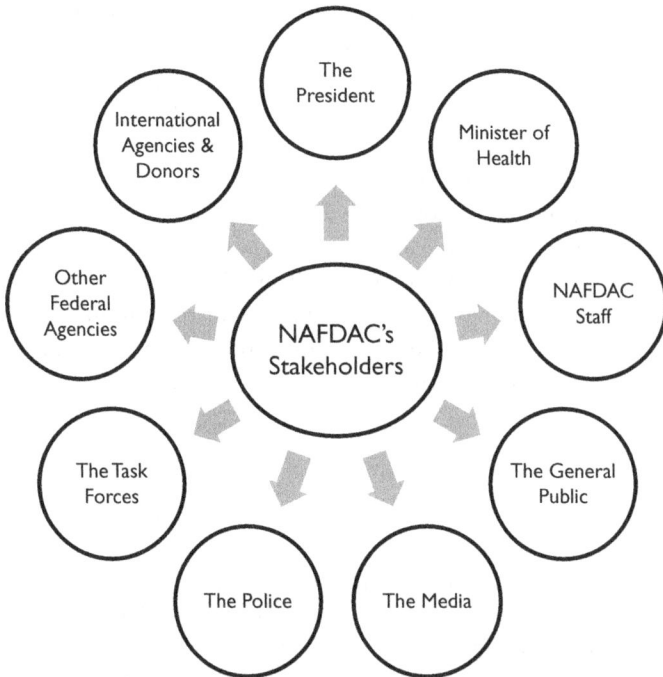

FIGURE 9.3 NAFDAC's stakeholders

Olori realized very earlier in his tenure that he needed the support of key stakeholders if he was to effect change in the government agency. As soon as he took charge of the agency, he identified the key stakeholders and began to develop a relationship with them. During his first weeks on the job, he met with several past chairmen of the agency. He thought that some members of the staff had loyalties to the past chairmen (there had been heavy board churn in the agency recently) so he decided to get them involved and also to learn from them. To provide some continuity, he asked the immediate past chairman the three things he had in the pipeline that he would have liked to implement and Olori implemented them.

Olori and his team also began a lecture series. They identified organizations that had been successfully transformed as key stakeholders from whom they could learn. The chairmen or director generals of these organizations were invited to the monthly lecture series to share their experience with the staff.

Alpha plc identified the Nigerian Stock Exchange as an important stakeholder of its restructuring exercise. Even as the change was being announced to company employees, the finance director was on the floor of the Exchange to communicate the restructuring plan and answer questions. The corporate affairs manager held a press conference and issued a press release in which he justified the restructuring. The human resource director canvassed the support of both the in-house and the national unions. The result was that the company's stock price remained stable and the articles in the press were positive in spite of the fact that 300 employees had been let go. Other companies, such as Shell Petroleum Development Company, are learning that the community and the environment are critical stakeholders for a sustainable business.

In summary: winning the commitment of employees and other stakeholders is important for successful change. Stakeholders are those who can affect the wealth-creating abilities and activities of the organization. Many of them have a stake in any major change initiative in the organization. Change strategists and agents should be assured of their commitment before they begin to implement the change. In the next section, the focus of the discussion is the change agents: those who have the responsibility of implementing the change initiative.

The Change Agent

In this book we have used the terms change agent or implementer to refer to those who have the mandate to implement change in the organization. While the change strategists define the vision and provide support for the change, the agents are the change facilitators. They act as consultants, advisers, counsellors (Caldwell 2003).

In some cases, the change agent is a single individual whose primary assignment is the implementation of change in the organization. For example, a multinational corporation in Nigeria employed a change agent to implement Six Sigma in the organization. However, there is a move towards change management teams. Very often, the team is expected to lead change while carrying out their routine jobs. Team members may be drawn from different levels of the organization or from senior management positions.

Whether the change agent is a single individual or a team, the personal characteristics of the agent are important for the success of the change. The choice of change agent is therefore an important decision. Doyle (2002: 493) noted that change agents 'are often selected on the basis of their competence in an existing role and may lack the added knowledge, skills and expertise to perform as effective change agents'.

Kendra and Taplin (2004) and Nikolaboau *et al.* (2007) pulled from the change literature the knowledge, skills and competencies change agents require to be successful in implementing change. These include: interpersonal skills, communication skills, collaboration skills, influencing skills and problem-solving skills. Nikolaboau *et al.* (2007) found in their experimental study that resilience (the ability to bounce back) was the most important characteristic of successful change agents. They also found that project management skills were positively related to team performance.

Lau and Woodman (1995) showed that locus of control is an important variable for success as change agents. Those change agents who believed that they could exercise control over their environment (those with high internal locus of control) were more likely to be successful than others.

Another personal disposition which has been found to be important for change agents is self-efficacy (Judge *et al.* 1999). Change agents with high self-efficacy are more likely to be successful in implementing change. Gabarro's (1987) work on taking charge suggests that experience in the organization (being an insider) did not matter for success though insiders make changes faster than outsiders. What did count was the manager's ability to build a team: his or her interpersonal skills.

Past research suggests that 'perceptions of competence and legitimacy are crucial for the role of the change agent' (Scurrah *et al.* 1971, cited in Nikolaboau *et al.* 2007: 307). The credibility of the change agent is important for winning support for the change. Change recipients want to be assured that the change agent(s) can deliver the expected outcomes. They research the background of the agents and evaluate their legitimacy and competence. If the general perception is that the change agent has no track record of performance and it seems that management is keeping the agent busy by giving him charge of the change initiative, recipients are not likely to commit to the change. If management is serious about change, they would choose people who can do the job.

Although Dora Akunyili had an impressive curriculum vitae – she was a university lecturer, had served on several senate committees, was active in the Pharmaceutical Society of Nigeria – President Obasanjo chose her to lead the transformation of NAFDAC for one reason: she was honest. He had heard that Dora had returned about £12,000 to the state after doctors told her she did not need the surgery for which the money had been given to her by the government. The chairman of the government agency she was working for at the time wrote her a commendation letter. The story was carried by a national newspaper.

Dora's success at NAFDAC can also be explained by her background. In spite of the fact that her parents were middle-class folks, she had had a rugged childhood. She grew up with her maternal grandmother in the village. She woke up at 4 am daily and walked 5 km to fetch water from the river. According to her: 'My

TABLE 9.1 Choosing Change Agents

The change strategists will need to find answers to the questions:
1. Should we select a change agent or a team?
2. Is this a full-time role or a part-time one? If full-time, are there any career prospects for the person(s) after the change has been institutionalized?
3. Should we use external consultants? If so, how do we ensure we own the project and that knowledge is transferred from the consultants to our staff?
4. What criteria should we use in selecting change agents?
5. How do we support the change agents politically, emotionally?
6. How many change projects or initiatives do we have on our plate?
7. Should we limit the number of initiatives any one employee/manager can participate in as a change agent?

upbringing helped me a lot. I have very good health. I can work long hours without getting tired. I am street smart' (Ovadje and Utomi 2007: 13). One of her managers commented on her self-efficacy and resilience: 'for her, most things are do-able; obstacles have to be overcome' (Ovadje and Utomi 2007: 14).

In 1994, Equity Building Society was declared insolvent by the Central Bank of Kenya. The management pleaded for time to turn it around. The Central Bank asked them to find a change agent. They put forward James Mwangi's name and the Central Bank acquiesced. James had had a brilliant career. He joined PricewaterhouseCoopers upon graduation. He moved to Ernst & Young after a few years and later to Trade Bank where he rose very quickly to the position of Group Financial Controller. In 1994, James Mwangi was one of the most senior Kenyan bankers in the country. He was also one of the three major depositors who accounted for 85 per cent of Equity's total deposits. James took a huge pay cut (one twelfth of his salary) to join Equity as the chief financial officer and change agent. In 2006, when the bank went public, James had transformed Equity into one of the largest and most profitable banks in Kenya.

Dora and James worked with their respective teams to transform their organizations. They embody some of the qualities of successful change agents. They pushed for results while caring about the people. They were not overwhelmed by obstacles; rather they were convinced that the changes could be successfully implemented.

Some change agents begin the change implementation process with a lot of enthusiasm and energy but over time their fervour cools and change recipients easily fall back to their old ways. A challenge change agents face is how to maintain their passion and energy during trying times. Sometimes change takes a toll on the persons driving the change. Buchanan (2003) researched the characteristics, demands and pressures of change agents. He found that change agents experienced a lot of stress (due to uncertainty regarding their role, increased workload, pressure to deliver results). They also had to deal with the pain of others (people who were let go or hurt by the change initiative).

The change agent is not impervious to negativity. Sometimes, feedback is negative, resistance is strong and results are slow in coming. The change agent herself or himself may be overwhelmed and be tempted to throw in the towel.

One change manager found a way to keep the flame burning. When the going was tough and he was feeling discouraged, he called some of the change champions to his office, talked with them and got some inspiration from them to keep going.

Some others post the vision, the goals, slogans, etc. on a notice board in their office as a reminder. They use entertaining symbols. Change agents also recognize that they need time off to get a balanced existence, refresh and get the energies they need to continue to push for the change.

Change creates greater levels of visibility and learning opportunities for change agents. If change agents have developed knowledge and skill, it could propel them into new career trajectories (Buchanan 2003: 680). On the other hand, change can be very difficult and messy. It could lead to stress, even burnout and negatively affect the career of change agents.

Summary

Change agents may be individuals or teams. They may be assigned the responsibility of implementing change on a part-time or full-time basis. They may be senior managers or be drawn from different levels of the hierarchy.

The choice of the change agent is very important as it can affect the success of the change initiative. Research suggests that the characteristics of successful change agents include: interpersonal skills, influence skills, problem-solving skills. They also tend to have high self-efficacy and are credible.

Change is difficult and could be messy. Change agents may suffer from high levels of stress and bear a lot of pain (personal and others' pain). The change agent role is a highly visible one. The learning opportunities presented by the change and the change agent's role prepare them for new career opportunities.

Key Success Factors for Winning Commitment to Change

In this last section of the chapter, we discuss some of the critical success factors for winning the commitment of stakeholders to change.

Choice of and Support for Change Agents

We have seen that the choice of change agents is a signal as to whether top management wants the change to happen or not. The credibility of the agent, her or his commitment to the change and her or his tenacity are important for successful implementation. Top management should beware of using performance on the job as the only criterion for selecting change agents; high performers do not necessarily have the competencies required of change agents.

It is important to realize that change agents are human; they get tired and sometimes get discouraged. The change strategists should provide them with the emotional and psychological support they need to stay the course.

Credible Communication

To make change happen in an organization, the change recipients must see the need for change. Change agents should communicate the need for change using several media. One CEO, who was hired from outside the organization, held a town hall meeting every month. Senior managers were not allowed at the town hall meeting. Employees could say just about anything during the meetings without fear of reprisal. The CEO used the town hall meeting to communicate his strategy and to obtain feedback from his troops.

Another change agent held town hall or village square meetings. These are reminiscent of the meetings held in many African villages. Participation is open to all and the purpose of the meeting is to promote the good of the collective. Focus groups, one-on-one meetings, notice boards, the Intranet, are all means of getting the message across and getting feedback from the staff.

The Intranet and other non-face-to-face communication media may not be sufficient in the African cultural context. In fact, in some situations it may be considered an insult. Mangaliso (2001) tells the story of a dispute in a mining company in South Africa. The lack of appreciation of African values by the management led to a two-week strike. The workers asked the management to address them on the issues which led to the conflict. The management refused to address the staff. Instead they sent envoys to meet with the workers and posted written statements on bulletin boards. The workers' response was to go on strike. Mangaliso (2001: 23) explained: 'For the group of African employees in the case, face-to-face communication was an important aspect of dispute resolution. To them, addressing someone in person is a sign that you respect and care for them.'

Change agents should tell the story of the change in such a way that the recipients see the big picture and what they need to do to make it happen. Great communication requires the use of words, images and emotions. Story-telling has been in use in Africa since time immemorial. The culture and values of the people are transmitted through stories and proverbs. Each story has a moral, a message. Change agents will do well to tap into this rich history.

Role-modelling the new way sends a powerful signal to the organization. It is not enough for the change agents to be role models. Top management and the immediate supervisors are important referents for employees. Senior management and key influencers should lead by example. Lawson and Price (2006: 34–5) emphasized the importance of role models at all levels of the organization: 'In any organization, people model their behaviour on "significant others": those they see in positions of influence. ... So to change behaviour consistently throughout the organization, it isn't enough to ensure that people at the top are in line with the new ways of working; role models at every level must lead by example.'

An expatriate managing director of an oil company in Nigeria was unable to cut costs significantly during his three-year term. When he arrived, he got himself an expensive car, and lived what employees considered a flamboyant lifestyle. His successor refused to get a new car: he said the three-year-old car of his predecessor was good enough. He ordered lunch from the same restaurant as his secretary. He ate groundnuts and boli (roasted plantain). When he asked for cuts, the unions cooperated with him and he succeeded in implementing the much-needed cost reduction initiative. The message from the staff was clear: lead by example.

Identify and Manage Key Stakeholders

Another key success factor is the ability to identify key stakeholders and develop a strategy for winning their commitment. Successful change agents know they cannot lead alone. They look for other change champions. Shell Petroleum Development Company Nigeria learnt the hard way that ignoring key stakeholders in the community could affect its reputation and revenues globally.

Support Personal Transitions through the Stages of Change

Finally, change agents should build the confidence and competence of recipients as they go through the stages of change. They should appreciate the different perspectives of change and develop strategies to get as many people on board as possible.

Summary

Winning the commitment of employees to change is a very important choice that change strategists and agents have to make. Without the commitment of the troops, the change initiative is not likely to be successful. Sometimes, employees do not see the need. They believe that the organization is in a stable environment: a zoo. Meal times are sacred, visiting hours are known, and one is taken care of. A major challenge change strategists and agents face is how to get employees to leave the zoo and work in the real world. As Mike Macharia put it: 'Entrepreneurship is a journey: you are running to eat or to avoid being eaten. An entrepreneur lives in the jungle. At a global level, I see myself as a gazelle; I am trying to stay alive. At the local level, I am a lion. If I don't wake up and run, I will die. The entrepreneur's challenge is to get the employees to leave the zoo and join him in the jungle.'

10

EVALUATION AND REFINEMENT

Introduction: Why Evaluate Performance?

Change leadership involves a series of choices. In this chapter, we discuss choices regarding evaluation and refinement of the change initiative. Evaluation is necessary for successful change. It helps focus attention and ensure that the change initiative is on track. Through regular evaluation, the organization takes stock and tracks performance on a variety of metrics. It provides answers to questions such as: where are we on the change journey? What milestones have been achieved? Which events were successfully managed? Nevertheless, research suggests that change is not often evaluated formally and systematically (Doyle *et al.* 2000).

If the change strategists and agents know where they are going (the vision is clear), and the success measures have been identified and agreed on, tracking progress can be relatively easy. Evaluation provides concrete information for decision-making regarding various aspects of the change. Without evaluation and consequently corrective action-taking, the vision may not be actualized. As Pettigrew *et al.* (2001) noted: change initiatives tend to run out of steam. Yet, little change evaluation is done (Doyle *et al.* 2000).

Some change initiatives are begun with enthusiasm but, as the pressure for results increases, many are abandoned or simply fail. As the managing partner of a consulting firm in Nigeria put it, people expect the change drivers to demonstrate that the changes are yielding results. They want the change agents to show that the improvements in say the bottom line are due to the changes being instituted in the organization. If change recipients do not see the expected results, they easily fall back to the old ways.

The change trajectory is often nonlinear: sometimes there are delays and unexpected consequences. Amis *et al.* (2004: 33) found in their study that change in organizational elements did not occur in a linear manner. They found 'oscillations, delays and reversals' though some of the organizations they studied did appear to move in a linear fashion. These challenges can be expected to be more acute in environments characterized by high uncertainty: in these environments linear transformations are rare. Change agents have to be prepared to change even the change vision itself if the need arises. In order to do this, they need information about how much change is really taking place and what is facilitating or constraining the change.

Change affects people differently. Those who feel a deep sense of loss may attempt to truncate the process altogether; some others may use their position and clout to reverse some decisions around the change. Change agents have to re-think, re-assess, and re-strategize to ensure the organization arrives at the desired destination (which itself may be somewhat altered as the change progresses).

Evaluation provides the organization with concrete performance information. This helps in motivating the change recipients. When milestones are achieved, there is cause for celebration. 'We did it!' is often a great motivator to higher levels of performance. Take the case of the manager of a beverage plant in Nigeria. The manager and the packaging team tracked their performance.

The team set the goals, held regular performance reviews and agreed on how to improve performance. Whenever the targets were met, the manager celebrated with the team: he bought puff-puff (a snack) and drinks. He managed individual and team performance. In just a few months, the results were impressive; within six months he had turned around the factory. He won the Manager of the Year Award and the factory won an award that year. As this case shows, a major reason for performance evaluation is to identify performance gaps and design interventions aimed at closing the gaps.

Evaluation also helps change drivers to win the commitment of some of the most sceptical change recipients. To win their commitment, some objective evidence that things are changing is sometimes critical (Skinner 2004). Evidence that change is happening – that it has happened in some part of the organization – may be the major reason why some sceptics will choose to join the change train.

Evaluation and refinement involves a review of the change plan and performance metrics, performance monitoring and, finally, action-taking.

What to Evaluate?

Evaluation is about performance management – reviewing objectives and monitoring and performance.

The outcomes of change initiatives are usually not immediately evident: they take time to become reality. A challenge of change evaluation is what to evaluate. If change agents wait to evaluate the final outcomes, they may never see these outcomes. As discussed in Chapter 5, change strategists and agents track certain signs that the outcomes will be achieved in due course.

Change agents may evaluate the change model, the impact of the change on people, the stages of change, reactions to change and the development of change capacity.

Evaluating the Change Model

The model presented in this book is a decision-making model. Throughout the book, we have emphasized the need for alignment or consistency among the choices around change. During evaluation, change agents try to find out if the decisions have been implemented and the results of such actions. For example, to actualize the vision of CMC Connect, decisions were taken to renovate the office, become affiliated with one of the best PR companies in the world, and overlay a project structure on the current organizational structure. During change evaluation, change agents and strategists want to know how well the organization is doing regarding the change. See Table 10.1 for typical questions they may want to ask.

During evaluation, the change agents investigate how well the organization is doing regarding the plan. All the decisions which were taken regarding the vision, change targets, success measures, leadership style, pace, and winning commitment to change are reviewed. Jick and Peiperl (2003: 91) stress that visions need to be adaptable. The environment is complex and uncertain, change strategists and agents have bounded rationality; they cannot foresee all possible circumstances. They therefore cannot assume that the change plan will be implemented without

TABLE 10.1 Evaluating the Change Initiative at CMC Connect

How well are we doing in actualizing the vision? How are we doing regarding the success measures we agreed?

How many blue-chip companies do we have in our customer portfolio? What share of the market of the blue-chips in West Africa do we have?

Regarding the activities and work plans:

Certain events and interventions were supposed to happen at certain times. Did they happen? Why? Why not?

Are we delivering according to plan? Why? Why not?

Have we dedicated the required resources to the change effort? Which resources are not available? Why? What can be done to make them available?

Are we communicating effectively? What kind of feedback are we getting from the troops? What are their major concerns?

Is the coalition growing? At what rate? Why? Is it powerful 'in terms of titles, information and experience, reputation and relationships' (Kotter 1995: 62)?

Is the pace and sequence of change right? Is the change in a lull? Why? What can be done to re-invigorate and revive it?

Is the leadership style effective?

Do we have an evaluation schedule? Do we take corrective actions? Have we communicated these actions clearly and effectively?

any changes to it. Evaluation and refinement is necessary because it incorporates learning as you go.

As the change is implemented, all change actors (strategists, agents and recipients) learn. As we will see later, this learning can be positive or negative. Change agents may, for example, come to the realization that some change targets were inadvertently omitted and should be added if the vision is to be actualized. The change style may not be effective and may have to be changed. Change agents will ask themselves several questions as they review the information they have gathered and what they have learned about the organization, the change process itself, themselves, etc.

Evaluating the Impact of the Change on People

This is a very important aspect of change, yet it is often ignored. Change affects people. One reason for the failure of change initiatives is the lack of attention to people issues. Take the example of Bunmi who worked for Bank A. A merger between Bank A and two others was announced. All employees were told they would have to interview for a job in the new organization. For Bunmi it was a traumatic experience. She waited in the office till 11.30 pm to be interviewed. No food or drink was provided. It was assumed they were lucky to be interviewed. One morning a few days later, employees were told that if they had not received a letter from the Human Resource Department that meant they had been fired. Although Bunmi was retained, her commitment to the bank waned; she left as soon as she found another job. Change recipients like Bunmi can frustrate a change effort because of the way they were treated.

It is important to track peoples' reaction to the change. If there is resistance, what is the source of the resistance? What are the naysayers telling us that can help move the agenda forward?

Some years ago, Alpha Nigeria plc decided to restructure its activities: the company outsourced all non-core activities. As a result, about 300 people were let go. The management was aware that by this decision they had changed the psychological contract between the employees and the company. Before this time, employees believed that so long as you performed, you had a job in Alpha. All of a sudden, employees saw their colleagues (good performers) being asked to leave the organization.

The management decided to shut down the factory for a week in order to make some structural changes and to give people time to recover. When employees came back to work the following week, they were welcomed with posters; the top managers met informally with workers to re-assure them about the future. In addition, a questionnaire was distributed to all employees asking them to evaluate the restructuring exercise. Some the questions included: Was it necessary? Was it fair? Did the right people leave? The results of the survey helped management design interventions to correct some wrong impressions especially on the factory floor.

The Alpha case points to the importance of evaluating reactions to change at the end of change events. In the case of Bank A referred to above, if an evaluation of employee reactions had been done after the placement exercise, the low morale among the staff may have been uncovered and the change agents would have designed interventions to address the issues.

The Stages of Change

Evaluation can also be done as change recipients transit from one stage of change to the following. In the last chapter, we argued that change agents should design strategies that support people so they move from one stage of change to the next. During evaluation, change agents may want to review these strategies. See Table 10.2 for typical questions.

Tracking peoples' reactions as they go through change and taking corrective measures where necessary is important for organizational change success. These evaluations may reveal the barriers that recipients meet as they go through change. Knowledge of the kind and nature of the barriers employees face in different parts of the organization should help change agents design specific interventions aimed at overcoming these difficulties.

TABLE 10.2 Evaluation as People move along the Stages of Change

---

Pre-Contemplation to Contemplation Stage

Was the communication plan implemented? For example, were T-shirts, face caps and other communication materials delivered on time? Are employees using the suggestion boxes? Is dialogue in the organization around the change initiative? Is the initiative visible? How many converts are there among influential people?

Contemplation to Action Stage

Were the training programmes effective in building knowledge, skills and feelings of self-efficacy?
Have work tools been provided according to the requirement?
Is there a coaching framework in place? Is coaching happening? Where? Why?
Are there support groups? Is knowledge being transferred within the groups and between groups? What is facilitating this? What are the hindering factors?
Is communication constant? Is it a two-way process?

Action and Maintenance Stages

Is coaching and mentoring going on to avoid falling back to old ways?
Are the new behaviours being aligned with other systems such as the performance management system, the reward and recognition system?
Is communication an on-going activity?

One change agent in Kenya tracked both the inputs and the outputs of the change. The inputs included the training programmes: number of awareness and training sessions held, timeliness in delivering the standard operating procedures, number of weekly meetings held in the units and departments and the quality of minutes taken (she carried out a random check of the minutes). Performance on these criteria gave her a sense of what was really going on. Output measures such as adoption rates, proficiency rates, the speed of adoption and timeliness in delivering the project were also tracked (Table 10.3).

It is pertinent to note that the number of training sessions held may not be an indication that change is taking place. It may be necessary to assess learning outcomes such as the level of awareness or knowledge, the skills acquired, perceived usefulness of the knowledge and skill acquired. Other learning outcomes may include self-efficacy, job performance, knowledge transfer and organizational performance (Kraiger *et al.* 1993).

Care should be taken in interpreting evaluation results. A drop in performance may actually mean that change is taking place. Take the case of the integration of two banks in Nigeria. Integration teams were set up in Abuja and Kaduna. During the integration, the best managers and employees were withdrawn from their normal duties to work on the integration teams. The level of uncertainty and the fact that the best people were withdrawn from their usual assignments for several weeks negatively affected performance in the short run.

Evaluation of Stakeholder Reactions

In Chapter 9, we discussed the importance of winning the support of key stakeholders. Some change initiatives have direct impact on a number of stakeholders and the environment. Some of these stakeholders can influence the outcomes of the change: they may be so powerful that they alter the course of the change. It is

TABLE 10.3 Output Measures

Adoption Rates

How many people are using the new system?

Speed of Adoption

How fast are employees converting to the new system? How many converts on day 1? Day 25?

Proficiency Rate

This is a measure of accuracy. How adept are employees with the new systems and processes?

therefore important for change agents to assess and monitor the reaction of key stakeholders to the change.

The change initiative may have a negative effect on the company's reputation. The Press, for example, may have written very negative articles on the organization. The strategies which were developed with respect to how the commitment of stakeholders would be won need to be evaluated and their effectiveness assessed.

Evaluation of Change Capacity

The model presented in this book incorporates learning. As change agents and recipients implement changes, they learn. This learning may be positive or negative. All three change actors may acquire new knowledge, skill and competence. The change recipients acquire knowledge regarding the change, task-related knowledge and also some knowledge of the motivations of the change strategists and agents. They make judgements regarding the need for the change, the trustworthiness of the change strategists and agents, and the organization's capacity for change. They acquire experience which influences their openness or otherwise to future change initiatives.

Change agents also have the opportunity to build competence in the specific area (e.g., in IT or ERP) as well as change management competence. They learn and make judgements about top management commitment to the change and the organization's capacity to change. Great change agents reflect on their learning and develop as leaders.

An important question to be asked in change evaluation is whether learning has been mainly positive or negative. If learning by change actors has been mostly positive, organizational capacity for change will have been improved. If, on the other hand, learning was mainly negative, the capacity of the organization to implement future changes successfully may have been significantly reduced. We will come back to this topic when we discuss the role of trust in change leadership.

Finally, change agents may want to evaluate how much knowledge transfer is taking place within units and across the organization.

Performance Monitoring and Evaluation

There are three stages in performance management: setting objectives, monitoring performance, and evaluation. Performance monitoring is about driving execution: getting things done.

Take the example of Mike Macharia of SST: Mike was concerned about SST's execution capacity. He wondered if the organizational structure was right. It seemed that the middle management was obstructing information flow. He was also concerned about some aspects of the organizational culture. Perhaps his greatest concern was the number of foreign firms that were entering the African market. They had up-to-date technology and huge resources. To remain competitive, Mike was convinced that SST had to further develop its execution skills.

The change began with all the executive committee members calculating their utilization rate and developing an activity plan, a roadmap and a project plan with deliverables and timelines in line with the agreed key performance indicators (KPIs). These were cascaded down the organizational ladder.

Mike then focused on day-to-day execution. Each executive met with his team every morning for thirty minutes. At these meetings, the executives received feedback from their team members, and they in turn provided them with direction. Once a week, the executives met to discuss the issues that arose in the daily meetings and their link to the strategic dashboard. These evaluation meetings put the team on the same page. As Skinner (2004) noted, the evaluations facilitated shared learning and interpretation.

For James Mwangi of Equity Bank, performance monitoring and evaluation is an on-going activity. He uses the performance information which is available on the intranet to evaluate, monitor and follow through. Branch managers say it is common to receive a call from James asking them to explain why, for example, the branch had opened many new accounts that day. He asks for an explanation for success as well as failure. He has a sense of when one of the managers needs coaching or mentoring and makes out time to provide the necessary support.

Obtaining Information for Evaluation

Change agents used several means to obtain the information needed for the evaluation of the change initiatives they were leading. Alpha Nigeria plc carried out an employee survey after a major restructuring of its business. Surveys and focus groups are commonly used. The use of focus groups enables the change agents to obtain a deeper understanding of the issues. Focus groups can be of employees, customers, suppliers, and other relevant stakeholders.

Blogs, discussion groups on the intranet and communities of practice are other ways of facilitating communication while obtaining some information on the effectiveness of the change, the barriers to change and the helping factors for the change.

To monitor the change effectively, change agents establish performance reporting standards and timelines. For example, performance reporting may be daily, weekly or even quarterly. The choice of the frequency of reporting is important. Weekly reporting for example provides timely information for closer monitoring and action-taking than does quarterly reporting. At Equity Bank Kenya, for example, key performance indices are updated on a daily basis and are available on the intranet.

At a federal agency, Ken Olori agreed milestones with the transformation teams and the project steering committee. Weekly status reports were generated. This made weekly monitoring and evaluation easy. In one year, the agency had undergone significant change.

The Special Case of Disruptive Change

Developing country environments are characterized by high levels of uncertainty. Change agents in this context have to continuously scan the environment for trends which may affect their organizations. Evaluation implies learning, openness to the environment; it is being alert to environmental changes even while implementing changes in the organization. For example, competitors' reaction to the strategic changes being implemented may necessitate a re-appraisal of some aspects of the change initiative.

Some environmental changes may be disruptive. An exogenous shock, such as a natural disaster or a change in technology, may threaten the very existence of the organization. This could happen while the organization is undergoing change. For example, an organization may be implementing a culture change when a new technology is introduced by a competitor or a major international company enters the market. Change agents must be able to take these new realities into account. In some cases, the external drivers of change may be so disruptive that change strategists and agents go back to the pre-vision stage.

Given the new realities in the environment, they ask themselves if a new vision needed. They may decide to abandon the current change altogether and begin a new journey. The capacity to read the environment and to adapt to new trends and realities is critical for survival in a rapidly changing environment.

Executives are paid to lead organizations and deliver on the expectations of stakeholders. In uncertain environments they have to be both gazelles and lions. They are paid to take decisions that ensure the survival and the success of the organization. They have to guide their organizations through unbeaten paths in the rainforest.

Refinement

The purpose of evaluation is to provide information for decision making. Refinement involves action taking to put the change process back on track. The corrective actions to be taken may include a change in the vision, addition of change targets, or an increase in the speed of change. Take the case of Equity Bank: the vision was: 'To be the dominant microfinance provider in Kenya by the year 2005'. In 2004, the vision was changed to cover a wider geographical region (Africa) and the timeline moved to 2020.

Corrective actions take us back to the decisions we took regarding vision, targets, success measures, pace and time, style, winning commitment. New choices may have to be made (see Table 10.4 for typical questions).

Care should be taken at the refinement stage to avoid throwing away the baby with the bathwater. It is advisable to isolate the real problem from the symptoms. Take the case of the introduction of a new performance management system in an organization. After the first appraisals had been done using the new system,

TABLE 10.4 Refinement

Targets – Should we introduce new targets?

Pace and sequence – Is it necessary to rearrange the change sequence? Should we go faster? Slower?

Winning commitment – Do we need a new plan to deal with the sources and/or causes of resistance?

Should we shelve the change effort given the new priorities?

How can we make resources available in a timely manner?

How can we improve communication across the organization?

---

several managers and staff complained that the new system was not good. They proposed a change to yet another system. The change agent listened more carefully and identified three critical variables: the quality of the performance measures, that is, the performance objectives, the quality of the evaluators, and finally the quality of the appraisal tools.

The change agents decided to work on the quality of the evaluators first. They found that a big challenge was the lack of courage of the evaluators and the quality of the dialogue during the appraisal. The change agents put together a plan to further develop performance management skills and attitudes in the managers. Once the evaluators were comfortable with the new system, resistance was reduced.

Sometimes the expected performance outcomes are slow in coming. Performance may even drop at the initial stage. However, a negative impact of the change on the bottom line may not be a sign that the change is not effective. In fact, it may well be a signal that the organization is changing. Performance improvement comes with time: change recipients go through several stages, their awareness grows, they develop skills over time and when they have learnt the new ways and are committed to the change, the organization begins to see the results.

Besides, organizations typically put their best employees on the change management team. The short-term result may be a drop in performance as these individuals split their time and energy between their regular job and the change initiative.

The Challenge of Institutionalization

When can one say change has occurred? When the change has been institutionalized, that is, when the new way becomes the routine; when the vision has been realized. For this to happen, change must be sustained over a reasonable length of time.

Given the short terms of top executives, institutionalization is an important consideration. Olori was the head of a government agency for one year. During this time, he brought about visible and fundamental changes in the agency. Sustaining these changes is a challenge.

Dora Akunyili was Director General of NAFDAC for several years. She transformed the agency. However, appointment to the position of Director General is a political decision: she could not influence the choice of her successor. When she left NAFDAC, she hoped that the people would resist a new Director General who tried to turn back the clock.

In institutions such as GTBank and Equity Bank, the mission and culture are the glue that holds the organization together. A conscious effort is made to help new organizational members imbibe the culture and work towards the attainment of the mission. Over time, the mission and values are owned by the staff: they are no longer the property of the top management. In these organizations, it is easier to sell the need for change, implement it and institutionalize it.

For example, at Equity Bank's 2010 retreat, the branch managers complained about the support they were receiving from head office (HQ), the culture of a new division in HQ and the cost of HQ. The MD encouraged them to make suggestions. All their recommendations were implemented including the shutting down of the investment banking division and major reassignments. Because a large number of organizational members believed in the mission of Equity, it was easy to institutionalize changes that were aligned with the mission.

Summary

In this book, we have emphasized that leading change is about taking and implementing decisions regarding a number of change elements. In this chapter, we presented the last of these choices: evaluation and refinement. If evaluation and refinement is to be effective, change agents should bear the following in mind.

First, the responsibility for monitoring and evaluation should be assigned to a person or team. Ideally, it should be a deliverable for someone on the change management team. This person should be responsible for ensuring that the measures are tracked and information is available in a timely manner for decision making.

Second, the focus in evaluation and refinement should be on learning and taking corrective action and not apportioning blame. We have seen that learning is critical especially in an uncertain environment characterized by rapid change. Change agents must themselves resist the temptation of being attached to the change plan. The latter is often only work in progress.

Many change efforts fail because of a lack of attention to people and how the change affects them. It is important to capture reactions to change as people go through the change. Resistance is not always negative. Those who resist change are telling us something about that change. It is up to the change agents to listen closely, to hear the unspoken (Kim and Mauborgne 2000).

One reason why sequencing decisions are important is that learning from one aspect of the business can be transferred to another. Change agents should institute avenues for the sharing of best practices. Sometimes awards and recognitions create so much competition across teams that not much knowledge transfer happens.

Finally, from the cases we have discussed, it is clear that certain factors such as information technology and project management tools facilitate change evaluation and refinement. The information required for evaluation has to be captured at a reasonable cost and should be available in a timely manner.

The timing and frequency of evaluations are also important for the success of the change initiative. Frequent evaluations facilitate closer monitoring and action taking. Timely access to resources is also important as refinement may necessitate the deployment of resources. Evaluation is one of the choices of the model: it must be consistent with other choices.

Many change efforts fail. In developing country environments, we can expect the failure rate to be higher due to the higher levels of uncertainty characteristic of these environments. Changes in technology, ease of transport and market access make it impossible for an organization to be isolated. Change objectives may evolve with time as the change initiative is implemented (Hemper and Matinson 2009: 488). Whether change is slow or fast paced, the model we have presented in this book is relevant to all those change strategists and agents who want to make change happen in their organizations. Very often, not only their jobs but the survival of the organizations they run are at stake.

Finally, no matter how well conceived the plans are, how coherent the decisions regarding vision, targets, style, etc., change has some unexpected and unplanned consequences (Harris and Ogbonna 2002). 'Change agents should be alert to shifting conditions both inside and outside the firm, vary their actions if need be, and zigzag their way to the final destination' (Huy 2001: 613).

11

CONCLUSION

Characteristics of the Model

We have presented a model of planned change in this book. The model integrates a range of choices which have been shown to be important in the design, implementation and evaluation of change. It presents change leadership as a series of decisions.

Central to the model is the idea that, for successful change, the choices change strategists and agents make must be consistent. The consistency of choices increases significantly the chances of success of the change initiative. The model presented in this book is as much about decision-making as it is about consistency in these decisions.

An important aspect of the model is that it incorporates learning. Change agents are able to take cognisance of environmental changes (including disruptive change) even as they implement change in the organization. The model also recognizes the role of learning, both positive and negative learning, during change implementation.

Some Questions

Can choice opportunities be skipped? We do not think so. This model is comprehensive. Change is a complex phenomenon. By not taking decisions (making conscious choices) regarding some elements of the model, change strategists may be taking enormous risks.

Can decisions be taken out of the order presented in this model? Once the decision to initiate change has been taken, the next logical choice opportunity is the choice of the change vision. Choices regarding the other elements of the model need not follow the sequence presented in this book. What is absolutely important is that all the decisions are consistent among themselves and with the change vision.

Usefulness of the Model

The model fits the reality of organizational life; managers make decisions. They have options and they exercise their power to choose. The model encourages an orderly sequence of choices in decision making.

The model has the potential of getting managers out of the fire-fighting mode they often find themselves in (Mintzberg 1990). The study suggests that managerial decisions are often based on intuition rather than analysis. A framework such as the one presented in this book is all the more important if organizations are to achieve expected results from change initiatives.

The salient issues in change leadership are captured by the model. The model also provides a very structured approach to change. It reduces the complexity of change initiatives by providing a framework that helps managers plan for change and thus increase the chances of success.

The model broadens the perspective of change leaders helping them see more choice opportunities than are available in previous models. This should reduce the over-emphasis on some aspect of change while forgetting other critical choice opportunities. The model presented in this book should help change strategists and agents in designing and implementing any change initiative: transformational or incremental. It contributes to our understanding of change and helps managers (in both the private and public sector) to effect successful changes in their organizations.

The Role of Trust in Leading Change

Trust is central to change leadership. It is probably more so in the African context where people and relationships matter more than results. If trust is important in leading organizations during normal times, it is even more so in times of change. Trust facilitates change; change is also an opportunity to build or strengthen trust.

Where there is no trust, employees may comply with instructions but they are not likely to commit to the change. They may spend an inordinate amount of time second-guessing the change agents. The lack of trust may exacerbate already high levels of uncertainty. Rumours will abound and the atmosphere can become toxic.

High trust levels facilitate organizational change. How change recipients interpret information and communication from management and the change agents will depend on their a priori perceptions of the credibility or otherwise of these change actors. If change strategists and agents are perceived to be credible, change recipients are likely to believe the information they are given. They feel certain that the data presented is correct, and there is really a need for change. Change recipients are likely to have positive feelings about the organization and the top management. This should be evident in their commitment to the change.

When there is mutual trust between employees and management, there is openness to communication: transparency. Honest answers are given to employee queries. Employees are confident they will not be taken advantage of so they discuss their challenges with the new ways (the change) freely.

Building Trust through Change

While trust may be a relatively stable affective state, it does change (Rune *et al.* 2005). High levels of uncertainty usually accompany change. Employees rely on change agents for information and support as they go through the change. The quality of decisions taken by change agents, the pace of change and the leadership style may affect trust levels in the organization. For example, a negative impact of the change on stakeholders may erode trust levels between change recipients and the top management. If the quality of decisions made by the change agents is poor, employees may begin to doubt their competence to lead the change and this could lead to resistance to the change.

Each change initiative is an opportunity to strengthen trust in an organization. If, on the whole, the right decisions have been taken and the choices are consistent, change recipients are likely to think that management is competent. This builds trust.

If employees feel that the benefits of the change will be enjoyed by investors and the top management alone, they are likely to feel they are being taken advantage of and thus resist the change. Trust levels are likely to fall.

As the change progresses, employees make judgments regarding the trustworthiness of the top management and the change agents. Fairness or procedural justice as well as concern for people are particularly important for trust building or erosion. Decision criteria should be clear and consistently followed. In this way, employees feel their bosses can be trusted. Change agents should also keep their commitments. Resources should be provided when needed; reward and recognition programmes should be administered as agreed.

Open communication and participation build trust. For example, taking action on suggestions made by employees (or letting them know why the suggestion cannot be implemented at that particular time) is important for maintaining and building trust in times of change.

Finally, supporting people as they go through change is critical for the maintenance or development of trust. Ovadje (2012) found in her study of trust in West Africa that if subordinates feel the boss is mainly concerned about results, they are not likely to trust him or her. The extent to which the boss is able to look beyond the individual's contribution to the person himself or herself is critical for a trusting relationship.

Let us go back to some of the cases presented in this book. Why were James Mwangi, Tayo Adenirokun and Dora Akunyili successful in changing their organizations? One of the reasons for their success in leading change initiatives in their organizations is the fact that they were trusted by their followers. James lived the mission. He said: 'My role is to live the mission and vision; to set the example, to the best of my ability. I never do anything even subconsciously that goes against the mission and vision.'

The late Tayo Adenirokun was highly respected by his staff. He was considered a professional to the core. He lived and breathed the values of the GTBank. A new employee and a manager had this to say about Tayo:

> Tayo refused to cut salaries and fire people during the Banking crisis; he respects his people and cares about their well being. I can talk to him about anything; I can even report a management staff. There is plenty of freedom to express oneself.
>
> Uncle T is amazing. He is not afraid of anything; he has nothing to hide. He does not go around with escorts. You don't have to carry his bag; he would refuse. He is simple. He takes decisions based on the facts available. He drives the culture of the bank. He is not an angel but he gets the balance right – he has a business to run and he is working with human beings.

Dora Akunyili attributes her success in turning around NAFDAC to the fact that she led by example. Since she was not corrupt, it was difficult for her staff to be corrupt. Besides, she got the board to fire several people who were found to be corrupt including a relative.

She carried out the crusade without fear or favour. She shut down the bakery of the wife of an ex-President of Nigeria because the bread was found to have bromate. The first company she sanctioned was the subsidiary of a large multinational. Dora received visitors in her office in groups. The door was left open, thus there were no private discussions.

James, Tayo and Dora had a lot in common. They were credible: they lived what they preached. They were honest. They did not hoard information; instead they made it available to all. They lived the values. They subordinated themselves to the mission of their organization. They encouraged openness, candour. They were caring – they saw employees as persons not instruments of production. It is not surprising, therefore, that they were successful change agents.

An Expatriate Leading Change in Africa

In all the cases discussed in this book, change was led by Africans in African organizations. One question remains to be answered. Given the peculiar situation of African and developing countries, what should an expatriate with a mandate to lead change in an organization in Africa bear in mind if he or she is to be successful? This is a pertinent question given that a large number of multinational corporations operate in Africa and very often an expatriate CEO is sent to lead change in the subsidiary in an African country. Very often, these expatriate CEOs have 3 to 4 years to effect change in the business. Their ability to understand the local environment and work within it is critical to their success in this role.

We asked the managing partner of a global consulting firm and a few human resource directors of multinational corporations (all Nigerians) what they thought an expatriate needs to do to be successful in leading change in the African context. They identified some of the challenges and proffered some solutions.

A challenge of change leadership which was identified by the respondents is sponsorship by the executive suite. Getting people in the top management to change can be very difficult. This is because of what one of the respondents called the 'oga' or 'big man' syndrome. According to him, 'whereas the average guy with less than six years tenure on the job can easily change, the managing director, executive directors and general managers do not see the need to model the change. They tell you: "Leave us alone and change them."'

The big man or 'oga' syndrome is perhaps due to the hierarchical nature of the African culture characterized by deference to authority, respect for positions and status differentials (Ituma *et al.* 2011). 'The big man' believes he knows the answers; he is not the problem. The problem is the followers. The task of the change implementers is to get people on the lower rungs of the ladder to change. An expatriate CEO may find it very difficult to get the support of senior managers for change. He will have to convince his team to model the change.

An expatriate coming into the African environment should also be aware that followers may appear to support a change but they may actually be indifferent to the change or even resistant to it. It is easy for an expatriate to remain at the surface, to be what one of the interviewees called a surface swimmer. He can easily float along thinking he has the support of the troops including executive directors and general managers. If he is to succeed, the expatriate must go beyond the enthusiastic reception (this is the culture: they clap for you even when they know you are not making a point!). Even executive directors and general managers may not question the judgement of the CEO so there is need to dig deep.

It is important to key into the culture of the people. One HR director talked about an expatriate CEO (an Indian) who got to know in a relatively short time when a subordinate said 'yes' but meant 'no'. He knew that even his lieutenants would not tell him his proposal made no sense even if they thought so. He had to dig deep to uncover the truth. He had to listen very closely. Over time, he understood the culture and knew when his lieutenants were solidly behind him. The inability to key into the culture of the people is a major challenge for an expatriate working in the African culture.

For an expatriate to lead change successfully in the African context, he or she must understand the macroeconomic environment. In a number of these countries, the poverty incidence is as high as 50 per cent. In these environments, people have a lot of baggage. Even executive directors have to pay school fees for the children of relatives; board members may want cash to meet several extended family obligations (they may not be interested in perks such as trips abroad for holiday). The members of staff want to know what is in it for them if this change is successful. The change strategists must show how extrinsic and intrinsic motives will be satisfied during or at the end of the change initiative.

One expatriate CEO connected very well with the people; he was able to touch the fears, aspirations and hopes of the staff. He knew the typical African can have a lot of baggage. He travelled to a city in the north of the country to see the operations and listen to the presentation by the regional manager. The CEO interrupted the presentation and asked for the numbers. The regional manager mentioned an abysmal low figure as the profit target for the year. The CEO did not respond. He simply took his briefcase, walked out of the meeting and left for the airport. This frightened the staff in that city who thought the operation would be shut down and they would lose their jobs. They worked hard and they produced very good results. The CEO knew they could do more and wanted to communicate this to them dramatically.

Many books on change leadership emphasize the importance of quick wins, of celebrating small successes. This is an opportunity to appreciate those who have shown commitment to the change and to show everyone else that change is taking place. In the African context, this is perhaps even more important. An expatriate who is able to show a quick and significant win is likely to get the support of followers throughout the change effort. One respondent told the anecdote of an expatriate CEO who was able to identify very quickly the source of the company's misfortunes. After this, he could not do anything wrong in the eyes of the factory workers. The latter and their union became his supporters and they enabled him carry out much needed change in the organization.

A foreigner trying to lead change in Africa must learn to be patient. As one respondent put it: 'What could take 6 months in the US could take 18 months here.' The environment is tough and there is a lot of uncertainty. The expatriate cannot come with a global agenda and try to work within a global time frame. Pushing it, trying to rush it, often leads to failure. He or she must appreciate the reality of working in a developing country. Sometimes, this means it takes more time to get results.

Finally, beyond the financials and other metrics people are concerned about the impact of the change on their colleagues. The change strategist must show an appreciation of the impact of the change on people. Employees want to know that the change strategists and agents are considerate and will take care of them.

CMC CONNECT

The Challenge of Realizing the Company Vision

Franca Ovadje prepared this case as the basis for class discussion rather than to illustrate either effective or ineffective handling of an administrative situation. The assistance of Eva Okolie is appreciated. Copyright © Lagos Business School, 2007. Reprinted by permission of Lagos Business School.

Yomi Badejo-Okusanya (YBO), the Managing Director of CMC Connect, was attending a programme for owner managers at the Business School. His enthusiasm for his company was infectious. His classmates considered him an extrovert and a visionary. He spoke about his company at every opportunity. He shared his dream, his plans and his frustrations:

> Late last year while on holiday, I read a book which changed my life completely. When I came back to the office, I did an analysis of the company. Where are we? Why are we where we are? I looked at the situation dispassionately. I found that some things were good, some bad, and others, ugly. I evolved a new vision and strategy for the business. We will be the best public relations firm in the west coast of Africa. I began the 'Regaining Lost Ground' Initiative.
>
> We have a Board of Directors. We are going to increase our share capital fourfold. Most of it will be paid up. We want to be in the PR Industry what FRA is among the law firms in Nigeria. We are doing bigger things. We want to pay our people more. I want to attract the best people. CMC must be the best company to work for in the industry. Our database should be full of CVs of top talent.
>
> We have just moved our office to a bigger and better building. I think that people who came to our old office were disappointed. We are perception

managers; our image must reflect who we are and what we do. We have called the new office: 'The Bridge House.' We act as a bridge. We take people from obscurity to fame; from hatred to love; and from misconception to reality. The Bridge to us is what the Stallion is to Union Bank.

We are going to decorate our offices with pictures of bridges from all over the world. The 'Pako' bridge in Aguda will not be left out. There is going to be so much excitement. Our reception, each office in 'The Bridge House,' will communicate something. We will have an 'African Room' close to the reception area. It will have the 'African Heroes Corner.' When people enter our offices, they will wonder what we do here.

We have a new logo. I had been looking for this logo for 3 years. I wanted something unique. We are going to launch it. We will inscribe it on lapel pins, cuff links, etc. It is part of our new identity. The logo means connection. We are going to paint the bottom of the pool with the new logo.

'The Bridge House' has a swimming pool, a tennis court and a gym. It used to be a fitness club. We want to create an environment where our people will love to work. If an employee comes in the morning and wants to swim, there is no problem. If another wants to work by the pool he or she is free to do so. There is no dress code. You dress to suit what you are going to do that day. What I am particular about is results.

One of our corporate values is fun. We enjoy what we do. There is laughter. We eat 'boli' (roasted plantain) and we fool around. The other values are enterprise and innovation. We must do everything fresh and new. We must add value to our stakeholders.

We have a theme song. It was a popular song in the 1980s. This song captures how I feel about the company. We do aerobics with this song. More than a fitness drive, it helps us see the importance of falling in line. Together we can make our vision a reality. If someone slows down, harmony is destroyed. Aerobics helps us communicate this to our people.

I recently employed an HR person who is a charger. She is young and open minded. She fits the environment I want to create in the company. She and I developed the 'Octagon': the eight dimensions of the CMC person. We will launch it soon.

We have been using the notice board and every meeting and opportunity to communicate the new vision. We are going to make T-shirts and face caps with our logo and vision.

There is a lot of potential in this country. We are going to make a quantum leap. Things are about to open up. These are very exciting times. So much is happening. New opportunities are opening up. International affiliation is a new vista for us. We are looking at a company that operates in over 80 countries. In terms of positioning, we have the right standing. I see business opportunities all the time. I am a born PR person. It is my passion. I see areas that others don't see. That is why I am pushing the company into areas like corporate social responsibility. We have come up with the idea of perception audit. If companies audit their accounts, audit their staff, why not audit their image too?

We have blue chip accounts. I have not even started looking for business. Prospects are good. I have built a personal profile which I am pulling back in order to build the CMC Connect brand. I am creating a small business unit called the 'Strategy and Business Development Unit' which will work directly with me.

I have come to the realization that the quality of our people will determine how far we will go. The area of business we are in is right and our strategy is right. The challenge is our people. The other day, a young man we employed a few months ago walked away. He was a journalist. We trained him and gave him freedom to act on a very important project with a major client. He got the job done. I praised him. But, on Monday morning, he walked away. Why would someone walk away from this dream? This is a good place for him to learn if nothing else. Is he seeing something I am not seeing?

How can I take my people to the next level? Do they share the vision? I came across this saying, 'leaders take people where they want to be. Great leaders take people where they ought to be.' I have it in a plaque in my office. I am trying to take my people where they ought to be. What I hear from them is, 'YBO, that is a great idea'. But then, they don't implement. One of my close lieutenants agreed with me on an issue in a meeting but later told his colleagues that what I said is not possible; it cannot be done.

Do they see the vision and all the things I am telling them as building castles in the air? 'This "bobo" has started dreaming again kind of thing?' Am I the problem? I have found that when I am around a lot gets done. When I travel, the pace slows down. How can we make the vision a reality? To be honest with you, I am not sure I won't have egg on my face down the line.

Company Background

It was at the tail end of his youth service year in 1988 that YBO faced the dilemma of what to do next. The options open to him were to go back to school to study Law or enter into the labour market. The former did not appeal to him considering the time he had already spent in school and the fact that many of his contemporaries were already earning salaries. He asked himself what he could do with a single honours degree in History from the University of Benin.

He decided to go into a field that would give him some comparative advantage based on his perceived talents and natural propensity. Several people had told him he had excellent people relations skills. He had always been keen on conveying the right perspective of issues to various audiences. In his university days, he often went out of his way to court the friendship and understanding of diverse groups in order to build bridges of communication and understanding among them. Many friends had told him that he would make a fantastic public relations practitioner. He also wanted a profession that would enable him to make his mark within the first 10 years of practice. He decided to become a public relations practitioner. His vision was clear from the beginning: 'to set up the leading public relations firm in Nigeria'.

Initially, he did not want to work for anybody; there were no public relations firms in existence anyway. At that time, public relations was an appendage of advertising. When Cornelius Tay of CT&A offered him employment in an advertising firm he accepted it; it was the closest to his dream.

After 4 years with CT&A, YBO founded Capital Marketing and Communications (CMC) with a share capital of one hundred thousand Naira. In his words: 'I was fired up enough to believe that my sheer determination will see me through'.

His office was the living room of his flat in Ikeja. He employed two people from the start and soon after recruited an additional person. Getting briefs proved to be a Herculean task. Bills began to pile. On one of his marketing calls, he met the Managing Director of ABG Communications who had recently set up a satellite retransmission business and YBO thought he could get the account. Instead, the MD asked YBO to become one of his agents even while running his PR practice.

Working as an agent of ABG had some benefits. 'I was able to raise enough cash to rent an office and to move away from the brink of poverty.' He was making money installing satellite dishes and no longer bothered to write public relations proposals to firms. But he did not find fulfilment in this. 'I knew that installing technology was not my call, and, sooner than later, I would have to pack it up and face my area of core competence.' When he eventually gave up the agency relationship to focus on this PR firm, he found that he did not even have a clientele portfolio from ABG. He began again from scratch.

His breakthrough came when his offer to manage the 25th Anniversary of the Manufacturers Association of Nigeria in April 1997 was accepted. His mandate was to source funds from the Association's members, organize the anniversary activities and share the profits accrued with the Association. The project proved successful.

It seemed to YBO that the advertising agencies were taking all the PR business even though they were not exactly competent to do the job. The options were to fight the advertising agencies or make friends with them. He decided to invite some of the agencies such as Lawson Thomas & Colleagues (LTC) to invest in CMC. LTC accepted and brought in fresh capital. CMC was thus able to lease new office space, recruit more staff, and competent people from LTC joined the CMC team.

Two years later, two other leading advertising firms, STB McCann and Centrespread FCB, also bought into CMC. The business name was changed to CMC Connect (Perception Managers).

CMC Connect (Perception Managers)

YBO realized that a clear and well communicated vision was not enough to bring about the changes he wanted. Having repositioned the company in the mind of the public, he went to work on the organizational structure and the people.

Structure

The business had grown significantly in the last several years. YBO found that he was spending all his time supervising subordinates, coaching and training them, looking for business, making presentations, etc. There was a need to delegate some of his duties to competent people. One of the managers commented: 'CMC used to be a one-man show. If the MD was not around, not much work could be done. The MD travelled a lot. In the past, we waited for him to get things done. He has now recruited professionals. This reduces the burden on the MD. There is now a structure. It is a company.'

There were four departments: Events, Media, Public Affairs and Image & Reputation. Four group heads and an associate director together with the Managing Director made up the management team. Three of the top management team joined the company within the last twelve months. Everyone was aware of the structure though an organizational chart had not been drawn up. The Top Management Team met every Monday morning to review the performance of the company and coordinate activities. Once a month, they had a 'Business Leaders Meeting' during which they tracked the progress of the company vis-à-vis the vision and agreed on corrective actions to realize the vision. The meeting was sometimes held in exciting venues outside the office such as Sheraton Hotel and Chopsticks Restaurant.

Some employees at the two lower levels of the organizational structure resisted the new structure. One manager explained: 'It is really difficult to put the structure in place because people don't see the need for it. We are a pretty small company in terms of number of employees. It's really hard for employees to understand the need for a structure. From the top, we still have to make them understand that the MD means it when he says he is not running a one-man business; that he wants a structured business. From the employees' perspective it is a one-man business and this is how it has been.'

One employee commented: 'I don't see it as a one-man business. The MD is not around now but things are still going on. But because of his temperament, if he walks into the office, the atmosphere changes. He is not around right now and everything is still in order and if any emergency comes up, the business leaders can handle it.'

While managers were encouraging employees to follow the reporting lines, some employees felt that only YBO had the authority to act; going through the managers seemed a waste of time. According to one employee, 'every decision to be taken gets to the MD's table. Even though we have Heads of Departments, they don't have the authority to take decisions. The MD signs all cheques.'

Although there were different departments, employees worked in any area their services were needed. One employee commented: 'I see some Media guys doing Events jobs. When I joined the Events Department, I thought I was going to be doing purely events work. I find myself doing some business development work. It is good, it is building me personally, but somebody is supposed to be doing that.'

A manager commented: 'Even though I do not work in the Events Department, I have conceptualized events and organized them. May be the Events Department has too much on its table. Media people are expected to conceptualize events and also take care of media. The MD calls on anyone to do whatever is needed. Of course, it is a form of training and this makes us multi-skilled. However, clarifying responsibilities and deliverables would help.'

Employees complained about the emphasis on business development. Each employee was expected to bring in business. Many of them were of the opinion that it was the MD's job to bring in business. One of them complained: 'I was not hired to work in business development. Business development requires some skills which I do not think I have. The MD and the Business Development department should scan the environment and bring in business. The rest of us are expected to take it from there. It is the responsibility of the MD to feed the business.'

Human Resource Management

The HR manager and the MD drew up an employee handbook which was yet to be printed and distributed to employees. They called it: 'Rules of Engagement'. 'It's like getting married', the MD explained. A cartoonist inserted cartoons and sketches as illustrations of the policies. A Recruitment Manual had been drawn up. It was to form the basis for recruitment and selection. It covered the eight dimensions of the CMC person (the Octagon). The Octagon was derived from a list drawn by the MD and the HR Manager of the fifty things a CMC person should be able to do. The MD planned to discuss the Octagon with all employees. The qualification, experience, skills, etc. required for each position in the organization were included in the Recruitment Manual. It was, thus, easy to know where a new employee would fit in the organization. There was a bias for sportive people. YBO felt that such people were likely to be more competitive. He explained, 'People who play some sport like to win and that is the kind of spirit we need in our business.'

The entry level position was that of Assistant Business Executive. There were four grade levels between this position and that of Managing Director.

The number of years of experience required for promotion from Assistant Business Executive to Managing Director was clearly stated. It was hoped that there would be fast trackers. YBO often gave his employees the example of the MD of Access Bank, who started as a National Youth Service Corp member in Guaranty Trust Bank and was promoted to the position of executive director in less than ten years.

Training programmes were organized regularly. Every employee knew his/her training group and schedule. All junior staff attended at least one training programme a year. Other members of staff were scheduled for at least two programmes annually. The MD regularly facilitated training programmes for staff. The Bridge House had a training room. The plan was to let it out to training institutions when no in-house training programmes were scheduled.

Salaries were paid in arrears between the 25th and the 28th of each month. However, many employees felt that the salary they received was not commensurate with the effort they put into the job. One employee elaborated: 'we do not receive bonuses. If we get a contract and it works out well and the company pays up, staff should get a percentage of the total profit even if it is 5% or 3%. As it is, no matter how well we perform, I get my monthly salary. So we say, "Ah! which one concerns me? Shey na salary dem go pay me!!"' (Is it my business? I will receive my salary.)

Another employee commented: 'I am motivated by someone saying to me, "well done" when I have performed exceedingly well or made some extraordinary effort. When I came to CMC, my goal was and still is to learn. I do not look at the salary for now.'

Some members of staff had been with the company since the inception of the company; they had never gone on leave. They had hoped that the appointment of an HR manager would change things but little had changed. They often worked during weekends to meet deadlines. The Group Heads frowned at leave requests and even scolded their colleagues for allowing their subordinates time off.

> Some policies are not pro-people at all. For example, one policy stipulates that an employee travelling out of Lagos on official assignment is given feeding and accommodation allowance but does not receive the out-of-station allowance until the client has paid for the job. I find this policy annoying. I am risking my life for the company. The company does not appreciate the risks involved and the role I play in my family.
>
> I use my car for official purposes and receive a fuel allowance of just N6000 every month. It costs me N3000 to fill my tank. How far can N6000 take me?
>
> My job requires me to call clients regularly. The company gives me N3000 per month for recharge cards! We sometimes run out of credit on the landline. You have to shout so often to get the resources you need to work. These things frustrate you.

The Culture and Management Style

The CMC culture required employees to use their initiative. They were expected to do what it took to deliver on different projects. Rigidities were avoided. There was no dress code for example.

According to one manager, 'I dress formally most of the time because I inter-face with clients. What we do here is perception management. So our dressing, our comportment must signal the impression we want people to have of us. We must dress appropriately. Employees have good command of English language, are articulate and confident. They must be able to convince people that they are the solution to their problems.'

A veteran manager noted: 'We make sure that new employees imbibe our culture. We make presentations in a particular way. There is a CMC way. We train all employees including our drivers and cleaners on how to present themselves. New employees are taken through it on a weekly basis. The MD worked hard to build a culture, a specific way of doing things. He loves uniformity.'

The case writer asked employees to comment on the MD's management style. Manager A:

> MD is very passionate about the company. He knows that people are his greatest asset. He has a deep passion for them. He is a visionary. He is trying to infect the staff with his passion for the company. When I joined this company, I didn't have the passion. After a few days here, I felt sure I was in the wrong company. Today, I am passionate about my job. I actually love my job so much that I turned down a job offer recently that paid more. What is keeping me in CMC is my passion for this job.
>
> I came from a multinational company where I was earning more but I wasn't happy with my job. There were many people who were not satisfied with their jobs in that company. CMC Connect has a healthy environment. I don't know how the MD does it. He does not know the impact he has made on the lives of people. He is adding value and knowledge to his staff. He is very intelligent. MD is an open person. He is welcoming; he plays the father role. I don't know how he does it. Several times, he has rebuked me, but, at the end of the day, I was sorry I did not get it right. When someone chastises you, and you know that person wants the best for you, you take the correction. He is obviously knowledgeable; he earned his respect from his staff. He is a leader.
>
> MD is very demanding; he is a perfectionist. He pushes hard. He is a bit abrupt sometimes. He is very creative; it seems there is a free-flowing chan-nel from a creative source into his mind. MD is a teacher; you can learn a lot from him. I personally do not have a problem moving at his pace though he is very tasking.

An officer in X department:

> The MD is a workaholic and a very intelligent man. He is considerate and compassionate. He has a good relationship with everyone in the office. The relationship is not that good between the staff and their Group Heads, that is, between the subordinates and their bosses.

An employee in Y Department:

> The MD always tells us that he is the boss and whatever he says is important. However, if you have a superior argument he listens to it. You have to prove beyond reasonable doubt that your alternative is superior. He travels a lot for conferences, marketing, etc. I think he should let some of the other Group Heads do a little bit of the international travelling as well. That would be nice.

An Officer in Z department:

> I see the MD as a mentor. He is always ready to teach; he wants to impart something to you. He believes you can do anything. That is his style of leadership. People I appreciate are people that want to stretch you beyond your perceived potentials, and he does that. I don't see him as a bossy person probably because I am not in the management level where they take decisions. But, at my own level, he is not a bossy person. A bossy person is a person that comes and says, 'this is what I want you to do. Whether you like it or not, just do it.' He asks for people's suggestions. I see him as a leader.

A new employee:

> There is a perception here that he uses his position as the MD to influence certain things. Some of the workers frown at this. He could walk into the accounts department and instruct that some of the suppliers who have a relationship with him (church members, friends, etc.) be paid and others not. He gets personal in some of the decisions taken.
>
> On my previous job, I could contest some decisions made by my boss. When I am running events, I don't want my MD getting involved. If you have employed people you have confidence in, leave them to work. At my former company, I reported to my GM weekly, not on a daily basis. He had that confidence in me. MD should have more confidence in his staff and empower them. He has Group Heads; let them do their jobs and let them report directly to him.
>
> Getting the MD to follow the rules is a challenge. A few days ago, the MD introduced a young man who was interested in a business development

job with the company. We told him the guy was a media guy, not a business developer, but he insisted. We told the MD we wanted to meet the guy. So, the top management interviewed him and came to the conclusion that he was not the right person for the job. 'He is smart and intelligent, but we need an expert in business development'. Some members of the team felt the MD may bring the guy in anyway and wondered why they were wasting their time interviewing.

One employee contrasted the MD's style with that of the managers: 'many of the business leaders or group heads have never led a team before. The MD talks big and some of the employees feel lost. They try to identify with their managers but feel intimidated by them. They would rather work with the MD because of his style.

Vision and Communication

The case writer asked employees to comment on the company vision. Below are the responses.

I think we should first take the lead in Nigeria before going out to the rest of Africa. There are PR companies that are well respected in Nigeria. They will not just sit there and wait for CMC to take over the market. The question is: 'what are you doing to make CMC Connect the company to be emulated; the company good PR guys out there want to work for; the company clients want to work with?' What makes a PR company is the quality of its accounts, how well you take care of them and your perception in the market. We have some really good accounts. We need to grow the client base.

The MD thinks really big and he goes faster than everybody else. We try to catch up. He wants us to do this; he wants us to do that. The members of staff find it hard to catch up with him, let alone walk at his pace.

I believe that it takes time to realize a vision. There should be landmarks and performance indicators. There are some silly mistakes that are uncalled for in the quality of our jobs and I think everything boils down to the quality of people; the background of the staff.

I trust that the MD will take us where we think we should be. The vision should be realized within the next two years.

All employees know the company's vision; the MD goes on and on about it. He communicates the vision at every opportunity. But I don't see it. Okay, you want us to be the best in West Africa, to be the best in this, to be the best in that. But the other day, I said I needed money to buy credit for my phone so that I can make business calls and that was a problem. Everything doesn't fit together.

The company organized aerobics sessions every fortnight. During these sessions, employees worked out to the rhythm of the company theme song, 'Ain't no stopping us now. We are on the move'. Several people commented on the theme song and work-out sessions:

> The theme song is simply disco; it does not motivate anyone. It provides entertainment for people. The MD likes it and wants us to take it seriously.

> It is a nice song. We all know it. Once you hear it, you remember your target. It is the CMC song.

> To be frank, it really motivates me. 'Ain't no stopping us now' reminds us to start doing something.

> I don't know the words of the song. I don't know if it is motivational or not. I don't really like music. My MD has a vision. There are challenges. He believes that by singing that song, the vision will get into our head and nothing will stop us.

The Challenge

Since the 1990s, a number of PR companies have been set up in Nigeria. Competition was stiff (especially for the accounts of the multinationals). Some of the advertising companies had their own PR firms. In spite of the stiff competition, Yomi Badejo felt the company had some very good accounts and the prospects were very good. He had started negotiations with a multinational PR company that wanted to invest in CMC Connect. He was concerned about the future.

> I am beginning to think I have few people who can help me berth the vision. Others are not just there. Everything slows down when I am not around. When I told them months ago that we will be moving to the Bridge House, some of them thought it was just a dream. Why do they lack passion? When I started the business I could not afford to pay the salaries to attract good people. I hired those I could find and trained them. Many left. Now, we hire good people, and yet, I am not getting the results I expect. We are making huge investments in our offices. We have to deliver extraordinary results. What is wrong?

> I called my office this morning. The receptionist answered the call with a lifeless 'Good Morning, this is CMC Connect'. How can a person pick up the phone on a Tuesday morning after a long weekend (Monday was public holiday) and sound so terrible. It is demoralizing. How can this be? How can our receptionist receive calls without an upbeat attitude? At 8.30 in the morning one should be ready to go.

> Years ago, I realized my inability to carry this vision alone so I got others to buy into the company. I knew I needed strong hands to make it

a reality. Now, we have a Board of Directors and the money to become the big fish in the big ocean. The challenge is the people – our employees. The vision is strong and clear, but we are still struggling to get there. The people we need are those who are highly driven, passionate, knowledge-able, result oriented, enterprising and vision minded. We have chosen to play premium in this market and as such we cannot accept anything that will compromise this goal.

DORA AKUNYILI AT NAFDAC

The Challenge of Changing a Government Agency

Franca Ovadje and Pat Utomi prepared this case as the basis for class discussion rather than to illustrate either effective or ineffective handling of an administrative situation. The assistance of Eva Okolie is appreciated.

Several groups massed outside her office. Members of staff were waiting to sort things out, several representatives of groups were anxious to persuade her to be keynote speaker or guest at an event, and reporters were waiting for their turn when the case writers arrived. She worked the group with practical ease clearing out the queue in a few minutes before settling down to the exercise of reflecting on six years as Nigeria's Food and Drug Regulation Czar.

From a pariah agency, NAFDAC had been transformed into a respected agency both within Nigeria and in the international community. The World Health Organization, the European Union, and Transparency International were just a few of the bodies that had recognized the achievements of NAFDAC. Many West African countries had lifted the ban on 'Made in Nigeria' drugs. Nigerian pharmaceutical companies were now exporting to the West African sub-region.

What gave her most satisfaction was the transformation that had occurred among NAFDAC employees. They were committed to the mission. They had demonstrated that it was possible for a government agency to truly serve the public. She smiled as she remembered several managers who had gone through a paradigmatic revolution. They were now professionals and so proud of themselves.

It was also gratifying that President Obasanjo had asked the management of several parastatals and government agencies to go to NAFDAC to learn how to turn around their organizations. In 2004, a team from the Central Bank visited NAFDAC for this purpose.

The threats to her life, especially the assassination attempt, had scared her family. They exerted considerable pressure on her to resign. Her little son was worried about her. Some of his friends teased him at school because his mother ostensibly destroyed their father's businesses. They were dealers in fake and adulterated products. Though she saw the dangers, she did not believe that anything would happen to her. This job had to be done and she had been picked to do it. Her arguments convinced members of her family for some time. Now, they told her she had done the job; it was time to rest. She had succumbed to the pressure and given notice of her intention to leave at the end of her term due in 2006 and probably go back to academia.

As she prepared to leave the agency, she recalled the conversation she had had in 2001 with the Nigerian President, Olusegun Obasanjo. The mandate had been clear. In mentally reviewing what her team had done, many questions came to her mind: What specific impact had NAFDAC had? By how much had the quantum of fake drugs reduced? Had she built an institution? Could NAFDAC resist a DG who did not share the same values and passion for safeguarding the nation's health?

The DG's appointment was a political one. The President had one more year in office. Was the change sustainable? What else could she do in these last months to further institutionalize these changes? This was more than a job; it was about safeguarding the health of her people.

Introduction

The National Agency for Food and Drug Administration and Control (NAFDAC) was established by Decree No. 15 of 1993 as amended in 1999 to 'control and regulate the manufacture, importation, exportation, distribution, advertisement, sale and use of food, drugs, cosmetics, chemicals/detergents, medical devices and all drinks including packaged water'. Prior to the establishment of the agency, the Directorate of Food and Drug Administration in the Federal Ministry of Health was responsible for the control and regulation of food, drugs, cosmetics and other regulated products in Nigeria. Though it had functional laboratories and carried out inspection and enforcement activities, its mandate did not include drug and product registration. Civil service bureaucracy and corruption, etc. rendered the Directorate ineffective.

The Pharmaceutical Society of Nigeria advocated the establishment of task forces to eradicate fake drugs from the country. The decree establishing the Federal Task Force on Fake and Counterfeit Drugs was promulgated in 1989 and amended in 1999 to include Unwholesome Processed Foods. The Decree also established State Task Forces that would be responsible for enforcement in the States. Their activities were to be coordinated by the Federal Task Force. The Task Forces could impose penalties, issue compliance directives or even shut down an establishment. In spite of these efforts, fake drugs and substandard products continued to be imported into and manufactured in Nigeria.

When in 1993 NAFDAC was established, the hope was that the agency would improve the situation. The task forces were expected to work with the agency in the area of enforcement. The law provided that the chairman of the task force be an officer of NAFDAC of not lower than deputy director level. A regulatory structure was established. This structure was used by Ghana as a blueprint in establishing its Food and Drug Board.

However, when Prof. Dora Akunyili assumed office on the 12th of April 2001, Nigeria was rated one of the countries with the highest incidence of fake and counterfeit drugs in the world. Expired products and counterfeit cosmetics were dumped into the country. The agency was ineffective. NAFDAC staff were disillusioned and poorly trained. The orientation was that of a public service bureaucracy. Employees had been transferred from the Ministry to NAFDAC when the latter was established in 1994. They collected bribes from companies for registration.

At a meeting of the Director General (DG) of NAFDAC with the Nigerian Economic Intelligence Committee and the Minister of Finance during the Abacha Administration, Prof. Aluko, the Head of the Commission, is said to have told the NAFDAC's DG that his agency was corrupt and they were to be sent out of the Ports. NADFAC was subsequently expelled from the Ports.

The culture of NAFDAC was that of a civil service in which procedures and systems had been overridden by military fiats. Many *bona fide* pharmacists, industrialists, etc. found the agency unapproachable. A number of consultants positioned themselves as middle men between the agency and those it was to regulate. The consultants mystified NAFDAC to the public. Information was not accessible; registration forms and procedures were unclear. Product registration and testing was a very complicated and time consuming process.

The NAFDAC offices lacked basic work tools. For example, most offices did not have functional photocopiers, vehicles, fax machines, air conditioners, generators, etc. When documents had to be copied, a member of staff was sent to a business centre. If the office had a functional copier, they could wait until electricity was available to make a photocopy. The buildings were dilapidated. The Abuja head office was located in a rented block of flats. The laboratories were not well equipped though some equipment was purchased for the laboratories with money from the Petroleum Trust Fund.

Some attempts were made before 2001 to fight the preponderance of fake products in Nigeria. The strategic focus was litigation. The problem however was that it took years to get a judgment. Conversely, it was easy to obtain a court injunction to stop NAFDAC from carrying out its functions pending judgment on the case. Meanwhile, the business owners continued to operate with impunity.

Dora Takes Charge

In 2001, President Olusegun Obasanjo was looking for a new Director General for NAFDAC. A close friend of his, Dr Onolapo Sholeye, mentioned a lady who had worked until recently with the Petroleum Trust Fund. While she was Regional Coordinator South East of PTF, she had applied for £15,000 for surgery in the United Kingdom. After some tests in the UK, it was found that she did not need the surgery. On returning to Nigeria, the lady had returned the balance of £12,000 to the PTF. The story had been reported in the Press at the time. The PTF Chairman, General Buhari, had written her a letter of commendation. The President asked Dr Sholeye to look for the lady. They found Dora Akunyili at the University of Nigeria Nsukka.

Her resumé was impressive. She had served on several senate committees at the University. From 1992 to 1994, she was a member of the State Hospitals Management Board of Anambra State. She was very active in the Pharmaceutical Society of Nigeria. She was the National Vice President of the Association of Lady Pharmacists between 1992 and 1995 and President of the Enugu State Branch of the Association for six years.

President Obasanjo called Dora directly to offer her the job of Director General of NAFDAC. The mandate was clear: 'turn around NAFDAC'; achieve effective food and drug regulation with special emphasis on the eradication of fake, counterfeit drugs and other regulated products from Nigeria. Dora saw very clearly the hand of God in this appointment.

On the 12th of April 2001, she took charge as the Director General of NAFDAC. She knew it was a big challenge but was not prepared for the rot she met. The offices were drab. Dora felt miserable but resolved that day to move the head office to a better place.

Within six months of taking charge of the agency, Dora asked her managers to organize a retreat for management staff and the members of the Governing Council of the Agency. The purpose was to work out the mission, a vision and the strategies the agency should implement to effect the changes. Vision and mission statements were developed during the retreat. The vision of the agency is: 'To safeguard public health' and the mission: 'To safeguard public health by ensuring that only the right quality products are manufactured, imported, exported, advertised, distributed, sold and used in Nigeria.' It was agreed that the agency's first goal be the eradication of fake drugs and other substandard regulated products.

Structural Changes

The whole of the top management of NAFDAC had been fired before Dora was recruited. There was, therefore, an urgent need to reconstitute the management team. The laws governing the agency vested the power of appointments, promotions and discipline on the Governing Council of the agency. Dora worked with the

Council to fill the vacancies at the top. Two directors were selected from within the agency; others were brought in from the private sector and an international agency.

The new management realized that staff posting in the past was not based on qualification. Some employees were, therefore, unable to do their jobs. A team of consultants was employed to identify the competencies of staff and ensure proper placement of staff. More people were employed as the activity level increased. Consultants were used for effective screening of candidates. Within 2002 and 2003, the number of samples analysed by the agency was more than the number analysed in the whole history of NAFDAC. Firings due to corruption created many vacant positions. These were filled from outside the civil service. By 2006, the ratio of old staff to new staff was 50:50.

Before 2001, task forces were responsible for checking compliance and giving sanctions. The organization was divided into directorates. There were six directorates. The Inspectorate Directorate was responsible for establishment inspection and, together with the task forces, was responsible for enforcement.

The new management restructured the agency into eight directorates. The Inspectorate Directorate was split in two: Establishment Inspection and Port Inspection. An Enforcement Directorate was created. It was to work with the task forces, the police and the NDLEA to ensure compliance with regulations. The DG recommended to the Minister of Health the appointment of NAFDAC's Director of Enforcement as the Chairman of the National Task Force. This facilitated coordination between the agency and the task force in the war against fake drugs and substandard products.

The other directorates were: Administration and Finance, Registration and Regulation, Laboratory Services, Narcotics and Chemical Control, Planning, Research and Enforcement. The Technical Department, Public Relations, Legal, Maintenance and Special Duties Departments were under the DG's office, which became a division. The Public Relations Department was properly staffed and the capacities of the people built. The Legal Department was strengthened to provide the legal expertise the agency needed to discharge its responsibilities.

Offices were opened in the twelve states of the Federation which had no NAFDAC presence. Special inspectorate offices were set up in the three large cities with huge presence of drug markets: Lagos, Kano and Onitsha. Each NAFDAC office carried out the task of all the Directorates. Six zonal offices were established to coordinate the activities of the State offices. The State offices were supervised by the Establishment Inspection Directorate but reported to the Director of Establishment Inspection and the Director of Enforcement.

Interdepartmental rivalry was a legacy of the government agency. Dora forced dialogue across departments. For example, she insisted on a meeting of the Directors of Registration & Regulation, Laboratory Services, and Establishment Inspection before a decision was taken on the bromate problem. Before any decision could be taken, at least two directorates had to be involved. Inter and intra departmental meetings were held in addition to the management meetings. No problem was to be brought to the attention of the DG unless and until at least two directorates had discussed it.

Increasing Revenues

The Federal Government's budgetary allocation to NAFDAC could not fund the activities of the agency. It could not even pay the salaries of the employees even though salaries were very low in 2001. The agency had been starved of funds for years. Functional laboratories were needed, offices had to be equipped and both human and institutional capacities built. To attract and retain good employees, salaries and benefits had to be reviewed substantially. A plan was developed and pursued aggressively.

The tariff the agency charged for product registration was fixed in 1994 when the exchange rate was $1 to N22. The exchange rate in 2001 was $1 to N111.23[1]. Decree No. 21 of 1995 stipulated a penalty of N50,000 for producers and importers of fake and unwholesome drugs and other NAFDAC regulated products. NAFDAC Decree No. 15 of 1993 stipulated a penalty of N5,000 for obstructing an officer from entering suspicious premises.

In May 2001, the new management hired regulatory consultants and legal experts to review the existing laws and make proposals to the agency's on a new tariff structure. In November 2001, the proposals were sent to the National Assembly to be enacted into law.

While the consultants worked on the new tariff structure, the management called meetings of stakeholders to sell to them the need for a tariff review. Workshops were organized for stakeholders by trade: patent medicines, customs licensed clearing agents, herbal traditional practitioners, flour millers, bakers, etc.

The tariffs and sanctions for non-compliance were thus significant and revenue was boosted to such an extent that the agency generated about 70 per cent of its income; Government allocation accounted for the remaining 30 per cent. Sanctions and penalties accounted for most of the internally generated income of the agency.

Building Capacity

Each year, a budget was drawn up and agreed with the Governing Council of the agency. Most of the income was spent on public enlightenment and staff training. In February 2003, President Olusegun Obasanjo commissioned the NAFDAC head office in Abuja. The agency used internally generated funds to buy and furnish the building.

Training programmes were organized for all categories of staff. The new directors were properly inducted and expectations were clearly communicated to them. Other members of staff attended specific training programmes designed to equip them with the skills to perform their function. For example, employees in the Regulatory Department attended training programmes on: NAFDAC Laws, Registration Requirements, Registration Forms, etc.

The DG made heroic efforts to get staff to attend training programmes abroad. She spent hours on the internet searching for training programmes that staff could benefit from. Since funds were not available in the early years of her tenure, she asked several organizations for sponsorship. A number of NGOs and donor agencies sponsored many of the programmes. As the agency improved its financial situation, internally generated funds were also used to fund overseas training programmes.

Apart from building human capacity, the management saw a crying need to build institutional capacity. It was the usual practice for offices to pick up samples from companies and store them until they could be sent to the laboratories (a few laboratories served the whole country). Many of these samples were to be stored in a very low temperature environment. Yet, there were no functional refrigerators and deep freezers in many offices. The situation was immediately addressed and all offices were equipped with new refrigerators and deep freezers.

Up-to-date analytical equipment was purchased for the laboratories. Modern laboratories were being built in Port-Harcourt, Calabar and Agulu. These laboratories were to be equipped with the most modern equipment. The Port-Harcourt Laboratory was complete; the others were near completion. Specialized laboratories were built within the old laboratories.

Communication was a big challenge. The telephone lines in many regional offices did not work. Communicating with the head office and among offices was very difficult. Once the GSM network was available in the capital of a State, the head of the office was provided with a GSM telephone. In a short time, all offices had telephone lines. To facilitate inspection, regulation and enforcement, new vehicles were purchased for all the offices around the Federation. Even chairs and tables were replaced; carpeting was laid in many offices. Functional air conditioners and generators were also purchased.

The State offices had been starved of funds. They received a quarterly impress of N6,000; their activities were very limited. The new management very quickly raised the impress fourfold depending on the level of activity of each office. Since almost all the equipment installed in the offices were new, maintenance costs were expected to be low in the first few years.

Changing the Culture

When Dora took charge in 2001, many employees were hardly to be found in their offices. The common excuse was: 'I am going to the bank'. She introduced a movement register. Members of staff had to write down when they came in and every time they left the office and returned. The register was checked by management. Two people who were found to be out of the office too often were fired.

Dora felt the need for a cultural revolution in the agency. Even the way members of staff dressed to work was important to her. A new dress code was introduced. She explained: 'If you don't dress well, how will you be respected as a regulator?'

If the fight against fake drugs and substandard products was to be won, the agency had to shed its reputation for corruption. A new policy was introduced which stipulated that sanctions could not be given by one member of staff alone. A policeman, a driver and two members of staff visited the company as a team and imposed the sanction. When fake drugs were found, they were destroyed publicly. The employee who reported the case witnessed the destruction of the consignment. Word soon spread round the organization that management acted on reported cases.

Dora commented:

> At the beginning the staff tried me. They wanted to see how serious I was about the change. When I recommended my brother-in-law for dismissal, they were shocked. Another brother-in-law imported unregistered margarine. When he was apprehended, he asked the officials if they did not know that his wife was the DG. He was sanctioned and I advised him not to spoil my work.
>
> One day, a Priest came to the office to pick some registration forms. He did not have enough money on him to pay the registration fee. One employee came to my office to ask me if the fees should be waived for the Priest to avoid his coming back just to pay the fee. I knew they were asking me to do this because I am Catholic. I called the Priest, gave him some money from my pocket and asked him to get a bank draft and pay the registration fee.

In 2005, NAFDAC came down hard on bakeries that used bromate in their bread. Miriam Babangida, the wife of an ex-military Head of State, owned a bakery in Minna. Tests of her bread showed that the loaves contained bromate. The ex-First Lady called Dora to ask her to do something. Dora got the bread sent to another laboratory for testing. When it was found to contain bromate, the bakery was closed down.

Dora's in-laws are from Agulu, a small town known among other things for its bakeries. During the fight against bromate, many bakeries in Agulu were closed down for violating the regulation. A member of the extended family told Dora a proverb: 'A snake does not kill a snake. When you finish this job, I hope you will come back home.'

Dora instituted rewards for any member of staff who reported a colleague for negotiating or receiving a bribe or failing to report a violation to the management. The DG sent a letter of commendation to the person who had sent in the report. In addition, the whistle blower was sometimes promoted and was sure to be sent on a training programme abroad within the year. The estacode paid during this training was very attractive. Members of staff soon became nervous. The story is told of a customer who came to NAFDAC to collect his cheque and offered the Chief Accountant a mobile phone. The gift was apparently unsolicited. The Chief Accountant not only refused the phone but immediately reported the incident to the DG explaining that he did not ask the customer for the gift.

An employee who reported a violation was also rewarded with a training pro-gramme abroad and a letter of commendation. Some employees did heroic things to report violations. One pursued a truck carrying fake drugs from the Port with his old car. When the truck driver stopped to refuel, the NAFDAC employee parked his car, punctured the tyres of the truck, and went to get the police to arrest the driver. The truck was apprehended and the fake drugs destroyed. The young man, who had spent only two months in the agency, was rewarded with a training programme in Europe.

A Disciplinary Committee was set up to investigate cases of bribery and cor-ruption among the staff of the agency. The committee met every month in 2002 and 2003. Employees who were found guilty were recommended for firing to the Governing Council. The Council approved these recommendations and the employees were fired. The DG's brother-in-law was one of the many employees who were dismissed. In 2002 and 2003, many members of staff were fired. In 2005, the Disciplinary Committee met only twice. All decisions proposed by the Disciplinary Committee and approved by the Council were communicated at the Monday morning meetings of all staff.

The DG often received many visitors at a time and dealt with the cases and problems in public. It soon became part of the culture to discuss issues in public. An Igbo chief led a delegation to the Director of Enforcement over an alleged breach of the law. The Director of Enforcement received the delegation in the visitors' waiting area and in the presence of other visitors (including the case writer). He explained to the Chief that a NAFDAC official had been directed to carry out an investigation of the case. If the Chief's statement was found to be untrue, the NAFDAC official had powers to detain the Chief. Minutes of meet-ings with stakeholders (whether singly or in groups) were taken. Her speeches were made available to all staff. Questions during promotion interviews were sometimes drawn from her speeches.

Rewarding Employees

Salaries were substantially increased. Employees of NAFDAC earned higher sala-ries than those in the civil service. The agency also paid staff a 13th month salary in December. Employees enjoyed free medical care in both the public hospitals and some private clinics. The agency rented houses for staff of certain grade levels. New staff buses conveyed staff to work and back home. The directors and the inspection teams were given new company cars. NAFDAC employees enjoyed fast track banking services anywhere in the Federation. They also received some financial assistance for weddings and funerals.

The hours of work were extended. Employees were in the office at 8am. While the closing time was 4pm, they stayed an extra hour to clear their desks and prepare for the next day. The staff buses left at 5pm. Managers often worked longer hours.

Foreign travel was a big favour in the old dispensation. Dora made it both a reward for performance and integrity and an opportunity for all staff to be exposed to best practices.

Members of staff were scheduled for assessment of Good Manufacturing Practice both locally and abroad whether they worked in the Inspectorate Directorate or not. For example, a team made up of employees from the Inspectorate Directorates, Laboratory Services and Administration would go on a GMP Inspection. This helped to create a team spirit across departments. It also enabled employees earn extra income in the form of estacode.

A manager who has been with the agency from inception commented: 'Now, when we go out, people look at us with respect. I have represented the DG in a number of fora. I find that questions raised in such fora about NAFDAC are answered by participants. I do not even need to respond. I now feel part of a successful organization. Employees are proud to work for NAFDAC. Our system today recognizes hard work. People do not need to be corrupt to earn a good living. Every year, the DG presents plaques to employees who performed exceedingly well during the Night of Excellence Award.'

Winning the Battle Against Fake and Substandard Products

The first sanction from NAFDAC was imposed on Nestle Nigeria plc in 2001. The company imported some raw materials which, though not expired, were very close to the expiry date. This meant that if used in the manufacturing process, the raw material would have expired before consumers bought the product. The agency not only imposed a huge sanction on Nestle but made it public. Several newspapers carried the story. The war had started. Between April 2001 and June 2004, NAFDAC destroyed counterfeit and substandard products worth N7.2 billion. Forty convictions had been secured at the courts and over forty cases against violators were still in court in 2004.

Management realized that the drug distribution system was chaotic. Drugs were distributed like other commodities. The poor regulatory and enforcement environment led to the emergence of drug markets in Aba, Onitsha and Kano. These markets received the products they sold from importers and the local pharmaceutical firms. Traders in the drug markets not only paid cash but bought in large quantities. They were, thus, the favourites of the pharmaceutical companies and the importers. Though the markets were illegal, they had been in existence for many years and were patronized by pharmacists. Dora and her team felt strongly that the drug markets had to be at least regulated if not closed down altogether.

The Director of Enforcement decided to carry out an inspection of the Ariara market in Aba. He informed the traders of his plan to visit the drug market for a routine check. Getting armed policemen to accompany him was a challenge – the drug lords had such a terrible reputation. On entering the drug market, the policemen and the Director were stoned with water sachets. They had to leave the market. For nine days, he worked with the Commissioner for Health in the State and a small committee to close down the market. On the agreed day, 200 policemen occupied the drug market at 4.30am and shut the market. The Kano market was shut down with 56 policemen.

After the markets had been shut, the enforcement agents went from shop to shop checking for fake and adulterated drugs. Two billion Naira worth of goods (US$14 million) were destroyed in the Onitsha and Lagos markets in July and October 2001.

The drug traders resisted strongly. The DG and some of her staff received numerous threats through mail and telephone. Fetish objects were deposited in the DG's office. In August 2001, six armed men invaded the DG's residence, but fortunately, she was out of town. On the 29th of August 2002, NAFDAC's laboratory in Oshodi, Lagos was vandalized and most of the equipment destroyed. In December 2003, an assassination attempt on the DG was miraculously foiled as the bullets went through her headgear without causing her any harm. On the 7th of March 2004, NAFDAC offices in Lagos were set ablaze. Office equipment and files were completed destroyed. Three days, later the Kaduna laboratory, with equipment only recently purchased, was destroyed.

Winning Over other Stakeholders

Dora recognized that the agency could not win the battle alone. They faced a public that did not know its rights; a public that did not understand the importance of the 'best before date' in any drug or food item. Fighting the companies was not enough. The public and other stakeholders had to be educated. The fake drug trade must be attacked from all fronts. The fundamental issue according to the DG was behavioural change. Consequently, a massive public enlightenment campaign was adopted as the strategic focus of the agency.

NAFDAC regularly published the list of identified fake, adulterated and substandard products. The agency also published the list of blacklisted companies, both local and international, that produced substandard products, did not conform to WHO certified Good Manufacturing Practices, etc.

The agency embarked on a massive public enlightenment campaign on TV, radio and the print media. Jingles cast in English language and the local languages were aired in both TV and radio stations nationwide. Billboards were erected in strategic locations, posters and stickers were distributed all over the country. The *NAFDAC News* magazine and the *Consumers' Safety Bulletin* also helped spread the message. By August 2001, the NAFDAC website was operational. The website showed a list of blacklisted companies and banned products. The website also educated the public on the definition of adulterated drugs, fake drugs, counterfeit drugs, unwholesome processed foods, etc. and their harmful effects when used or consumed.

Workshops were organized in all states of the Federation. Ultimately the goal was that every Nigerian, even children, would check the registration number,

NAFDAC number and 'best before date' before consuming any drug or packaged food. An annual essay competition for secondary schools was being instituted. Consumer Safety Clubs were planned for all secondary schools in the country.

Management realized it needed whistle blowers who would provide information for action. If people knew their rights and obligations and were encouraged to provide the intelligence that NAFDAC needed so much to win the war against fake drugs, a lot could be achieved. In the workshops, advertisements, and the DG's several presentations, members of the public were encouraged to report transgressions of the law to NAFDAC. NAFDAC telephone numbers and the addresses of its offices nationwide were publicized. Seizures and destruction of fake drugs were televised and shown on the network television station. A good number of the seizures made by NAFDAC were made possible through information provided by members of the public.

According to the Director of Enforcement, 'Our phones are on 24 hours. I have three mobile phones and I never put them off. We receive information from the public about violations. In fact, most of the intelligence we get is from the public. Our information sources have never leaked. We check the veracity of the information, not who sent it. The DG can call at 2am to give you some information she has received or to follow up on something. She sometimes calls throughout the night to follow up particular cases.'

The need for collaboration with other agencies and bodies was recognized very early in the change process. According to Dora: 'The lack of teamwork among NAFDAC, Customs, National Drug Law Enforcement Agency (NDLEA), Standards Organization of Nigeria (SON), Nigerian Ports Authority (NPA) etc. creates a fertile ground for counterfeiters to escape detection arrest and sanctions.' To build the necessary bridges, advocacy visits were made to various stakeholders. The Inspector General of Police agreed to partner with the agency. Officers from Force CID worked with NAFDAC duty officers on all its regulatory and enforcement activities. The collaboration produced immediate results. In July 2001, about 1 billion Naira worth of substandard products were destroyed in Onitsha market. In October of the same year, approximately the same value of fake drugs was destroyed in the Kano market.

The advocacy visit to the Chairman of NDLEA led to a collaborative agreement by the two agencies. The NDLEA agreed to provide NAFDAC with security back-up for NAFDAC's enforcement activities, training of NAFDAC's enforcement personnel and access to NDLEA's anti-drug facilities.

The management was aware that many of the fake drugs and substandard products were imported. The importers made false declarations regarding the contents of the containers. When NAFDAC officials issued 'stop or seizure' notices on the containers, the Port Authorities did not obey. Although administrative guidelines for importation of drugs into Nigeria had been issued in January 2002, the management saw the need to work closely with port authorities to stop the importation of fake drugs and substandard products into the country.

The Director General made an advocacy visit to the Comptroller-General of Customs seeking his assistance in actualizing the vision of NAFDAC. As a result of the new cooperation, NAFDAC inspectors were involved in the examination of regulated products; they removed samples for laboratory analysis and the 'stop and seizure' notices issued by NAFDAC inspectors were honoured by Customs officials.

The visit to the Minister of Aviation, and the Managing Director of the Federal Airports Authority of Nigeria produced the expected results. A new policy was introduced which stipulated that any airline that brought fake drugs and substandard products to Nigeria would be prosecuted and the aircraft grounded.

The team also visited embassies of countries with high incidence of fake drugs in Nigeria such as India and China. Standards Organization of Nigeria, The Pharmaceutical Council of Nigeria, Association of Food and Beverages Manufacturers, etc. were also visited. The DG and her team shared with these bodies the vision of NAFDAC, the need to cleanse the country of fake drugs and the role the stakeholders could play in the war. Collaborative agreements were reached with these organizations. Where NAFDAC felt that these organizations lacked capacity, the NAFDAC Management organized training programmes for them.

The importers, pharmaceutical companies and others involved in the business of producing, importing and/or distributing drugs and other regulated products were not left out. Management saw the need to educate the companies they regulated as to the requirements of the law and the need for quality and safety. To this end, workshops were organized according to industry or product groups for pharmacists, pharmaceutical companies, etc. As early as 2001, workshops were organized for manufacturers of sachet water (popularly known as pure water). Participants were taught simple and safe methods of production. They also saw the effects of producing in an unhygienic environment. They were told they could walk into any NAFDAC office to make enquiries and obtain any information they required. The addresses of NAFDAC offices and telephone numbers were publicized.

Stakeholders' fora were also organized. In these fora, management listened to the stakeholders. One concern expressed by the stakeholders was the inadequacy of NAFDAC's guidelines. The management employed the services of a consultant who worked in a committee with NAFDAC staff to review the existing guidelines and set up standard operating procedures for the agency. The new guidelines included the registration of locally manufactured and imported food and drugs, the importation and exportation of regulated products, the registration of vaccines, etc. Registration forms and procedures were simplified. The results were impressive. While in seven years, 5,735 products had been registered, in one year 3,630 products were registered.

The DG developed a good working relationship with the Minister of Health and the members of the Governing Council of the agency. According to Dora:

Neither the President nor the Minister of Health interfered with what we are doing in NAFDAC. The Council has been very supportive. Getting approval from the Council and the Minister of Health has been very easy. When the Council knows that you are doing the right thing and you are not compromising yourself, they support you. If we were destroying the system, they would have helped us destroy it.

When we seize products, the owners usually go to the Council members to put pressure on me. The Council members never bring up those issues with me. I think they are afraid I will blow it up to the Press.

From time to time, she met with President Obasanjo to brief him on what the agency was doing and seek his support for some of its activities.

Dora developed a very cordial relationship with the press. Workshops were regularly organized for journalists. The themes varied with the focus of NAFDAC at the time. For example, before a vitamin A deficiency campaign, members of the press were invited to a workshop during which they were educated on the role of vitamin A. Every time the agency seized fake drugs or food, the press was invited to the scene of the destruction.

One director commented: 'Dora went out of her way to develop a relationship with all the Editors of the newspapers, the features editions, journalists who reported on health issues, etc. This relationship helped NAFDAC a great deal as the journalists often wrote articles which helped the war against fake products at no cost to the Agency.'

Dora Akunyili is arguably one of the best known public officials in Nigeria. She has received over 180 awards including the Order of the Federal Republic in 2002 and the Integrity Award in 2003.

Dora's Background and Leadership

Dora Akunyili was born into a middle class family. At the age of ten, she left her home in Makurdi for Isuofa village where she lived with her maternal grandmother and uncle. The move was a big shock for her. There was no electricity and pipe borne water in the village. She woke up at 4am daily and walked 5 km in the company of other children to the river to fetch water. When there was no moonlight, they walked in pitch darkness. On her return from the stream, she swept the rooms and the compound, warmed some leftover '*akpu*' from the previous day for breakfast and walked to school.

After school, she fetched fire wood and did some gardening. Dinner was usually some boiled yam with oil or vegetables. She studied at night with light from a lantern. Commenting on this period of her life, Dora said: 'I spent all year working. I remember being happy when it rained because I could rest a little in the afternoon.' Even though her father sent more than enough money for her upkeep, her grandmother felt that eating well was a luxury; good things spoilt children.

According to Dora: 'I had a rugged childhood; a childhood of intense labour. My upbringing helped me a lot. I have very good health; I have never had tooth problems. I can work long hours without getting tired. I am street smart; people cannot deceive me.'

Her family home and her grandmother's were deeply Catholic homes. She learnt at home and later at school to love God and to live a virtuous life. Her Catholic upbringing was further reinforced at school. She attended the Holy Ghost Primary School in Makurdi, and later the St Patrick's Primary School in Isuofia. She was awarded the Eastern Nigeria Government Post Primary Scholarship. She obtained the School Certificate from the Queen of the Rosary Secondary School, Nsukka and studied pharmacy at the University of Nigeria, Nsukka.

A number of employees of NAFDAC commented on her management style:

> She is very pushy but caring. She appreciates small things and this make people feel really good. Saying 'thank you' and 'well done' come easy to her and this motivates the staff, even the directors. She is compassionate. She recognizes that we all work very hard and many of us very long hours.

One manager said he was having some problems with his wife because he was not seeing them often; the family lived outside Abuja. Dora would go to him from time to time and say: 'hey, you have not seen your family for some time. Do you want to travel?' and she would give him time off to travel and spend time with his family.

Employees who showed drive and who performed were recognized. Dora sometimes bought gifts for the wives of staff. She often went with senior management staff to meetings with the President. One manager commented: 'The DG asked me to accompany her to a meeting with the President at the Villa. Naturally, I told my wife about the visit. The next day, my wife told her friends that her husband attended a meeting at the Villa. She was so proud. For some time, she did not bother about my late hours in the office.'

> The New DG is accessible. You can reach her 24 hours a day by email, telephone or simply through an SMS if she is not in the office or during the weekend. She responds to you within an hour. You don't get this kind of commitment in the civil service. Her accessibility has created room for people to feed her with information. This makes it possible for her to make better decisions. Some directors were embarrassed by her knowledge of what was going on in the company. She often asked them specific questions on issues they had not even heard of in their departments.
>
> She has passion and stamina. A nap of 15 minutes and she can run another 12 hours. Dora is a workaholic. For her, most things are doable; obstacles have to be overcome.

Dora trusts us. She does not wait for a memo and signatures to take decisions. If a matter is urgent and you send her a text message, she can take a decision with the recommendation you gave. She is very good at recognizing what each person is good at. When she joined NAFDAC, there were many round pegs in square holes. She looked at our competencies and tried to take advantage of them. In the organization today, talent is where it should be. So, this change is sustainable.

Dora puts everything into the job. She is passionate about it. She sleeps and wakes NAFDAC and how to sanitize the environment. The passion robs off on you. We have to remind her to rest.

I have the authority to do my job. When, for example, I saw the need to shut down the Ariara market because of their refusal to cooperate with us, I of course carried along my boss. But, it was not a question of asking for permission at each stage before taking a decision. The DG knows you know the job and trusts you to do it. The Council gave me a plaque for shutting down the Ariara market. I am sure the DG suggested that action.

A leader must lead by example. If Dora were corrupt, we would not be where we are today. She does not steal; she does not support destructive attitudes. She is straightforward and reacts immediately to things that need quick attention. She really listens. She consults before she makes decisions.

Note

1 *Sources*: World Bank, Economist Intelligence Unit (EIU).

GTBANK

Doing it Right and Doing Well

Franca Ovadje and Rose Ogbechie

Dr Franca Ovadje and Rose Ogbechie prepared this case as the basis for class discussion rather than to illustrate either effective or ineffective handling of an administrative situation. The assistance of Elohor Ovadje is appreciated.

It was December 2009. Tayo Adenirokun, the Group Managing Director of GTBank plc was sitting in his office. He had just read an email from an employee. He recalled the growth of the bank from its inception in 1990, the values upon which the organization was founded and the unwavering passion each 'Guaranty Trust Bank' employee applied to every single task. Doing well while being an ethical institution had been very challenging but now things were changing. Since the Central Bank of Nigeria (CBN) announcement in August 2009 and the subsequent takeover of ailing banks, new accounts had been flowing into GTBank. If the CBN had not guaranteed deposits and barred government agencies from moving their funds, there would have been a disaster in the banking industry. The bank ballooned in a few weeks. The customer base grew so much that the systems were stretched and some downtime was experienced.

GTBank had done exceedingly well: profit after tax was N36.51 billion in 2010 compared to 23.85 billion the previous year; return on average equity (ROE) of 18.55 per cent was up from 12.96 per cent in 2009. The local rating agency, Agusto & Co. had given the bank triple A (Aaa). Standard and Poor gave the Bank a double B minus in 2009. GTBank was the only Nigerian bank with such a rating.

Euromoney named GTBank the best bank in Nigeria in both 2009 and 2010. The list of awards and recognitions was impressive. GTBank emerged the most

Customer Focused Bank in both 2009 and 2010 (KPMG Banking Industry Customer Survey). It was arguably the most respected bank in Nigeria.

The reason for Tayo's gladness was the content of the email he had received:

> Now we understand what you were telling us. We can hold our heads high in the industry and everywhere. People tell us, 'you guys are different'. It is a nice feeling.

Even though the journey had been long and arduous, Tayo felt it had been worthwhile. And now external events had validated the *GTBank way*. He was happy that they made all the effort to do things properly from the beginning. He knew that remaining on course would continue to be a challenge. He wondered what else the bank could do to further strengthen the bank's values especially among new recruits.

The Beginnings

GTBank obtained a banking licence on 1 August 1990. Once they had the licence, the founders, Fola Adeola and Tayo Adenirokun, started looking for investors and employees. They were very clear from the beginning about the kind of bank they wanted to create.

According to Tayo:

> We wanted to create an institution; one that will outlive its founders. We noticed that there was no Nigerian owned and run organization that had seen two generations. We had seen the model; one rich man bankrolls the banking licence and shareholding and has a dominant influence on the Bank. I worked for six months in a merchant bank owned by a money bag. It did not work; a professional could not work there. We wanted to avoid this mistake. We wanted to be successful, even rich; we wanted to make our mark on our profession. We wanted to make a difference.

In the beginning, their dreams were rather modest. Fola said to the young men and women who joined the bank in 1990 that the bank would make 500 million Naira some day.

Fola, Tayo and the new recruits spent six months preparing for the opening of the first branch. They had recruited a core group of people most of whom were young graduates. They organized training programmes for the staff. The founders resisted pressures from competitors to open their doors and start making money. They maintained regular contact with the investors and explained their plans. They used the time to refurbish the building which was to house their first branch. They organized a strategy session involving all employees. At the end of the session, the group had agreed on a vision statement and the way they would live their lives; the organizational values (see Exhibit I for the vision and mission).

Two senior managers, founding members of staff commented on the vision:

> Fola and Tayo told us what the Bank was about and we came up with the Vision. We challenged every word, brought out a dictionary and argued until we reached a consensus. Our vision is about perfection; it is something we live. Every time we have a strategy session we look at the vision again but we find it is still very relevant today.
>
> *An executive director*

> The Bank did not have any specific targets at inception. We just provided great customer service. We wanted to be a reference point in what we do. Being the biggest is nothing. The purpose was to create role models in society.
>
> *A senior manager*

From inception, the management shied away from the public sector where ethics would preclude the bank from getting a significant share of the market. Over time however, they realized that there were some islands of sanity in the public sector and GTBank entered this sector. Public sector however, remains a relatively small part of the Bank's portfolio.

Corporate Governance

Once Fola and Tayo had obtained the banking licence, they went on to choose the initial investors. They looked for professionals they felt comfortable with; people they had worked with in their careers who could understand the vision, and share the values of the bank. According to Tayo:

> There were no money bags on the Board that could tell us what to do. We set up with little money from forty-three shareholders. No one felt he owned the Bank.

The board members were from different fields: there were lawyers, economists, financiers, people with varied experience in business, etc. The board had several committees all of which were very active. A number of board members commented on the functioning of the board:

> Memos are given to Board members in good time so they can study them and take a position. The committees do their work. We meet to discuss the proposals. We put our heads together and we arrive at a consensus. Board meetings do not last the whole day. Many of the Board members have

been on the Board for many years; at least 3 of them since inception of
the Bank.

A non-executive director

We have well orchestrated and mapped out strategies. The founding
Managing Director (Fola) left after twelve years; no one forced him to leave.
We have had 3 Board Chairmen; there have been no fights on the Board.

An executive director

According to the chairman of the board:

The Board does not interfere. We are on the Board to contribute to the
work of the Bank not to bring people in for employment. Even if you
recommend someone to the Management, the person must follow the
recruitment process. The past Chairman's child failed the pre-employment
examination; he was not employed. What is important is that the Bank as a
corporate entity is doing well; there are other places where your children
can work.

I was on the Board for ten years before I became the Chairman. There is
a lot of debate, of discussion on the Board but always in a very cordial
atmosphere. We are very peaceful, united and friendly. There are no cliques,
no meetings before the meeting. This is how I met the Board. We don't vote.
It is how the founders set it up. We have no-holds barred discussions. We
don't push things aside; we tackle them. Everyone is allowed to speak and
there are no meetings before the meeting. We are convinced that
Management has nothing to hide. They are doing their job well so we try
to cooperate with them unless we see something is going wrong.

The allowance paid to Board members is not significant considering the net
worth of the board members. According to one non-executive director: 'we joke
that GTB is very stingy but if an organization gives you gifts for nothing, ask
yourself where the money is coming from'.

The chairman commented on the culture:

We have a long term perspective but of course we look at the short, medium
and long term. I think conservatism has its virtues. We don't jump into
things; we consider them thoroughly. GTB has a strong sense of morality.
Aggressiveness may mean giving people patronage and that is something
GTB will never do. We have lost business because we play by the rules. It is
not always easy. We lose business and others wax strong.

The bank had internal and external auditors who independently briefed non-
executive directors through the risk and audit committees. In the 20 years of the

bank's history, there has not been one case in which CBN queried GTB for presenting a false audit; there have been disagreements about classification but not misrepresentation. Complying with the laws of the land was considered very important at GTBank.

Organizational Structure and Processes

In the first 15 years of its history, GTBank focused on corporate banking. It expanded slowly to different parts of the country. The bank opened subsidiaries in English speaking West Africa and in London. When it entered the retail market seriously in 2006, it expanded its branch network rapidly.

The operating units of the Bank were the Strategic Business Units (SBUs). These were structured around industries. For example, an SBU served the airline industry; another served financial services, etc. Each SBU had a team leader. In 2002, the bank had been re-organized into six regions: Southeast, Southwest, North Central, Northeast, Northwest and Lagos. Each region was headed by a divisional head who resided in the region.

A team leader observed:

> We work in teams. No team member visits a customer alone. We work to lift each other up. I think that is the reason the Bank has done so well. Team members have different qualities so we complement each other; one member is good with relationship management, another brings the deal, yet another is great with the desk work.

A manager commented on the level of empowerment:

> You are the MD of your business. I can get a COT concession signed in 30 minutes because of our flat structure. In my former bank it took a month. I cannot work in another bank after this. If I leave GTB, I will go into farming.

A new employee elaborated on the work relationships:

> Job functions are well spelt out. We are crafted into a team and that becomes family. We have a platform for exchange of ideas; the network is perfect. We have the tools to do our job. I enjoy my work every day.

Although the structure was clear, reporting lines were not strictly followed. According to a team leader:

> I can call my group head to go with me to see a customer. I can even call the MD. We get enough resources to run our business.

A number of employees commented on the processes and systems in the Bank:
A team leader:

> You have to imbibe professionalism, you have no choice. Controls are in
> place and this makes it difficult for you to do what you should not do. You
> do not have funds available to you, everything is tight. Some people say they
> cannot cope with the system and they leave.

An ED elaborated:

> In many places people are doing things and don't know why they are doing
> them. Our system does not require you to see the MD because there is a
> process.

There are clear service level agreements (SLAs). Each team generated its liabilities
and assets. At the monthly performance review (MPR), they were assessed on their
contribution to the bottom line. The focus was on the performance of the team.
The team leader assessed individual contribution during the appraisal exercises.

At the end of the month, each SBU's profit and loss statement is published on
the intranet. One manager elaborated:

> The figures are there; it is difficult to cook them up. You can get everybody
> talking to everybody on the intranet. Teams that achieved their targets are
> rewarded with cash, plaques and/or verbal commendation.

The MPR and the operations review (OPR) were very important management
systems in GTBank. The reviews are done at three levels: group, divisional and
branch. The profit centres made presentations at the MPRs. One manager
elaborated:

> You come out to tell everyone what you have done, the strategies that led
> to your success, the challenges you face and your proposed solutions.

A senior manager:

> During the MPRs and OPRs, we tell them you cannot do this or that. We
> give examples of how we did it in the past. We sometimes come up with a
> communiqué which is published on the intranet.

Senior management saw the reviews as an opportunity to instil the bank's
values while pushing for results. No one was allowed to use the ethical stance
of the bank as an excuse for not achieving their goals. As one senior manager
put it:

The budget is cast in stone. In cutting the budget, you are expected to scan the environment. You look at what you can do given the environment and the way we do business.

A manager who joined GTBank after some years with another bank commented:

GTB is rigid in many positive ways. Everything is structured. In my former bank the branch manager had some discretion. Here there is nothing like that. What applies in branch A applies in B. There are things I could do in my former bank which I cannot do here. There, the manager was the alpha and omega; he could order a teller to pay a million Naira to a customer. Here the operations staff will not carry out that order. Besides, the marketing people do not evaluate the performance of operations staff so the latter are likely to do what is right.

A non-executive director:

In the early years, I was sitting with the Chairman in Fola's office when a customer called him. He told the customer the facility will be ready at such a time and asked her to call back. Fola called the young girl in charge of the account and asked her if the facility was ready. She said the facility could not be given because certain conditions had not been met. Fola called the customer immediately and apologized. He said there was nothing he could do to reverse the decision. I was impressed.

GTB is run by systems; everybody does his work. A number of people sign off on a facility before the final signatory. There is an unwritten rule that certain things are not permitted. Non-executive Directors do not breathe over the necks of management. I introduced my cousin to the Bank but he was not hired.

A Commitment to Customers

The bank had a reputation for good customer service. It has won several awards. It conducted customer satisfaction surveys regularly. Customers were encouraged to lodge a complaint by dialling a telephone number which was displayed in the banking hall.

One corporate customer commented on the quality of service:

The effort they put to deliver service is striking. They seem to respond much better than other banks. From the security guard at the gate to the manager, you get the impression of a conscious effort to provide service. We had one deal that went really bad though. They made sure subsequent ones were double checked.

Employees often went to great lengths to recover customers whenever a service failure was reported. One customer talked about his experience: someone had withdrawn money from his account using an ATM machine. He complained about it but was not satisfied with the response from his customer relationship person. So he escalated the problem. He was astonished when a senior manager called him to book an appointment to see him. The senior manager came to the meeting with the account officer to apologize for the delay in solving the problem.

A corporate customer talked about the challenge of banking with GTB:

> Sometimes, their ethical stance is challenging. Those of us who do business with government say gosh! You assume GTB will frown at certain transactions. I call it the GTB snob. It strikes your conscience.

Several employees commented on the service culture of the Bank.

> Here in GTB you are not allowed to argue with a customer. This is something you don't see elsewhere.
>
> *A manager*

> If you want to do the right thing and sustain your business, you cannot go wrong with our model. We seek first to understand the customer. The first question we ask the customer is: how is the business? What are your headaches, your future plans? We start a conversation.
>
> Branches hold customer service meetings weekly. We share best practices. We tell the customer how we can add value to his business. We render service and make legitimate money. It means hard work, intelligent work. If I give a bribe, I have not added value.
>
> You come up with a bespoke service offering for the customer. If you are not well trained you can't help them. There is no information you want that is not available on our intranet. Cars are available, remuneration is okay. In spite of the crisis in the industry, we have not cut salaries; we have not sacked people.
>
> *An executive director*

> I have done a lot of public sector work. We attack it from a value-adding perspective. We look for the 5 to 10% who appreciate value and we work with them. If we had done business like others we would have been much more profitable but that is not value adding.
>
> *A manager*

> We hold our own in this environment. We are satisfied with the share we get considering we don't give patronage. We have diversified the income base; we have corporate banking, commercial and retail banking so public sector is not significant. If the bulk of your income comes from a volatile

public sector you will have problems. Some public officials make ten times their income on a monthly basis.

Customers sometimes ask for things we don't do. They threaten to call Tayo. They feel we have more bottlenecks but we are simply doing the right thing. There is a Standard Operating Procedure. Tayo pacifies them but we do not change the procedures. Once he said to us: 'you know we cannot do that but you could have been more diplomatic about it'.

A manager

Only those who are lazy or who look at business from a shallow perspective talk about bribes. You have to know your bank and the market you are playing in. We were taught in training school who the real managers of the business are. We focus on what we can do to enhance the customer's business.

A manager

GTBank was known for innovative products. In fact, flawless service delivery and innovative products were very important aspects of its customer value proposition. It changed the banking hall hours in Nigeria in the 1990s; it was the first to introduce on-line real time banking. Even the social projects it sponsored were innovative.

Organizational Culture

GTBank has a distinctive culture. One of the case writers carried out the following exercise on three occasions. She projected a slide with the values: Integrity, Professionalism, Customer Service and Friendliness and asked participants to name the company. They chorused GTBank. The participants were from a firm in the oil and gas sector; an insurance company and a group of HR managers who were attending a conference.

Several members of staff and a few board members commented on the bank's values:

A senior manager:

The core value is integrity. It is hammered into our brains on a daily basis. Professionalism and customer service are others.

A non-executive director:

GTBank stands for integrity. We are not going to look for profit at all cost. There was a time during the military regime when GTB suffered a loss of income because we were not ready to play ball with the people in government.

A pioneer staff:

> Even when banks were dealing in free funds we did not. Two people who did it against the rules were sacked. They told us from the beginning that to build an enduring organization we should not be in a hurry to make money.

A manager commented:

> Tayo insists that we cut a budget and we compare ourselves against that budget not against another bank's budget. He tells us not to get carried away by the figures our neighbours have published. Last year, staff harassed Tayo to make loans available for customers to buy shares. Many other banks were doing it. He kept us in check.

GTBank had a code of ethics. But the code was not written at the beginning. According to Tayo:

> At the beginning, we did not have a code. We just lived our life that way. We were just being natural.

Years later, the code was written and communicated to all staff. Every new member of staff received a copy upon joining. Since 2009, an electronic copy is sent to the mailbox of employees every quarter. They are asked to read it, agree to abide by the code by signing it and submit it. Signed copies are sent automatically to the legal team and HR.

Breaches of the ethical code were punished. The sanction depended on the gravity of the offence and varied from forfeiture of promotion, suspension without pay, to dismissal. Very senior people in the bank had been asked to leave for issues bothering on ethics. In several cases, the police was invited. An executive director elaborated:

> If there is a case of fraud, the Systems and Control Unit investigates and builds a case on it. People read the case. Branches and teams meet to discuss the issues. We also make presentations on the impact the breach had on others so the staff can learn. The steps taken are communicated, the name of the person(s) involved are given. The loopholes are reviewed and blocked. Sometimes the matter is taken to the police.

A manager:

> Whistle blowing is encouraged here and it is anonymous. We have CCTVs everywhere. The MD will sack you if you give a bribe of five thousand Naira to anybody.

Another manager:

> I always wanted to work with GTB. I took a salary cut to join. One day after a visit to a customer, I called my boss to tell her that the Finance Director of the company had asked me to sleep with him. She told me clearly: 'we don't want dirty money here.' I never heard that in my former bank. In my former bank, we distributed money to public servants. I was not comfortable with it so my boss left me out. Colleagues in other banks get business and you have to struggle but you are better off and they know it. This environment makes you tough and determined.

Tayo elaborated:

> In the beginning, it was tough; we looked unreal. How can you do business this way? This is Nigeria! But customers do not throw you away completely. We sell professionalism and good customer service. When customers need to do something that requires professional thought, they remember GTB. We don't do a lot of government business; it comes with all that baggage. We don't have a fat account of any government. But if a state government wants to issue a bond they come to us because they want to do it professionally. They know we can do real things for them.

A corporate customer of the bank told one of the case writers:

> What I would offer to my other bankers without batting an eyelid, I would not even discuss with GTB. They have created an impression; there are some things one would not even discuss with them. You go to GTB for regular transactions. If we have to cash a huge some of money we don't use our GTB account. I don't want them to ask questions so I use my other bankers for such transactions.
>
> The members of staff make an extra effort to provide service. They have a snob effect too. I would rather dine with a GTB staff. He has more breadth; he can discuss Nigerian art, Renaissance architecture etc. They make a conscious effort in recruitment; they are rounded individuals not just bankers.

Employees talked about other values of the GTBank culture:

> Candour is a key success factor in this organization. You are not punished for expressing your opinion. You defend your position and no one thinks you are saucy. It is a very open environment so people are not frustrated. People who are frustrated do great damage in a service business. Uncle T, like Fola, encourages discourse. You can tell Tayo that you don't agree with him; that you want to be convinced. Everyone talks at the credit committees.

A manager:

> When I joined I had issues with expressing my opinion until I discovered that you can really challenge what your boss says. However, because you are dealing with very intelligent people convincing them is not easy; you have to be prepared and you must be articulate.

A senior manager:

> You don't have to go to your manager's house. We have clear targets and appropriate processes. I don't remember when last I visited Tayo. There are no threats, the work environment is peaceful.

An employee with just over one year's tenure:

> We are true to ourselves and customers. What we tell them they will get is what they get.

A manager:

> I could have brought in a huge sum of money. I was almost frustrated in the process and the ED told me to calm down; this may not be my money. The customer will give us some of it because we are a safe bank. He said to me: 'if you are going to look for money and meet integrity on the way, pick up integrity and go back home. We don't have to do every business.'

A new hire:

> When you are in an organization where the leaders are doing things ethically you have to follow suit. You can't do otherwise.

A senior manager commented on the mutual dealings among employees:

> We show genuine interest in the well being of others. We try to look out for each other as best we can. We go to the market with a lot of knowledge and not short skirts, light-skinned girls, etc. We go with substance.

A few others highlighted some of the challenges:
A manager who left the Bank and was re-hired:

> When we started it was easy to know a GTB person. Over time, we have not done enough to ensure the culture permeates and is as strong as it used

to be. We are working on it. The old generation are never late to meetings; the younger people arrive late and are not hiding in shame!

Tayo:

GTB has a very strong culture. Our people are not friendly to outsiders. We have a challenge at this level. The success rate for middle to top level hires is 30%. The MPR can be very brutal. Some people don't understand that there is no ill-feeling. I don't hate you but if you bring a stupid credit I will ask you if you are dumb. We work harder than most in our industry. We have had to work harder to get where we are today.

An executive director commented on how the values are passed on to new employees:

It is the responsibility of the supervisor to improve the skill level of his people and pass on the culture. A lot of things get passed on at meetings and in training sessions.

Leadership Style

The case writers asked several employees to comment on the leadership.

Tayo is very simple and down to earth. He is friendly. No one calls him sir. We call him Tayo and those who feel they cannot call him Tayo call him Uncle T. If you call him sir, he tells you immediately that his name is Tayo. He is approachable and in touch with things. Even the lowest cadre of staff can go to him with their problems. The top management encourages openness. Even those who joined and were not so open have become more so. The culture rubs off on them and they become more personable.

A manager

Tayo refused to cut salaries and fire people during the Banking crisis; he respects his people and cares about their well being. I can talk to him about anything; I can even report a management staff. There is plenty of freedom to express oneself.

A new employee

Uncle T is amazing. He is not afraid of anything; he has nothing to hide. He does not go around with escorts. You don't have to carry his bag; he would refuse. He is simple. He takes decisions based on the facts available. He drives the culture of the bank. He is not an angel but he gets the balance right – he has a business to run and he is working with human beings.

A manager

Tayo and Segun are irritated by the expression: 'what other banks are doing'.

A manager

[Tayo] gives you a free hand; he watches you from afar for a while. He is a real guy who is not surrounded by sycophants. He still eats in the lunch room with everyone else. He asks questions. He lets you go about your business.

[He] drives himself at weekends. He is not obnoxious or pompous. He is the humblest person at that level that I have seen. I admire his style; it works. Some bosses are afraid of their subordinates because they feel threatened. That is not common here.

Tayo is a good judge of character. Based on continuous assessment he tells you exactly what he feels about you but he does not keep malice. Not many people are like that. He comes from a disciplined family.

An executive director

An executive director commented on the leadership style of the senior management:

We lead by example. I will not ask you to do what is not right. There is nothing you are doing that I am not willing to do with you. We have a relationship with the people; we share experience with them. It is difficult to tell you not to drink if I am drunk.

People Management

A lot of the responsibility for the management of people was devolved to line managers. Managers were considered business leaders and were therefore expected to deliver results and manage people and resources. They took decisions on people issues and the Human Resource (HR) Department implemented these decisions. However, recruitment and selection was managed by HR. According to the Head of HR:

We cascade a lot of HR functions to line managers. Regional and Group heads handle people issues. Everybody is an HR person. We send them on leadership courses.

Many new initiatives regarding people management started in different divisions. If a practice yields good results, it is shared and sometimes HR takes it up. For example, the Corporate Banking Division began a mentoring programme. A year later, HR introduced a formal mentoring programme which gives mentees unlimited access to a senior manager.

Recruitment and Pre-employment Programme

Most employees joined the bank fresh from university with little or no work experience. They went through gruelling tests and a series of interviews. GTBank tried to attract the best people. Those who are selected joined a rigorous orientation programme of 3 to 4 months. During the programme, they are taught the basics of banking and more importantly the vision and values of the Bank. Top management facilitated at some of the sessions. They shared the vision and way of life. Other courses taught on the pre-employment programme included: customer service, personal grooming, dress sense, table etiquette, and use of English.

An executive director spoke about the recruitment and selection strategy:

> Our recruitment strategy is unique. We attract fresh graduates; people who can be moulded. We sell the vision to them. They believe they can make a difference and become role models. We empower them and give them all the resources they require to excel. We groom them to serve the customer. The customer is the focus of the business. Satisfied customers bring other customers. The best people, best environment and best resources bring the results.

Employees were enthusiastic about the programme. Many believed they received the training to be bankers on the programme. Three employees shared their experience:

> We had fun. The MD took us to his house for a treat. He blew our minds. He gave us books, branded T-shirts, etc.
>
> *A new hire*

> The training school was the foundation. We were exposed to the culture of the Bank; we were taught self management, managing your finances, etc. We were taught to be role models. Most of the sessions were taught by GTB staff. My husband told me they brainwashed me at the training school but he liked it.
>
> *A manager with 10 years' tenure*

> We were taught how to relate with people, manage people, provide service, etc. We are taught to save for the future, to have a budget – even for telephone recharge cards.
>
> *A manager with 6 years' tenure*

Senior managers talked to the new recruits about the history and culture of the bank. One manager commented:

The Group Managing Director and the Deputy Managing Director give sessions on the Induction Programme. They are very passionate about the Bank's values. You know they hold these values close to their heart. It shows in their work, speech, attitude, etc.

New hires visited a prison during the orientation programme. One employee commented on the experience:

They told us what it would be like to be caught. We saw bankers who had been fraudulent. We met prisoners; spoke to the wardens, District Police Officers, etc.

Some fun activities were also organized during the programme. A half day on the beach was one of the favourites.

Stories of the beginnings of the bank are told at the training school. One story that is often told is that of a customer who was shouting in the banking hall asking to see the MD. Unknown to the customer, Tayo was at the customer desk. He apologized to the customer, said he was sorry that the MD was very busy and he would like to help.

At the end of the orientation programme, the new recruits sat for examinations. Those who passed the examinations were hired by the bank. The others were immediately hired by GTBank's competitors.

Training

GTBank committed huge resources to staff development. Every member of staff was entitled to some days of training each year. Employees had an input into their own training; they could recommend training programmes they would like to attend. Training programmes were organized regularly. Contract staff and interns were not left out. If anyone felt he had not received the required training he sent an email to HR and he/she was quickly nominated for the programme. Employees went on leave each year. If anyone forfeited his annual leave, he forfeited the leave allowance.

Contract staff also attended an induction programme and training programmes organized by the bank and by their employers. One of the contract staff commented:

Here they make you feel that being a contract staff is not something so bad. You don't have to have a contract staff mentality.

Performance and Reward Management

Performance was appraised on both quantitative and qualitative measures. The ability to meet profit before tax, balance sheet targets, etc. in addition to leadership skills and interpersonal skills were appraised.

According to the HR manager, 'we do not pay the best salaries; we offer a great environment to work'.

However, remuneration was very competitive and many members of staff were shareholders of the bank. A bonus system had been instituted. The system was transparent. As Tayo put it:

> If you make your budget you get your money. There are no arguments, and you know you earned it. We can all make money in a transparent way.

The salary structure is flat. There are a number of salary levels but no steps within the levels. Managers on a particular level earned the same salaries and enjoyed the same benefits. The Head of HR elaborated:

> We are big on welfare. We believe everybody is equal. All AGMs are the same. It is a fallacy but I am willing to live with some of those discrepancies. There are no steps within the levels. We do Mother Theresa type of things here.

GTBank was known to take care of its employees. If an employee fell ill, the medical bills were paid; even if she had to be flown abroad. A manager who does not work with the bank told one of the case writers this story. His sister, an employee of GTBank had an accident and was hospitalized. They paid all the medical expenses but what impressed the family most was the fact that the GMD sent her a get well message.

Corporate Social Responsibility

GTBank has been innovative in the type of social projects it supported. In 1996, the bank adopted The Massey Street Children's Hospital in a poor suburb of Lagos. It has continued to support the hospital with infrastructure development and purchase of equipment. Later, other healthcare projects were added.

The bank has supported various projects in the Arts including exhibitions, drama, festivals, etc. Perhaps the single area where GTBank has invested a large sum is in education. It has adopted 10 schools in different parts of the country. It renovates the school buildings; provides basic utilities such as water and electricity; supplies books and other equipment and beautifies the environment.

Some of its social projects were aimed at developing capacity in the public sector. For example, the bank sponsored senior government officials to training programmes regardless of whether they did business with them or not. Other social projects were linked to the business. A manager in the public sector desk explained:

> We went to the Governor of one of the states and we said to him: 'this is a new state and you have just been elected. The State needs hospitals, roads,

an airport, etc. We told him what we can do for the State. We financed the airport and projects in five local government areas in the State. We told the Governor that we were going to carry out a social responsibility project. We renovated a secondary school in the capital with five million Naira but we did not give five Naira bribe. We left our sign posts there. Everyone knows we did that project. We were part of the success story of that State. We have done similar projects in other states. We enter into a partnership to move the state forward.

The Challenge

Tayo was approaching the end of his self imposed tenure as Group Managing Director of the bank. He was satisfied with what they had built so far. GTBank was an institution that was well respected and admired. The Orange Rules campaign had brought to the public the values of the bank. The goal had always been to create an enduring institution, owned and run by Nigerians according to the highest professional and ethical standards.

A manager in the Corporate Affairs department had recently talked about the bank as an iconic brand. The statement had generated a lot of debate. Many of the senior managers believed that the bank was not an iconic brand yet. One of them commented:

> We have less than 200 branches in 6 countries. People do not know us outside these countries. Yes, we are a strong and visible brand in our chosen environment. Our website is the 3rd most visited in Nigeria but we are not an iconic brand.

GTBank had subsidiaries in London and in Anglophone West Africa. Plans were underway to expand to the Francophone countries. If the bank was to maintain its culture, more attention had to be put into the development of new hires.

A senior manager commented:

> I see a big challenge with the young generation. The societal values are reflected in the young people. When we bring them in, we bend them to our way. The educational system is not what it was 10 to 20 years ago. We mentor them and help them learn. But we are not immune to the environment.
>
> Those days, we came into the system with lower expectations. Today, the average employee wants a car and a home tomorrow and does not ask how his peers got them. We tell them things don't work that way. You have to pay the dues. I used to go to CBN at 2am to lodge cash. Before, it was taken for granted that if there is a queue everyone will help out. Now we have to insist.

Between 2002 and 2006 we grew very fast. We brought in fresh graduates into the training school in batches. We also brought in middle managers. It takes much more to change managers.

A Generation Y new hire commented on his colleagues:

My generation has ethics but we have issues with commitment. I think we are lagging there. We don't match the way the guys up there do things; they are professional to the core. They are very serious about many little things like lateness to meetings, how you communicate, going the extra mile to serve customers, etc.

A middle manager concluded:

At different times people review their lives and where they are in an organization. The younger ones are a little bit more aggressive about themselves, what they want to do, how fast to get there, etc. But in terms of culture some are doing very well; you would think they started here twenty years ago.

The events of August 2009 reinforced our values. They show that there is a reward for taking the straight and narrow path. CBN is trying to promote what we are already doing. When we go marketing we don't have to say anything; they tell us they know our Bank and that they invited us to the meeting.

Our branches are busting; we have seen a phenomenal growth in new accounts. Some customers I have been marketing for six years opened three accounts just like that. Ethics is not a limiting factor anymore. The environment is changing.

EXHIBIT I Guaranty Trust Bank

MISSION STATEMENT

We are a high quality financial services provider with the urge to be the best at all times whilst adding value to all stakeholders.

VISION STATEMENT

We are a team driven to deliver the utmost in customer services. We are synonymous with innovation, building excellence and superior financial performance; and creating role models for society.

Source: gtbank.com

EXHIBIT II GTBank Financial Statements (2007–2010)

Five Year Financial Summary

Balance Sheet	Dec 2010	Dec 2009	Dec 2008 (10 months)	Feb 2008	Feb 2007
	N'000	N'000	N'000	N'000	N'000
ASSETS					
Cash and balances with CBN	27,017,683	34,890,767	62,579,450	38,969,734	32,346,472
Treasury bills	141,775,484	29,405,616	52,715,562	63,105,768	124,794,434
Due from other banks	204,567,931	202,810,278	191,187,296	64,224,277	96,593,552
Loans and advances to customers	—	—	—	—	4,443,719
Other facilities	563,482,281	538,137,569	413,983,817	291,530,777	113,705,183
Advances under finance lease	—	1,288	23,835	18,091	—
Investment securities	46,356,435	134,126,992	86,616,909	115,240,952	40,739,800
Investment in subsidiaries	30,115,862	29,774,817	28,274,817	15,022,241	4,536,594
Deferred tax assets	—	—	—	—	—
Other assets	7,631,958	9,478,730	46,866,078	94,581,049	41,453,189
Equipment on lease	—	—	—	—	—
Property and equipment	45,815,129	41,285,479	36,030,992	31,652,460	19,749,488
TOTAL ASSETS	**1,066,762,763**	**1,019,911,536**	**918,278,756**	**714,345,349**	**478,363,061**
LIABILITIES					
Share capital	11,658,593	9,326,874	7,461,500	6,839,708	4,000,000
Share premium	119,076,566	119,076,566	119,076,565	119,076,565	21,391,928
Reserves	74,432,647	60,072,348	53,012,660	35,136,791	22,041,260
Customers' deposit	713,080,374	662,261,026	445,740,212	357,006,128	290,792,372
Due to other banks	3,320,059	1,083,016	27,965,203	324,844	—

	Dec 2010	Dec 2009	Dec 2008 (10 months)	Feb 2008	Feb 2007
	N'000	N'000	N'000	N'000	N'000
Finance lease obligations	1,847,629	2,211,130	2,125,260	2,350,447	—
Current income tax payable	8,686,276	2,373,006	9,237,928	5,791,420	3,332,773
Other liabilities	43,243,089	81,284,082	186,892,178	127,740,385	72,196,921
Deferred tax liabilities	4,160,684	4,134,454	3,395,712	2,731,679	1,071,027
Dividend payable	35,785	—	—	—	—
Retirement benefit obligation	—	240,811	475,010	1,204,806	984,806
Debt securities in issue	66,387,400	65,515,655	48,838,125	—	—
Other facilities	—	—	—	—	4,488,605
Other borrowings	20,833,661	12,332,568	14,058,403	56,142,576	58,063,369
TOTAL LIABILITIES	**1,066,762,763**	**1,019,911,536**	**918,278,756**	**714,345,349**	**478,363,061**
Guarantees and other commitments on behalf of customers	401,745,825	316,381,113	389,543,782	322,462,234	115,000,398

Five Year Financial Summary

Profit and Loss Account	Dec 2010	Dec 2009	Dec 2008 (10 months)	Feb 2008	Feb 2007
	N'000	N'000	N'000	N'000	N'000
Net operating income	108,630,864	112,659,732	74,411,912	58,471,300	33,756,269
Operating expenses	(55,612,315)	(48,696,218)	(35,521,595)	(27,427,338)	(17,688,652)
Allowance for loan loss and other risk assets	(7,543,509)	(37,003,705)	(4,281,200)	(3,845,258)	(717,386)
Profit on ordinary activities before taxation	**45,475,040**	**26,959,809**	**34,609,117**	**27,198,704**	**15,350,231**
Taxation	(8,963,412)	(3,111,748)	(6,535,865)	(5,708,819)	(2,337,085)
Profit after taxation	**36,511,628**	**23,848,061**	**28,073,252**	**21,489,885**	**13,013,146**

Continued

Five Year Financial Summary

Profit and Loss Account

	Dec 2010	Dec 2009	Dec 2008 (10 months)	Feb 2008	Feb 2007
Extraordinary income	—	—	—	—	—
Profit after taxation and extraordinary income	**36,511,628**	**23,848,061**	**28,073,252**	**21,489,885**	**13,013,146**
Earnings per share (unadjusted)	157K	128K	188K	173K	163K

EXHIBIT III GTBank Financial Statements 2004–2006

Three Year Financial Summary

Balance Sheet	2006	2005	2004
	N'000	N'000	N'000
ASSETS			
Cash and short-term funds	72,305,298	46,293,166	30,861,568
Short term investments	103,806,539	28,477,211	20,417,590
Loans and advances	83,476,852	65,035,248	43,675,606
Other facilities	4,460,852	—	—
Advances under finance lease	920	5,682	—
Other assets	16,677,604	16,593,043	15,788,347
Long term investments	12,622,734	3,856,213	3,697,206
Equipment on lease	1,250	241,967	1,229,433
Fixed assets	11,729,436	7,399,936	4,022,808

	2006	2005	2004
Total assets	305,080,565	167,897,704	119,698,240
LIABILITIES			
Deposits and other accounts	212,833,770	95,563,587	74,222,497
Other facilities	4,505,911	—	—
Other liabilities, including tax and dividend payable (restated)*	37,857,757	29,256,293	28,981,961
Long term borrowings	9,237,585	6,909,788	3,525,804
Total liabilities	264,435,023	131,729,668	106,730,262
Net assets	40,645,542	36,168,036	12,967,978
CAPITAL AND RESERVES			
Share capital	3,000,000	3,000,000	1,500,000
Share premium	21,391,928	21,391,928	2,172,666
Other reserves (restated)*	16,253,614	11,776,108	9,295,312
Shareholders' Fund	40,645,542	36,168,036	12,967,978

Three Year Financial Summary: Profit and Loss Account

Three Year Financial Summary

Profit and Loss Account

	2006	2005	2004
	N'000	N'000	N'000
Gross earnings	31,970,318	23,833,771	18,053,377
Profit on ordinary activities before taxation	10,024,936	7,004,243	5,029,725
Taxation	(2,119,430)	(1,673,447)	(973,168)
Profit on ordinary activities after taxation	7,905,506	5,330,796	4,056,557

Continued

Three Year Financial Summary: Profit and Loss Account

Three Year Financial Summary

Profit and Loss Account	2006	2005	2004
Extraordinary income	772,000	—	—
Profit after taxation and extraordinary income	**8,677,506**	**5,330,796**	**4,056,557**
Earnings per share (unadjusted)	145K	110K	135K
Declared dividend per share**	70K	62K	60K

Source: GTBank 2010 Annual Report

EXHIBIT IV Comparative Analysis of Selected Banks in Nigeria

	GTBank		First Bank		Zenith Bank		UBA	
	2009	2010	2009	2010	2009	2010	2009	2010
Total Assets (in million)	1,019,912	1,066,763	2,172,346	1,957,258	1,573,196	1,789,458	1,400,879	1,432,632
Total Equity	188,476	205,168	309,558	340,735	328,383	350,414	187,719	187,730
Total Operating Expenditure (in millions)	48,696	55,612	88,397	107,392	89,074	103,410	109,380	82,557
Total Compensation Expenditure (in millions)	15,220	15,120	39,275	50,982	103,410	89,074	34,054	28,457
Total Customers Deposits	662,261	713,080	1,236,599	1,330,771	1,111,328	1,289,552	1,119,063	1,216,464
PAT (in millions)	23,848	36,512	1,275	26,936	18,365	33,335	12,889	2,167
PBT (in millions)	26,959	45,475	7,689	31,491	31,753	42,957	22,989	16,359
Staff Number	2,566	2,569	8,221	7,603	7,393	7,190	11,791	10,651

Source: Annual Reports of GTBank, First Bank, Zenith Bank and UBA

EXHIBIT V Guaranty Trust Bank: ORANGE RULES

The **Orange Rules** are principles for progression, success, relationships and life. They guide GTBank's approach to banking and everything they do. They include:

1. Simplicity: 'The sense of reducing to the simplest possible terms every problem that besets us.' *Sir Henri Deterding*
    'Simplicity brings clarity, understanding and progress. We are straightforward, direct and easy to deal with, making the complex uncomplicated. Complexity leads to confusion, discouragement and a feeling of helplessness.'

2. Professionalism: 'is knowing how to do it, when to do it, and doing it'. *Frank Tyger*
    'We are thorough and efficient, always inspiring confidence. People have tremendous respect for professionals. They are relied on, trusted and believed in.'

3. Service: 'To give real service you must add something which cannot be bought or measured with money, and that is, sincerity and integrity.' *Donald A. Adams*
    'Our major strength, we're constantly improving on our ability to delight our customers. Lend a hand. Be there when you're needed. Bend over backwards to please and serve.'

4. Friendliness: 'The influence of each human being on others in this life is a kind of Immortality.' *John Quincy Adams*
    'We enjoy working together to fulfil customers' needs, building mutually rewarding relationships. Unfriendliness is often seen as a sign of disrespect. But a friendly person warms the heart and is a pleasure to do business with.'

5. Excellence: 'Is an art won by training and habituation.' *Aristotle*
    'We stand out from the crowd, always refreshing, always beyond the ordinary. Excellence is the ability to strive for the best, to never settle for average. It is being best in class, a benchmark, an inspiration.'

6. Trustworthiness: 'No virtue is more universally accepted as a test of good character than trustworthiness.' *Sharry Emerson Fosdick DD*
    'We are reliable, what we say is what we do; trust us to always do what is right. Be honest. Be trusted with information and money. Be a confidante.'

7. Social Responsibility: 'It is easy to dodge our responsibilities but we cannot dodge the consequences of dodging our responsibilities.' *Sir Josiah Stamp*
    'We care, we believe in building and sharing for the good of all. Give back to society.'

8. Innovation: 'Innovation is the application of creativity and imagination in a business context.' *Jeffrey Immelt*
    'We care, we believe in building and sharing for the good of all. Give back to society.'

SEVEN SEAS TECHNOLOGIES

An Entrepreneurial Journey

This case was prepared by Franca Ovadje as a basis for class discussion rather than to illustrate either effective or ineffective handling of an administrative situation. The assistance of Ruky Esharegaran is appreciated.
Copyright © 2011 Lagos Business School. Reprinted by permission of Lagos Business School.

Introduction

From its humble beginnings in 1999, Seven Seas Technologies (SST) had become one of the major players in the ICT industry in Kenya. A private equity firm, Aureos, acquired 21 per cent shares of SST in 2008. With this acquisition, the company entered a new phase in its history. Mike Macharia, the founder/CEO was looking at the future:

> A number of things can happen in four years. First, we may be acquired by a global organization such as a systems integration company or we may go public. Our vision is to build a Pan African business. This will involve partnering with other IT companies in other parts of Africa. A private equity firm can put this together. A large firm like this can be listed in the London or Johannesburg Stock Exchange.
>
> We are now playing in a bigger league. These players are ruthless. The customers are questioning your value proposition. There is not much value from being a local company in Kenya – just a warm, cosy feeling. You must fight for your position. Local is sometimes perceived as poor quality. No one ever got fired for buying an IBM.
>
> Our long term dream is to become the Accenture of Africa. To achieve this, we must win the people game. Consulting and IT transfer is about

people – interfacing with people, credentials, authenticity, etc. How do we get these people? How do we restructure our brand? How do we share wealth with those coming in?

The entrepreneurial journey is very lonely. Some time ago, nine friends and I decided to drive from Nairobi to Mozambique. A week before the departure date, only 2 of us were ready to go and the second person was not part of the original 10! I took the road trip and my friends called to cheer me up. They stayed home!

Finding his Voice

Mike Macharia (called Mike by all the staff) founded Seven Seas Technology. He attended Strathmore School in Nairobi, where he was always in the top quartile of the class. He wanted to study architecture in one of the best universities in Kenya. During the one year between secondary school and university, he regis-tered for the CPA examinations. At the end of the year, he gained admission into the Ligarden University to study mathematics and physics. Although the univer-sity was in a remote part of the country and he did not like the course, he took up the admission when he realised it was impossible to change the course of study.

He spent a semester in the university. He commented on his experience:

> Coming from Strathmore School, I was shocked by the conditions; the classrooms were too small for the number of students, there were endless queues in the cafeteria, etc. There were 400 to 500 people in the Psychology class. I asked myself: if I spend 4 years here what will happen to me?

Although he excelled, he found mathematics and physics impractical: 'I asked myself: Who does this stuff? Is this relevant to my life? How do all these equations help me? Where is this taking me? And these lab coats…?'

During the semester break, he took a job in an information technology (IT) firm in Westlands, Nairobi and he continued attending classes in the evenings, in preparation for the CPA examinations. The break was a long one because the students had rioted and the campus was closed indefinitely.

Mike commented on his experience with the company:

> The company had a huge debt portfolio and my job was debt collection. I talked to the customers. They complained that systems they bought from us were not delivered on time; a job card had not been signed, the delivery note was not sent, etc. I got to know the problems and found solutions to them. The CEO gave me his big Mercedes Benz car for the job when he saw that the debt level was reducing. The customers picked my calls because I told them stories. I was always nice to them and they knew I would have interesting stories for them.

One day Mike called Nasir, the CEO of one of the companies on the debtors list, to follow up on the debt. They agreed to meet at 5pm that day. During the meeting, Nasir asked Mike to work for him. Mike replied: 'Pay me first and I will work for you.'

At the interview, Nasir gave him a cash box, told him there was X Kenyan Shillings in the box and asked him to reconcile the accounts. Mike found there was much more money in the box and said so, and he reconciled the accounts. Nasir gave him the job and Mike accepted a full time job with Nasir as the company accountant. He explained: 'I connected with him and said I would like to work for him.'

Mike's parents were unaware of his employment contract. They assumed he was doing a vacation job and hence, were surprised he made no preparation to go back to the university as the resumption date drew near. Since he had not been a difficult child, they assumed he would do the expected. While on his way to work one day, he informed his parents that he was not going back to school and remained adamant despite his parents' objection.

Mike rose very fast in the organization. He said:

> I knew I had a lot to lose. I took on a lot of responsibility in the organization. I was in the finance department but I met with customers. It was always about cash flow. The staff (between 35 and 45) came to me with their problems and I spoke to the CEO on their behalf. In no time, I became the person who could tell the CEO the organization's temperature.

Mike redefined his job. Though he was expected to do payroll, cash flow, etc., he added an operations role and got himself involved in vendor management. He also attended a lot of conferences. He said:

> The CEO soon took me to Board Meetings. The company was owned by Institutions so the Board members were drawn from these institutions. I learnt a lot from the Board meetings. The Directors asked very interesting questions. I learnt discipline, leverage (they leveraged their name), how to raise capital, etc.

Mike worked very hard and often carried work home at the weekends. 'I was living a double life – a teenage life with parties and concerts and a life of hard work. I used to carry the CPU home and work all Sunday afternoon.' His boss (a finance graduate from Manchester) was very hard working. They both celebrated New Year in the office while closing the company's accounts. Mike was very passionate about the business. He was hurt whenever someone said he was leaving.

Intrapreneurship

Mike saw an opportunity in the computer hardware business. He elaborated:

> Customers called us for computers but we did not sell computers. At the time, the margin on boxes was between 25 and 30%. If we bought in bulk and sold

to re-sellers we could make a 15% margin and allow the re-sellers a 10% margin. The challenges would be logistics, cash flow and the shelf life of the computers. We would have to sell pretty fast; before an upgrade was released. I proposed the idea to the CEO and he agreed. I was in charge in the Finance Department so the idea was housed in my department. We soon began to make money. Not only did we sell boxes, we organized training programmes for the re-sellers' salesmen and charged them for the programme. Our technical engineers ran these programmes and we paid them for the service.

This business soon accounted for 70% of the gross profit of the company. I proposed a new pay structure that allowed us earn commissions. In 3 years, I was the second highest earner in the firm. Because of this success, I was moved from Finance to Sales, but I still did some business consultancy for the Finance Department. We asked for shares in the business but the Board refused; they were institutional investors. The Board also refused to set up a distribution firm to run this business. They felt that the revenue was not realistic in the long term. The CEO was great. He allowed us [to] run a business within a business. He gave me a lot of leeway.

The Beginning of SST

Mike decided to go to the USA to further his studies. He had made enough money to pay his fees and live there for 2 years. He planned to arrive 3 or 4 months earlier so he could travel around the country before starting school. He told his boss he was leaving. While making preparations for his trip, Mike met the Chief Financial Officer of Rwanda Airlines. They decided to have dinner.

Mike explained:

> During dinner, he told me that they were setting up an airline in Rwanda. He asked me if I could handle the IT requirements. I said why not? I could finish the job and still be on time to start school in September. So I went to Rwanda in February 1999, did the study and sent him a proposal.
>
> I had no company so getting paid was going to be a problem. I contacted Rob, who at that time was running Desktop; one of the re-sellers I had done business with. We had agreed that we would do business together with a name that was global and not tied to IT. We hurriedly set up Seven Seas Consultants in March with 2 shares: one each. We were paid for the proposal and invited to implement the plan.
>
> I used my relationships from the past. I bought equipment from some of the re-sellers we had supplied in my former firm. They all knew me well. The habits and contacts I acquired in paid employment served me well.
>
> At the end of the project, I was 25 years old and I had enough money for my studies in the US. I was going back to Nairobi to close the business and sell my car and household items when I was again delayed by a new project.

Mike was having coffee one afternoon when a friend told him that the military in Rwanda had problems with paying the soldiers and an IT solution was needed. Soldiers had to go from all over the country to the central office to collect their salaries. They wanted a solution that would integrate all branches so a soldier could go to an office near him to withdraw money.

That evening Mike did some research on the internet on Wide Area Network and came up with CISCO. He immediately wrote a proposal and prepared a PowerPoint presentation. He called a colleague in Nairobi for the bill of quantities, mark ups, etc.

The next morning he went to the barracks to make the presentation. The Committee agreed to go ahead and asked him to see the Patron of the Micro Finance Institution (he later became the President of Rwanda). He ratified the solution. Mike elaborated:

> I called Rob and said I had a new deal. I thought I could do this deal and go straight to school. With the money I would make, I could even buy a home in the US! We immediately hired young people to do the accounts for us and contracted engineers to solve the problem.
>
> We later found that we had underestimated many things; by August the project was not up. The bank was calling for cash, suppliers were calling for their money and the engineers could not solve the problem. Someone referred me to a CISCO partner in India. I jumped on the plane and went to Bombay to look for an engineer who could solve the problem. I stage managed the platform: booked into a 4–5 star hotel and made sure I was looking decent. I paid the engineer upfront and he solved the problem. We created the first ISDN line in Rwanda. The military was happy and the cash flow problems evaporated.
>
> In 7 months, I had made $130,000. I decided there was an opportunity. I could make $600,000 in one year. What was I going to a business school for? I decided to stay and grow the business. So instead of closing the business, we hired auditors and began to put things in place. In one year, Seven Seas Consultants had grown bigger than Rob's business. Rob later sold this business to focus on SST.

The First Years of SST

SST moved into Rob's office in Nairobi. Mike saw an opportunity to sell network connectivity equipment to the ISPs so he repeated the business model he had used earlier in his career and sold to resellers who sold to the ISPs. He ran the sales, technical and finance functions. SST used bank loans and supplier credit to finance projects. Since Mike knew the suppliers and had been dealing with them for some time, they allowed SST credit term of 30 days which he pushed to 90 days.

Mike explained:

> They knew I would pay as soon as I could. I talked to them every day. They came to see me and I shared my vision with them. The entrepreneurs among the suppliers supported us. The finance directors of the large companies were more mechanical in their dealings. Some even threatened to sue us if we did not pay.
>
> We had nothing; no brand, no plush offices, and no fancy cars. Getting customers was not easy. The large companies did not want to work with us neither did people who have been in the industry for some time. To attract business and the right calibre of people, I inspired people with my plans for the future and talked to them of the project we executed in Rwanda.
>
> We entered into a number of partnership agreements with companies like Cisco Systems. We also signed an agreement with an Indian IT company to provide us with expatriates. They sent some of their people to work with us for 6 months. Because of our partners, some good people came to work with us. We wanted them to work for SST but this was a good starting off point.

The business model was simple; Mike got jobs, bought equipment from SST's partners and, for complex projects, recruited expatriates to implement the projects. Mike and Rob learnt from their experience in Rwanda that cash flow was critical for the success of the business. Access to bank loans for larger projects was impossible. More importantly, by 2003, the environment was changing. Mike felt that the future was not in selling bandwidth or equipment, but in creating value. They needed advice and money. They decided to invite Mr. Gachui to invest in SST.

The late Mr Gachui was a well known personality in the business world in Kenya. He had an impressive career and owned one of the ISPs. Mike travelled with Mr Gachui to Bangalore, India where they visited several IT companies including Infosys. Mike elaborated:

> We saw that indigenous corporations were running multi-billion dollar companies. The logo of one of the technology companies struck me. It was simply: 'applying thought.' I shared with Mr. Gachui my understanding of the future of the industry and my vision for SST. I told him my story and he said he would like to be in this business. He told me he was investing in me. He did not ask for the Balance Sheet or account statement. I told him I needed money and advice. In three months we had agreed. There was no valuation; we just went to the lawyers to draw up an agreement.'
>
> He became the Chairman of the company. He did not take Board fees; he never asked to be paid for his time, advice, etc. He brought credibility to the business. He guided me through the rough terrain. He did not get business for us but met people and introduced us. We 'met' almost every day.

Mr. Gachui commented:

> Some people think that Mike is my son. We are not even relatives. Mike came to me with a proposal for us to do business together. His business model was simple. He got customers, he had suppliers and he used bank credit to finance purchases. There wasn't much in the business. He had put in little capital but he had a lot of passion and energy. I did not look at the finances. I decided to invest in Mike so I brought in US$70,000 and provided a bank guarantee of US$200,000. The banks would not lend much to Mike but they knew me and knew I could pay. With the injection of capital, Mike was able to grow the business and shift from moving boxes to providing solutions.

Between March 2003 and 2008, Mike's mentor and chairman called him every weekday. According to Mike, this relationship was critical to the success of the company.

Mike explained:

> He was very busy but he called me daily. We talked for about 10 to 20 minutes. He validated my thought process. There are few inspiring stories for entrepreneurs. We read about fraudsters and the like in the media. Sometimes you are frustrated and you need some advice, a sounding board.

Mr Gachui commented on his experience mentoring Mike:

> We talked three times a week if not more. One should not stop the entrepreneurial passion. But I held the reins to keep him on course; on the road. I also introduced people to him. Though he was very young, he related with everyone confidently. His youth and his passion endeared him to many.
>
> He has a strong personality so working with him is challenging. To make sure he does not go off the road, I call him often to ask him how things are going. I knew he would succeed because he had a passion for what he did and he infected others with his zeal.

The Kibaki Government which was sworn in in 2003 changed the economic landscape significantly. With the new government, it became possible to get business without godfathers. The Kenyan economy also began to grow. New ISPs were set up and Safaricom, the first mobile telephone network in Kenya was awarded a GSM licence in 1999. Mike commented on these changes:

> If this had not happened, SST would have grown in Rwanda and Uganda and not in Kenya. We started transforming SST into a solutions provider.

The People Challenge

Mike believed that if employees are happy, they work harder and they satisfy customers. He had learnt from his experience that good employees bring good employees.

He explained:

> I could compromise my own happiness but not that of my employees. So I went out of my way to do things for them. I would meet employees in the evening, visit their families, etc. I paid salaries on time even if I had to borrow money to do so. I was not shy with information. In fact, sharing information relieves you in terms of what has to be done. I also shared the vision with them.

SST relied heavily on expatriate staff to provide solutions to complex technical problems. Some of these expatriates did not adjust and returned to their country. The cost of maintaining an expatriate staff was also very high. It seemed to Mike that no company in the market was developing talent. Instead, everyone was competing for the limited talent available. The few qualified Kenyan engineers moved from one company to the next and commanded a premium for their services.

In 2005, Mike decided to develop a crop of local engineers. He elaborated:

> One morning after a frustrating night overseeing a project, on my way to work, I detoured to Jomo Kenyatta University of Technology and asked for the IT laboratory. I requested the IT administrator to introduce to me a few students in the final year who had shown interest in the IT lab and who did jobs for him. He gave me 4 or 5 names. I met them during their break time, requested them to give me names of 2 or 3 of their colleagues who they would start a business with if I gave them capital. I invited all of them to my office on Saturdays for a Technical Forum. I told them that the technical knowledge they were acquiring in university was not relevant to industry. I advised them to prepare for certification examinations. They brought their colleagues and soon there was a good group of students attending classes in our offices on Saturdays.

Mike wanted to hire some of them upon graduation. He guessed that their parents most probably wanted them to work with multinationals. He also recognized that SST could not pay them the salaries they were looking for. So he decided to address the issues they were likely to face as young graduates on their first job.

He expatiated:

> Housing is a major challenge for this group of people. They cannot afford good housing and cannot afford to live close to the business district. They

spend many hours commuting to and from work (sometimes up to 4 hours daily). This reduces their productive time. They eat junk food because it is cheap and also because they do not have time to prepare our elaborate meals. This has a negative effect on their health. The infrastructural challenges in the environment (such as electricity and water supply) also make it difficult for them to put in extra hours of work or study during the weekend.

SST employed eight of these graduates as engineers and sales people. They were between 23 and 24 years old and they were single. The company rented three-bedroom flats for them. Three people lived in a flat. The flat was serviced; a maid did the cleaning and laundry and also prepared meals for them. Since the flats were a 5-minute walk from the office, the employees walked to the office. They often went home for dinner and were back in the office till late. Supper and all meals during the weekend were free of charge.

An employee commented:

> When I joined the company in 2005, only 2 people were married. The CEO was not married. The company provided us accommodation close to the office. This enabled us work late if we felt like it. They gave us the right environment to work and develop our career. Lunch was partially spon-sored, supper was prepared by a maid and there was tea in the office. The conditions improved with time. Now we have medical insurance for the family, car allowance, airtime allowance, etc. Instead of guest houses, we are given money for housing. These days only expatriates live in the guest houses. It is difficult to maintain guest houses for 49 engineers. People are also starting families. If someone is working late for a project, a taxi is assigned to him and the fare is paid by the company.

Mike asked the new recruits to spend 45 per cent of their time on personal tech-nical development. Incentives were provided for certification. Engineers could triple their salary on certification. They had access to all the resources needed to prepare for the examinations. Mike evaluated the experience:

> We needed certified engineers who could handle complex projects and reduce our reliance on expatriates from India. In Kenya at the time, it took an engineer one year to pass the CCNA and two and a half years to pass the CCNP. Our engineers passed the CCNA in one month and the CCNP in just one year. Our staff began to handle complex projects. They started to generate revenue very quickly. Overnight, we moved our partnership from low level to Premier.
>
> This first crop of engineers brought their friends. People began to queue to work with us. We became known as a place where you could develop your career. Our competitors started attracting our people. After about

3 years a few left to work for our clients, set up their own business, etc. Some of them came back. We encouraged them to come back. These people received a lot of executive coaching; they had the right framework. The model worked very well.

Several employees commented on their experience in SST:

> One of the biggest talents Mike has is his ability to share his vision. You can sit with him and be inspired by what would happen in the future. I joined SST upon graduation. I bought into the vision of what the company would be. We were a small team of engineers and we started taking on challenging projects with top customers. We were brave.
>
> During my last semester in university, I went to SST on Saturdays for the Technical Forum. Some partners from India were around and they helped us draw up a roadmap, a career plan for the next 5 years: what we would specialize in, what certifications we would need, etc. SST provided us with the resources we needed to achieve our individual plans. We got books, online resources and they also encouraged a healthy competitive spirit. Those of us who stayed have realized our career aspirations.
>
> I am passionate about technology. I am doing something new; something many people don't know. I feel I came back to family; I found my colleagues. I appreciate the drive in terms of visionary leadership, aggressive energy.

One employee had this to say about his early years in SST:

> When we were a small company, you went with Mike for a meeting with the CEO of a company. This was more motivating and you learnt more than sitting in a class on customer relationship management. Interns went out with experienced people and they learnt on the job. This is how we grew the company.

Another employee commented on his experience in SST:

> We had the opportunity to travel. We implemented projects in Ethiopia, Rwanda, Tanzania, and Uganda. We attended training programmes in the United Kingdom, South Africa, etc.

Growth Pains

By 2007, SST had grown from a small team to a staff strength of sixty employees. The human resource function was basically administrative and tactical. A talent manager was hired to make the HR function more strategic. Mike had come to the realization that he could no longer run the business without a team of managers. He said:

> The entrepreneur does not have the emotional bandwidth to handle all the personal issues of more than 30 people. You just cannot deal with all of them. They think you are their father and mother. You have to be there for weddings, etc. You need middle management to help you manage this.

A new organizational structure was created. A country manager ran the business in each country where SST had an office. The company was divided into divisions. A general manager (GM) headed each division. The GMs were recruited from abroad. A middle level management level was created; they reported to the GMs. Some members of staff were promoted into this cadre. Positions which could not be filled from within were advertised.

According to Mike, finding the right people was a challenge:

> We encountered a number of challenges. Our salaries were not very attractive, we did not offer mortgages and our name was not a household name. Convincing them to work for us was difficult. So we got people who were about to enter into middle management in other companies and made them middle managers.

There were high expectations of the managers and the new reporting relationship. The GMs were effectively mini CEOs. However, the results did not meet the expectations. The talent manager explained:

> The new structure created some problems. For example, we found that several divisions visited the same client for business. This was not good for client relationship. Besides, many of the GMs did not settle and went back to their country. This created a vacuum. Mike did not have the capacity to mentor all the middle managers most of whom were techies. Techies are not necessarily good with people. Some tell you they don't want to be in front of a customer. We decided to jettison the SBU structure and focus on client relationship.

Some employees commented on the organizational structure:

> Coming up with an organizational structure that is solid has been a challenge. Every year we try to come up with one but we do not have a good structure to sustain the company. Structure matters because people want to know where they will be in 2 years.

Growth and time brought other challenges. Employee demographics were changing; at the beginning almost all the members of staff were in their twenties.

In 2008, a few of the staff were in their forties and many were in their thirties. The health plan in place was for staff members only and there was no maternity cover. Mike and Angela agreed that the needs of the different groups were different and SST had to address these needs.

In the annual strategy session held in December 2007, a decision was taken to raise money and reduce the company's reliance on supplier credit. Consultants prepared the business plan and in two months an agreement was signed with a private equity firm, Aureos. They invested $5m in the business for a 21 per cent stake. Mike talked about the impact of the change:

> Our issues were very simple. The way of thinking of a private equity firm is very different. We have a 200 page Board agreement. I have a contract which stipulates that I can be fired. You need to move your ego out of the way. It is no longer about you, the entrepreneur. Before, I talked to my Chairman any time: on the phone, playing golf ... If we wanted to discuss a major issue, we had lunch. Now we have a Board with Aureos represented. Many things have changed.

In 2009, an executive management layer was introduced. The positions were filled from outside. Mike was always on the lookout for Kenyans working for world class companies in the industry abroad. He met with several and talked to them about going home to work with SST. He attracted a few of them to fill the executive management positions. He explained:

> You need their wealth of experience. They want to get paid and they want shares. No doubt, having a private equity firm on board and money in the bank made it easier to attract good people.

While Mike was convinced that he had the right people in the executive management cadre, giving them room to make decisions proved to be a challenge for him. He elaborated:

> You feel that your blood is everywhere. You see the company car sticker in traffic and you want to call someone immediately to find out why it is looking tatty. With so much passion you may be a bull dozer. I have to manage the emotion of letting go and allowing others run the business. I spend a lot of time with the executive management. The business needs to move from Mike to become an institution.

To improve communication and understanding between the executive management and the board (not all of them were board members), a number of strategy workshops were organized for board members and the executive management team. Mike explained:

We gave Board members information so they could understand what we were doing. I went to these workshops with a sheet of paper instead of my usual pile of papers and presentations. These changes have not been easy for me.

By late 2009, the executive management was settling into the organization but they were still in the process of becoming a team. They were very busy setting up systems and taking charge of their functions. The new Chief Financial Officer commented:

> The first few months were hectic. I was coming from an environment that had systems. Finance is black and white really. I found a sales culture in the Finance function. I brought in a new finance manager, set up a new financial system and we got moving. My catch phrase is: facts and data. Because of the amount of work we had to do, we have been working long hours and even on Saturdays. This is not sustainable. I see my role as giving guidance and creating future CFOs. A lot of people have potential. They need guidance.

Mike was concerned that as he let go, a vacuum was being created in the organization. The executive management was settling in but the managers below them were feeling alone. The informal organization was working very well but it was not integrating with the formal organization. It soon became clear that there was a disconnection between the executive management and the other staff. Some of the middle managers seemed to be undermining their authority. He explained:

> Your influence as an entrepreneur is very deep. The people feel connected to you. But I am now saying I may not have the bandwidth for you. Before I could see you and figure out if you had a bad night. Now the CEO/Entrepreneur connects with you through the executive management.

One employee commented:

> People might get lost in the crowd as we grow. At the beginning, we were visible and management took us into account. We gave 200% because we were visible. As we grow, engineers must be assured that what they are doing matters; that they are on the right path in terms of their career. They need personalized attention. They must not feel their voice is lost. There should be a plan for them. This is what makes us work hard.

SST had instituted a quarterly town hall meeting which all members of staff attended. The CEO used the meetings to communicate future plans, introduce new members, talk about exits, etc. Team building sessions were also organized half yearly.

As soon as Mike graduated from the Advanced Management Programme at the Strathmore Business School (the programme is run in collaboration with the IESE Business School), he decided to start a council. The CFO explained the purpose of the council:

> We have an executive management (EXCO) layer. People no longer have access to the CEO. They are probably wondering if they can communicate the same issues through EXCO. We wanted to understand the issues. We needed some frank feedback from the staff especially the middle managers.

Mike elaborated:

> People form a parallel organization in organizations. To know the climate, I need the council. I take issues there and I expect them to bring issues. We must understand the real issues in the organization: we need a feedback mechanism.

The Council had ten members from different functions and levels. Among the EXCO members, only the CEO and the CFO were members of the Council. Mike wanted the CFO to be part of the council because as he put it:

> There may be some financial implications to certain suggestions or some queries that the CFO can immediately address.

The First Council

The first council was held in November 2009. During the first 15 minutes, the CEO introduced the issue to be discussed. He said that communication between EXCO and the middle to lower levels of the organization was not as good as before. He asked if EXCO was facilitating communication or stifling it. He told the meeting that a lot was happening in the company that EXCO was unaware of. It seemed to him that EXCO was not taken seriously.

During the next 30 minutes, members asked questions. Some wanted to know if the job descriptions for the EXCO were clear and if members of staff were aware of them. Another asked if EXCO had powers to make decisions. Someone else commented that the organizational chart had changed so many times: middle management was top management before the change. Another told the CEO not to correct EXCO members in public.

The CEO was quiet while Council members gave their opinion. One member said that the CEO governed through position and relationship but now he was governing through position alone. They recommended that EXCO members lead by relationships too. Mike then spent the last 20 minutes addressing each point raised by the members and making some commitments.

He commented to the case writer: 'I made three levels of commitment. The first were my key discoveries. For example, I told them that I discovered there was an informal network.' His SMART Commitments included things he would do before the next council meeting. For example, he committed to ensuring that EXCO members spend time with their team, take them out for lunch or dinner. He would also document the Leadership Development Programme of SST.

Mike and the CFO left the meeting elated. The latter commented:

> You could see the maturity in the organization. The talent is there; the answers are in the corridor. They are willing to share the burden of carrying the organization to the next level.

The SST Culture

The talent manager described the SST culture in these words:

> SST is an amazing world; it is a world of collaboration. We pull in on each other's thoughts, ideas, experience, to try to make something work; to achieve what we want to achieve. If a deal does not go through, we feel it. We understand the connections. We now have to trickle this down so all the staff understand. We are doing this through the town hall meetings, the alignment of the balanced scorecards, etc.

In a meeting with Mike and two members of the EXCO, the case writer asked how the team made decisions. The meeting was in held in Mike's office, the 'Vision Room'.

Mike: We use the white board a lot. We have animated discussions. I do not keep problems to myself. I raise them in different ways with different people. I engaged many of the Strathmore lecturers. The white board gives clarity; one can see patterns. We don't bring in consultants. We also execute quickly; we do not procrastinate.

Angela: That has its pros and cons. When entrepreneurs want to have their way, professionals get frustrated. You keep trying to change them.

Mike: Yes. We get an answer but if we get a better solution in two weeks, we embrace the better solution.

Angela: We need a test bed. If you quickly roll out a solution without a testing platform you end up making many changes.

Martin: We do not have the problem of analysis–paralysis. We make investment based on what we want to achieve not what we have in the pot. We are a growing business. We have to spend money and hopefully get the blockbuster.

Mike: I would like to include Entrepreneurial Spirit among our core values.

Angela: But entrepreneurship is not for everybody.
Martin: We should be clear about the definition of entrepreneurship.
Angela: Innovation Leadership.

Some of the employees commented on the organizational culture:

> In the technical department, there is a culture of team work. We help each other. Between departments, there are some frictions. There is no friction between Finance and Technical though; they encourage us to work harder.

Rob, Mike's business partner commented:

> You try to create a relationship that makes people feel comfortable. We are warm, we are a family. We have created successful teams. We make people feel comfortable but we expect results. The same way you treat your child; you give her toys but school work must be done so you are tough on that.
>
> Our challenge is performance. We put a lot of pressure on people. Sometimes they do not have the strength and stamina. We all need stamina; one year may not be as good as another year. We are young people. We have a fighting spirit.
>
> We strive for excellence; to do it slightly better than needed. In 2009 we started the 212 initiative. 212 degrees Fahrenheit is boiling point of water. An extra degree (213) produces steam which can drive locomotives, engines, etc. In life you do the normal things but the extra adds a new flavour. The little extra helps you achieve more.
>
> We are living in a society where corruption is rife and people look for short cuts. We instil in our people the ethical way. We get the business we can get the right way. So we measure ourselves on performance, not patronage. We encourage our people to stand for ethics. Our Chairman insisted on this a lot. 'Value your integrity and value yourself' he said, and we appreciated this.
>
> Sometimes we don't get the deals. But our path is more sustainable. You cannot build a business on patronage. You raise your income on one deal and then the guy is moved and you are down again. We follow a hard path but slowly, slowly, brick by brick we will arrive.
>
> Being at the cutting edge of technology makes things very interesting; you are changing your environment. It is nice to be a part of the change.

Leadership Style

The talent manager:

> Mike is extremely inspirational. He can make you believe and get everyone to do it. Working with him can also be frustrating. He has his way. You have

to work hard to win him over the same way he works to win you over. He listens if you present your case well, you may need several sessions to convince him. You must have a value proposition. He is strong willed. When our ideas are in conflict, we go to the white board. He does not have an ego, this helps.

An employee who has been with SST for many years:

He is a fighter. He never gives up. That is why we are here today. I have seen him go through a lot of challenges but he has been able to rise to the challenges. Is he easy to work with? If you know his character, it is easy. Sometimes he is very tough. If you are not tough, you will give up under the pressure.

Another employee:

If you know him it is easy to work with him. We had a flat structure so it was easy to go to him. Now it is not ethical to bypass your line manager. You should talk to the line manager and HR. He used to walk into my office to talk about movies, projects, technical stuff, etc. These little things kept us going. He does not do this as much as before and the next level is not filling this gap.

Another employee:

Mike mentored us a lot. After a trip, he would tell us what he learned. He bought dinner, lunch or breakfast and we talked. He was there with us on the projects. He gave us management books such as *Good to Great* and he discussed them with us. This is still happening but to a lesser degree because the company has grown. I cannot remember when last I met Mike in his office!

Several employees commented on Mike's style:

Mike is a visionary leader who leads by relationship not position. You would expect a CEO to be someone you cannot approach. He is sociable; he breaks the ice. He listens. You can go to him with the issues you are facing in life. He stands out as a leader.

He is a go-getter. He is relentless. I have not seen Mike lose his passion or optimism. Even when we lose a good deal, he cheers us up.

He recognizes effort and achievement and talks about them proudly. He commends people.

Mike drives a hard bargain. He wants excellence. If you are not giving it to him, he finds a way. He does not settle for less. He lets you know if he thinks you are not getting there. Mike sees steps ahead and aligns people to take charge of the opportunities.

Mike has a good grasp of technology. He brings in a business angle and an understanding of the customer. Since he understands the customer and the technology, he knows how to position the solution.

He does not get involved in the details of execution. He delegates this and guides overall progress.

Mike is very dynamic in decision making. Consistency in decision making is important. He should stick to his decisions and live up to the promise.

One of the senior managers commented:

Someone called me to say that Aureos was looking for an executive for SST. He said to me: 'You must meet Mike Macharia. He has the Obama effect. I met him and I was impressed. He is very passionate about the business. His passion is infectious. Although he is young, he has the maturity and understanding of someone in his fifties. I was sold on his vision.

Mike does not take things too seriously. He can give bad news with a smile. He sells easily. Someone told me: 'Your CEO has too much energy. It is something they have not seen before. Mike is learning to let go. He does many things at the same time. I take my laptop with me to meetings with him. He often thinks of something and decides to call someone right in the middle of the meeting. So I open my laptop and start answering my emails until he is ready to continue.

Rob commented on Mike's style:

I have known him for many years. He wants to succeed; to set his own destiny. Sometimes he is too ahead of himself but he lands on his feet again. He has a lot of energy. He inspires. His drive moves the company forward. If results are not achieved he can be too aggressive.

The Challenges

The management of SST recognized the challenges in the IT industry. Competition for clients and for talent had intensified. Some of SST's technical partners had become competitors especially for big ticket projects. A number of large multinationals such as Ericsson, IBM, Accenture and Nokia had entered the Kenyan market.

On the people side, the competition for talent was intensifying. Clients were trying to poach SST engineers and managers. Zain/Airtel had entered the telecommunications market and seemed to be actively searching for talent in the industry.

A manager put it succinctly:

> Retention of technical people is a big challenge. Ericsson, Nokia, Siemens, Safaricom, and Airtel are all offering better packages. We have to get more business so we can pay engineers comparable salaries. You need to settle down so you need a good position, good structure so you can grow, and you need money.

Mike reflected on the current situation and the future of SST:

> I am very happy when customers call to tell me they want to do business with SST and ask who they should talk to in the organization. Our revenues are doubling every year. Our people costs are very high. We must increase revenues to cover the rising people cost. People tend to resign when there are no projects. We must ensure that we are constantly busy. Consultancy is the way forward. But to be significant players in this segment, we have to attract top talent; the Chief Information Officers or Heads of IT in the large companies. Many of them are in their forties. They will want a share in the business and some room for entrepreneurship. We must create a platform for them to join us. We must create an entrepreneurial organization within an entrepreneurial organization with independent and interdependent relationships. The company gets value and so do they.
>
> When you work in an environment where people are told the companies to work for are the MNCs, the only reason you can attract good people is faith and vision. How else can you motivate them to come? You must offer them a value proposition that is higher than the MNCs. You are playing from behind and you are in the talent game. How do we attract experienced IT people to our organization?
>
> I am reducing my personal stake in the business. We valued the company and offered employees an opportunity to buy SST shares. We would like them to buy into the long term vision of the company. If 40% of the staff buy into the long term vision, we are made.

Mike was in a hurry to get the transformation going. One reason for the sense of urgency was personal: he expected his family's demand on his time to increase in the near future. He shared his concerns about the future with the case writer:

> Initially, a large majority of our employees were in their 20s. With time, they moved into their 30s. We have brought in people into management levels who are in their 40s. By 2009, 20% of the staff were in their 40s; 30% in their 30s and 40% in their 20s. How do we manage the social dynamics within the organization?

You need the people; your brand is your people. To get people on the race, you must give them a vision. But how do you move your emotional soul for the business to your managers and get them to take the baton?

Our staff costs are huge and they are growing. I am wondering if everyone is fully utilized. Is the organization bloated? It seems to me that I am doing other people's work. Whose monkey am I carrying? Are we getting value from the people we hired? Do we have people who are pillars in the business?

Rob reflected on the journey so far:

SST has been successful. We broke into a market that was traditionally ruled by foreign companies. We have tapped into the talent of young Kenyans. Fiber has arrived; a boom is coming. A lot will happen in the market.

Has the journey been worthwhile? The people we sell our technology to have embraced our vision and are comfortable working with us. We get business because of our vision and energy. We have built a name. We now sell solutions with complex engineering requirements. We have added consultancy to our offering. The customer is getting more educated so how we present the value proposition is important.

Money is not the most important thing in business. In this business, you need to value the knowledge you transfer and help people make the move to the next level. The opportunities in Africa are huge. You need money but the purpose should be contribution. Money is not the purpose here. With equity capital, we are now able to provide solutions we could not take on before. You make lots of money by having a different purpose.

Although the challenges ahead were enormous, there was a general feeling that SST will overcome the challenges. As one senior manager put it, 'this company was built on courage'.

EXHIBIT I Seven Seas Technologies

Seven Seas Technologies is a leading provider of integrated business and technology solutions across Africa in the Financial, Telecom, Real Estate, Service Industry and Government, in partnership with Global Technology Industry leaders and collaborative synergies with Domain & Technology centric Eco-systems partners. We deliver business value to customers through a combination of process excellence, quality frameworks and service delivery innovation. Our core motivation is defining Service Excellence in Technology driven business solutions.

VISION

'To be an African company defining service excellence in technology driven business solutions.'

MISSION

'To help customers get the most from their investment in technology by driving optimal performance during its life cycle.'

CORE VALUES

Core values are the ideals and enduring principles that underpin our performance and culture.

- Service Excellence
- Innovation Leadership
- Passion for Success
- Valued Partnerships

SST Subsidiaries

Enterprise Networks

The Enterprise Networks Division comprises of a dedicated team of professionals, who provide value-added and high quality services in design, implementation and support of network security, wireless technology, converged voice, video and data networking technology.

Intelligent Real Estate

Seven Seas Technologies Intelligent Real Estate Division offers IT services integration with buildings' systems under one common IP network to provide more satisfied occupants, while reducing energy, maintenance, and operating expenses of the building.

Service Provider

The Seven Seas Technologies Service Provider Division is focused on offering technology solutions that enable telecommunications service providers to offer differentiated services to their customers that maximize the users' experience.

Business Applications

The Business Applications arm of Seven Seas Technologies is the preferred integration partner for custom business application solutions in Africa cutting across all the industry vertical markets.

Data Centre & Application Infrastructure (DCAI)

In partnership with the best data centre solutions providers in the industry, IBM, Sun, Oracle, Symantec and EMC, our solutions are designed to reduce the total cost of managing data centres while improving data availability in a secure environment.

Knowledge Transfer Centre

Knowledge Transfer Centre (KTC) is a leading provider of internationally recognized ICT and technology related business training, delivered in partnership with global technology vendors and service delivery partners.

TADE OYINLOLA

Franca Ovadje prepared this case as a basis for class discussion rather than to illustrate either effective or ineffective handling of an administrative situation.
The assistance of Ruky Esharegaran is appreciated.
Copyright © 2011 Lagos Business School. Reprinted with permission of Lagos Business School.

Background

Tade Oyinlola was born in Kaduna, Nigeria. He attended Federal Government College and Command Secondary School, both in Kaduna. He spoke Hausa better than Yoruba, his native tongue, and his closest friends while growing up were Easterners. During his childhood, he often complained about his position in the family; he was the third of five children. He was always the right age for most of the jobs that needed to be done around the house. He said:

> If someone had to wash or cook, it was me. My older siblings always seemed too 'old' for these jobs and my younger siblings, too young. So I ended up doing a lot of the hard work.

Over time, however, he became a focal point in the family and instrumental in decision making around family plans.

At a relatively young age, he was attracted to the army because he admired an uncle who was then a young officer in the Nigerian Army and also his older brother – now an officer in the Nigerian Army. Whilst at the Federal Government College Kaduna, Tade joined the WAI Brigade and later the Nigerian Cadet Force.

When he moved to Command Secondary School he continued his foray with the para-military organization, (the Cadet Force). According to him:

> I learnt the basic tenets of discipline in these organizations, I learnt to multi-task, and to obey instructions. I understood the impact of a 'weak link' in a chain.

Tade's father was an agricultural economist. He lectured at the University of Lagos for a few years before moving into banking and later agricultural management. His mother was a teacher and later became an education inspector. When Tade was very young, his father bought a Commodore 64 computer console. The children were not allowed to touch the console. Tade became very curious about how it worked and this probably influenced his choice of electronics and computer engineering as a course of study at the Federal University of Technology, Minna.

Tade shared some thoughts about himself:

> I like to think that I'm very much like my grandfather. Some colleagues and superiors who read my grandfather's biography gave me some feedback about some similarity in character and mien. He reigned as King of Okuku town, in Osun state from 1934 until his death in 1960. I grew up hearing loads of stories of his influence, networks, and business acumen; he ran a very successful business before he became king. He was credited with native intelligence, was known to be fair and people naturally deferred to his authority. He was highly respected by the traditional Council of Obas (Kings) within the Region and also the government establishment at the time.

Tade continued:

> I make friends easily, and I keep them. My mum was often exasperated with the number of friends I had as a child. She says I can make friends with anyone, irrespective of social strata and keep that friendship for life! My colleagues are sometimes shocked by the extent of contacts I have, from CEOs to security men. Three years ago, I went to IITA for an activity, and whilst waiting at the gate to register, I got talking to the gateman, got his mobile phone number, and kept in touch with him. A couple of years later, some colleagues were stranded at IITA gate and called to ask if I knew anyone there, and I promptly called the gateman friend of mine, who just happened to be there at the time, and was able to provide the much needed assistance my colleagues required. They were astonished!
>
> I am extremely outgoing, and try to live life to its fullest. I probably party as hard as I work. If you meet me at an event, party, or social gathering you will not believe I'm the same person who can get extremely serious at work. I am an extremely giving person. I give of myself without counting the cost but in the same vein, can get offended and emotional when I feel

I am being taken advantage of. I promptly withdraw access to an erring party when I see a devious agenda but I tell them how I feel.

Tade goes to the gym and plays squash every weekday morning before going to the office (when he is in town). He also rides horses and plays polo over the weekends, during the season.

Early Work Experiences

All through Tade's University days, he worked (part-time) in an entertainment facility, Al-amin Pictures in Kaduna that ran a cinema, music and video centre. He also during this time held a couple of catering briefs for parties particularly for graduating cadets of the Nigerian Defence Academy and somehow also got involved in campus politics and was elected President of the National Electrical and Computer Engineering Students Association (NECESA).

Tade wanted to spend the compulsory six-month internship during his penultimate year at university with an oil firm. He did not get a position and by a stroke of luck, he walked into the premises of an airline telecommunications firm that services the aviation industry, was invited to take a test, which he passed and was asked to start work there the very next day. It was at this company that he understood the basics of telecommunications and IT.

His dream at graduation, like that of most of his colleagues, was to get a job in an oil company. He worked with the Shell Petroleum Development Company as an airline dispatcher during his National Service year. After he completed the National Youth Service, he was given an award for meritorious service from the NYSC and the Lagos State Government. He then got an offer from Bristow Helicopters to work for Shell as contract staff. He did not stay there for long. He explained:

> I felt I was losing IT competence working for Shell as a contract staff. My engagement at Shell was such a disappointment, primarily because I was not doing what I studied in school and was not engaged in developing the much needed technical foundation I believed my career required. Instead, I was in the flight-booking department scheduling flights. I looked at people who had been there for years and even though they were financially comfortable, I could not picture myself in that light; one lady had been a contract staff for eleven years, and the supervisor had been on the job for seventeen years mostly doing the same or a similar job. At the end of my service year, I got retained at Bristow Helicopters, and working contractually on its operations with Shell. I knew it was only a matter of time, before I had to leave.

Three months later, he received an offer from Resourcery Limited (an information technology infrastructure and service focused company) for less than half of his salary (at Bristow Helicopters) and he moved to Resourcery. At that time,

Resourcery engineers felt they were the best paid, best dressed and the most competent in the industry. Tade got grounded and his character firmed up and his technical competence honed, at Resourcery Limited.

Tade started out in Resourcery as a product manager. He later moved to business development and then wireless networking. In 2000, he was invited to an interview with Ericsson. A friend of his who worked with Ericsson had recommended him. He elaborated:

> I waited at the gate for two and a half hours; there were no mobile phones then so I could not contact anyone in the office. My salary at the time was higher than what I heard this position would offer, and I asked myself why I was waiting to be interviewed for a job that will result in a pay cut. Besides, I felt I was still on a steep competence development slope at Resourcery and had a lot more to learn. Since I could not find a good reason to keep waiting, I went back to my office and emailed my contact person there to explain the situation.

A year later, Tade left Resourcery for Atlasco Technologies to start up their wireless offering – a metropolitan area network connecting base stations at Ikeja, Apapa and Victoria Island. He stayed there for a year and half. He said:

> We had 250 customers and 2 base stations in Ikeja and Apapa (we were unable to bring up the VI base station). As the Wireless Network Manager, I started my foray into the broad and interesting field of management. I invested a lot of time and energy into the setup. However, after an in-depth assessment of the attributes of the leadership and the structure and culture of the company, I concluded that it was time to move. Job descriptions were undefined; the culture was extremely lax and unethical. I had to look long term.

Tade at Ericsson

Tade left Atlasco to start his own business in 2002. He had a great time installing local area networks, wireless networks, supplying computer systems, network security boxes and solutions, etc. The customer base was growing; he was busy. Then the call came in January 2003. He elaborated:

> My friend at Ericsson had once again recommended me, this time for the position of Service Delivery Manager. He called me to tell me to seriously consider the job offer this time. He was confident I could do the job. We were in school together so we knew each other well. I interviewed for the position and was selected.

On the 10 February 2003, Tade resumed work at Ericsson. He later found out that the company had been trying to fill the position for some time but had not found the right candidate. His job was to ensure technical support services were delivered to clients in accordance with contractual obligations. He occupied this position for three years and in that time handled all customers in the West African region.

Tade commented:

> Not long after I joined Ericsson, both my friend and the manager we reported to at the time, left for one of the network operators. I could have moved with them but decided to remain in Ericsson, as there seemed to be potential for growth and learning. At the time, I had worked for four companies. The job at Ericsson aligned with my personal goals and I shared the company's values.

At the end of 2005, Tade became the head of Ericsson Local Support (ELS), a position previously held by an expatriate. This job was probably the most tasking (and thankless) job within the organization but also one that provided a very good view of all aspects of the business. The ELS had staff strength of 54 employees at the time – 18 Nigerians and 36 expatriate contractors.

Tade commented on his management style:

> I decided that to work well with the team, I had to get to know each of the 54 people who worked in the department, as well as possible. I developed a good relationship with each one. I look at what is best for the individual, not only what is best for the company. I sincerely care for what I do and the people I work with. I am concerned about the quality of our work output and the impact of my decisions on the people I work with. I think the manager has to get involved in the job. You get calls when there are problems. You may be called at anytime of the night and will have to respond on site or by remote connection and it takes more than just financial reward to get someone to do this. As Support Manager, I went to work at all hours of the day and night. So when I asked my staff to leave their home at 2am to solve a problem at a client's site, they did it. You cannot get a member of staff out of his house at that time of night by command or executive fiat. He will not do it for money or because you threatened him.

As he took charge of the job, Tade wondered if the department really needed so many expatriates. He began to work at replacing them with Nigerians. He stopped renewing the contract of the consultants and as a consultant's contract ended, he was replaced with a local. He prepared the local staff and urged them to show that they could do the job.

Tade recalled some of his experiences:

> In the course of managing this department, I have given warnings, enforced the rules, moved people into new roles, demoted a colleague, etc. but in all of this, my team knew I was fair. One has to reason things out. I don't follow

the instructions from my boss – hook, line and sinker. I secure buy-in where necessary and try to understand the issues. My boss once asked me to fire one of my subordinates for an operational error he had made. The man had been with the company for 12 years. I demoted the man and told him he had not demonstrated courage and competence on the job. I defended my action with my boss and convinced him that a demotion was a better option. The man who was demoted later told me he was happy; a burden had been taken from his shoulders. He was happy to be a contributor; he did not want to manage a team.

Tade valued the relationships he had built with his bosses, colleagues, and especially his subordinates. He said:

Many of them talk to me about their challenges, even their personal problems. Those who wanted to leave talked to me about it before putting in their resignation letter. I am still in contact with many of them today. Most of the expatriates have moved on but we keep in touch.

In 2004 he signed into the Ericsson Volunteer Programme, a disaster relief initiative, working with the United Nations and the Swedish Rescue Service Agency. Following the earthquake in Pakistan in 2005, he coordinated relief efforts with other volunteers in different parts of the world. He spent two weeks at the UN camp in Muzzaffarabad, Pakistan, in 2006 working as a volunteer providing voice and data communication services. Tade was the only volunteer from Africa in camp at the time.

In 2007 he joined the executive MBA class at the Lagos Business School. Tade explained:

I took responsibility for my development. I picked up the application form for the Lagos Business School's Executive MBA in 2002. I submitted the same form in 2006. I had since started saving for the EMBA and wrote in my development plan at the end of 2003 that I will do an MSc in 2005/2006 and the EMBA in 2007/8. I started the MSc at the University of Lagos but after two long strikes and the suspension of the academic session, I decided to opt out of the programme.

I had the option of going abroad for the EMBA but since I wanted to operate in this environment, an EMBA in Nigeria was a better choice to consolidate all available learning around the local environment, but with an international perspective. A former colleague at Resourcery had done the EMBA in 2001, and I had watched a couple of her group sessions. I knew that quality was definitely what I needed.

While on the EMBA programme, his manager nominated him to attend a course on finance for non-finance managers organized by Ericsson in Ireland. He turned down the invitation because he felt he had acquired the knowledge from the finance courses on the EMBA. 'That was cost saving for the company too', he noted.

In October 2007, Tade travelled to Sweden to make a presentation to the senior management of Ericsson. He explained:

> My boss was to go with the Chief Technology Officer (CTO) of one of the Operators but he was on vacation and I was acting head of the division at the time. One of my mentors, a Swede, and Senior Vice President was visiting Nigeria at the time. He asked me to accompany the CTO. It turned out that the CTO could not make the trip either, so I made the presentation to the 100 top managers from Ericsson's offices globally, on behalf of both the Operator and Ericsson Nigeria. My Manager later told me that before I left the stage, he had received a text message from his own Manager commending me on the content and quality of delivery of the presentation. The text message read: 'Tade is not just an ELS manager, he is worth much more than that; he has just delivered a brilliant presentation.' I met a few people that day including a Senior Vice President who is now the President of the Group.

By the end of 2007, Tade had transformed the department. There were 36 expatriates and 18 Nigerians in the support services department when Tade took charge. After two years, the department had 48 Nigerians and 10 expatriates. The financial savings were huge. Tade and his team did not set out to save. They believed they had smart people and they helped them deliver. The department became the third largest contributor to global performance with savings of US$12 million over two years.

The tangible results gave Tade and his team greater visibility. At the end of the year, the vice president of the services division moved competence development for technical staff from the human resources department to the operations department and asked Tade to drive it as Senior Manager, Competence Development – Services.

Tade loved his job and he loved Ericsson. He commented:

> I work in a company where people are free to make decisions. You are allowed to express and prove yourself. You take responsibility for the outcome of your decisions and you defend your actions, good or bad.

The Competence Development Programme

On the 1 January 2008, Tade began his new assignment as Senior Manager, Competence Development. He remained within the technical side of the business. He was to develop local staff and reduce the company's dependence on expatriates. The HR department was hitherto responsible for competence development of all members of staff. Some people wondered why Tade was doing HR work. He explained:

> I have a job to do. I was brought in to do this job. I focus on what I have to achieve. If in doing that someone feels I am not bowing as much as I should, too bad. I have learnt to pick my battles wisely.

Tade was clear about what he wanted to do. He was convinced that Ericsson needed people who understood the nature of the work in the different departments and could support them; people who could lean on each other. The silo mentality (à la Chinese walls) had to be broken. Technical people must be able to empathize – to bend over backwards to support a colleague when and where required. They will of course need the technical skills. The challenge was to get the expatriates to work themselves out of their job.

He elaborated:

> I had a budget and was given a free hand by the Vice President of the Division, to develop the concept (which we called the Ericsson Skills Acquisition Program – ESAP) and build the team. I know Ericsson well; I have worked with all the key departments. I listed some competencies we had to develop in the people: Ericsson needed people who had true empathy, mutual respect and who break silos. They also had to be dedicated and extremely hard working. I designed the programme, got approval, proceeded to put a team together and ran the implementation. Before now, many expatriates came with a lot of technical knowledge. This knowledge was not always effectively passed on to Nigerians though it was a requirement in the employment contract. Besides the developmental goals, it was costing the company a lot to maintain so many expatriates in Nigeria. The structured programme I put together was to develop the competencies of Nigerians to ensure that they replaced the expatriates in a short time.

He began from the premise that the new recruits were smart and they needed challenges to fire up their enthusiasm to learn and improve. He recognized that Ericsson was not the best paying company in the industry so retention might be an issue. However, for people who wanted to develop their competencies, this was an ideal place to be.

He wanted to recruit smart people but not necessarily first class graduates. However, he conceded when the HR director insisted on first class degree holders. He needed the HR director's support on a more important issue so he decided to go ahead with this suggestion. After three days in an assessment centre, an offer was made to 30 young graduates but only 18 accepted the offer. The salary package for this grade was deliberately set at an uncompetitive level. Tade wanted to attract candidates who were more interested in learning and growth than in money. Their salaries would grow over time.

Tade and his new team faced a number of challenges. First, he needed managers who would mentor the new recruits. He was a strong believer in mentoring. He had mentors. He elaborated:

> I meet with my mentors once in a while. Two of whom are Swedes. I had two mentoring sessions with one of them before he left Nigeria. I have two other mentors, one in Sweden and the other in Brazil. I keep in touch with them. I also have a former HR Director of a multinational in the brewery industry as a mentor. He was invited to the company to give us a talk some years ago, and I realized I could learn a lot [from] him so after the talk I asked him to be my mentor. I learnt a lot from my first Manager at Ericsson; the guy who hired me. His leadership style was fantastic. One of his stellar comments was: 'whatever you do, don't be a "boss"!!'

Tade often fed on people's experiences; his father-in-law was one of such people. He is a retired major general in the Nigerian Army. They talked often and he shared his experiences with Tade. He had been involved in every single career defining decision in Tade's life and this, Tade valued greatly. His mother-in-law was that voice of reason; gentle, quiet and full of guidance. Her wisdom always set Tade on track. Although Tade's biological parents were the anchors of his developmental years, he did not spend much of his working life in close proximity with them, largely because of the physical distance.

One of Tade's biggest challenges as Head of Competence Development Unit was getting the new recruits to see Ericsson the way he sees it, so they do not get carried away and lose focus after some time. He spent time with them in the first few weeks of their engagement during the foundation courses. He tried to give them a sense of purpose. At the beginning, some colleagues accused Tade's team of 'brain washing' the new recruits but Tade didn't see it this way. Tade's team only wanted to influence them; to help them see that competence was more important than financial remuneration especially in early career. They believed that competence guarantees the depth or size of one's remuneration over time. The team explained to the new recruits the relative theory of money. They told the young graduates to focus on life-long learning and assured them that Ericsson is a knowledge environment.

Following another arduous selection process, the second batch (of 30 young graduates) of the ESAP program resumed 3 months after the first batch.

Tade enumerated:

> We wanted them to know they could make a difference. Each one knew the impact of his/her actions or inactions on the bottom line. We did a lot of personal effectiveness and emotional intelligence stuff with them. Some of them (such as those who left KPMG and the banks) took pay cuts to join

the programme. We told them: 'you accepted this job with a lower salary because you feel your competence is important to you. You have to focus; forget your peers. It doesn't matter what your neighbour earns.' We wanted them to realize very early in their career the importance of focusing on what you want for yourself and not how much others are earning.

Tade had a reputation for 'jollofing'. He used this love for parties to advantage. After each milestone, there was some sort of celebration: the last day of the Assessment Centre, the end of the recruitment exercise, etc. The graduation party was grand. All 148 mentors who had been a part of the programme received a gift at the party. At the graduation party two directors of the company told Tade that they owed him an apology; they thought that the programme would not succeed.

Tade was very happy with the results. He said:

> The graduates know Ericsson better than I. Because they have worked in various departments, they understand what every part of the business contributes. We have learned that rotation is important for experience. The company wants to apply the model to other parts of the organization.

The success of the execution of this program could not have been possible without the support of Tade's superiors and the dedication and competence of his team of three colleagues.

In 2008, Tade Oyinlola's name was included in the Madison's International Who's Who historical society of professionals, a registry of executives and professionals who have demonstrated exemplary achievement and distinguished contributions to the business community. He was selected 'Member of the Year'.

A New Assignment

On the 1 April, 2009, Tade moved to HR to head the Learning Department. HR had been restructured into Staffing, Compensation and Benefits, and Learning. In a chat with the Regional Head of HR a month earlier, she had told Tade that what he was doing was an HR function and requested that he formally move to the HR organization.

When asked where he was 'going', Tade responded:

> I have always been strong on people development. I thrive there naturally. I am firm, I have a heart and I am fair. I think that my experience in operations will be valuable in HR. I have done everything in Services (Operations). If I were to head the Services division, in two years I will probably be done with services. In HR, I have a lot to learn and I could have an impact.
>
> I did not know I would get into HR; time and chance created the opportunity. I must point out however, that the people management

courses on the EMBA were the tools I was able to leverage on, in my conversion from technical to general management and Human Resources.

In November 2009, Tade was mapped as a management planning candidate in Ericsson so he attended an assessment centre at the company's headquarters in Sweden. After an arduous 5-day assessment, he was identified as an international candidate, with the potential for a position at a regional management level.

Moving on

Less than two years after Tade moved to HR, he was appointed Director, Learning and Competence Development for the Sub-Saharan region. He moved to South Africa to run a critical project during the first six months of his new assignment.

Before leaving for Johannesburg, he reflected on his career so far and shared some of what he had learnt:

> I got married at 27, which is early by some standards. My wife and I attended the same schools from Nursery through University. We are good friends and have maintained a great friendship, which we now share with our two children.
>
> I drove the same car for a long time. My level of contentment is probably higher than most people's. We spent a couple of years paying for a plot of land. At that time, my dad got worried. He asked me if we were not squeezing ourselves too hard. All we had went into the land and later, the building.
>
> You have to develop yourself to take advantage of opportunities when they come and step out of your comfort zone. At the end of the EMBA programme, I mapped out a five-year leadership development plan. I knew I needed some international exposure so towards the end of the EMBA, I signed into the optional one-week programme at the IESE Business School in Barcelona. Five months after the EMBA, I attended the High Potential Leadership Programme at Harvard Business School in Boston. A year after that, I attended 'The Leadership Journey' at the Wharton Business School in Pennsylvania. In the coming years, I will continue to focus on leadership development and possibly public policy and governance. I paid for all these programmes including the EMBA. Maybe the company will refund some of that money. I don't know and it does not really matter.
>
> One lesson I have learnt is that your career development is yours to manage. You have to latch on to the experiences of friends and mentors, old and young alike. Leaving your development or career growth to another person or your organization, could be counter productive, unless your organization has a strong focus on people development. Even at that, each individual has a lot of responsibility for his or her career.

Fear of the unknown has affected a number of careers, and some could throw away an opportunity to develop in the longer term, for short term financial benefit; others do all sorts of things to maintain a social class whether real or not. Both groups end up making many mistakes. If you work hard, very hard, financial reward will ultimately come to you. If on the other hand, you focus too much too soon on quick financial returns at the risk of developing and building strong foundation of core competence, you may not be able to sustain your lifestyle.

THE TRANSFORMATION OF EQUITY BANK

> There was a time when our colleagues in the industry ignored us during marketing drives. Equity was not even on the programme of events. If we were lucky, we were asked to greet the people at the end of the meeting. We were snubbed because they considered us a village bank. The humiliation our marketing teams suffered brought us closer together. We kept our focus on our customers; how to serve them better and how to retain them ... Today, we are one of the top three banks in Kenya. Many of our customers consider themselves members of the Bank. They make suggestions to us and they introduce their friends and relatives to the Bank.
>
> *Equity Bank branch manager*

Equity Bank had indeed been transformed from a moribund building society, with total losses of over KSh 33 million and a non-performing loan portfolio of 54 per cent in 1993, into one of the leading banks in the country. In 2008, Equity Bank was ranked the No. 1 Bank in the banking survey by Think Business. It won the Euromoney award for the Best Bank in Kenya in 2007 and 2008. At the Africa Investor Award ceremony held at the New York Stock Exchange in September 2008, Equity Bank was named the best performing public listed company in Africa. The list of awards won by the bank was long and impressive.

Instead of celebrating the bank's successes however, the main architect of the transformation, James Mwangi, was thinking of the challenges ahead. He wondered

if the bank could continue to meet the expectations of its customers in the homesteads all over the country and in the towns. 'This is not a bank. It is a movement.
It has given people dignity and self esteem. Our customers think we can solve any
problem. They think we are a panacea. They expect us to go beyond a socio-economic transformation. They feel they own this institution and they expect it to do
more for them. Some of them even want us to help them solve their marital problems. What should we do?' he wondered.

James Mwangi, the managing director, was also concerned about the fact that
in the last 15 years, the bank had not known hard times. He shared his concerns
with the case writer:

> We have not failed in anything. Our people are used to 15% to 20% salary
> increases every year. They have come to expect smooth curves, exponential
> growth in accounts, in deposits, etc. Our customers are proud of the Bank.
> They walk into the branches like chiefs. They even confront the staff if they
> feel they are not working the Equity Bank way. From a moribund institution,
> their bank has become the most modern bank. If there is an external shock
> in the economy and/or the industry, will Equity Bank weather the storm?
> Do we have the capacity to face an external shock, to confront failure?

Finally, as the bank began aggressive expansion in the East African region, James
wondered if the executive management had the experience to lead the bank into
the future.

Background

Equity Building Society was set up in 1984 to provide financial services to the
nwananchi – the ordinary Kenyan. From inception it had a strong social mission.
While profit was considered important, the founders were more concerned with
contributing to the social and economic development of rural Kenya by providing the poor with access to financing. The business model was simple: Equity
Building Society collected savings from customers and gave mortgage loans. In
just a few years, the company had opened five branches in rural areas.

However, Equity's growth spurt was short lived. The 1980s and 1990s was a
period of intense competition in the financial services sector in Kenya. Many local
financial institutions collapsed. These failures led to a crisis of confidence in the
sector. Between 1986 and 1993, Equity grew savings by only KSh 2 million and
loans and advances increased by KSh 5 million. By 1993, 54 per cent of Equity's
loans were non-performing and accumulated losses totalled KSh 33 million.
According to a report by Microsave, 'deposits were being used to meet operating
expenses. The liquidity ratio stood at 5.8%, way below the required 20 per cent.'[1]
Three major depositors accounted for 85 per cent of the total deposits of Equity.
One of them, the Kenya Ministry of Water, sued for liquidation of the company.

Equity was declared insolvent by the Central Bank of Kenya (CBK). According to the CBK report, the main challenges facing Equity Building Society were poor management and ineffective governance. CBK respected Equity as a financial institution that [had] touched many Kenyans in a special way[2]. It was therefore reluctant to ask the Registrar of Building Societies to close the company. When Equity's management pleaded for time to reverse the company's fortunes, CBK asked them to find a change agent. James Mwangi's name was put forward. At the time, James was one of the three major depositors of Equity and was a well known banker. The CBK acquiesced.

James Mwangi joins Equity

James Mwangi joined Equity in 1994 as the finance director and change agent. He converted his deposits to shares and became a major shareholder in the fledging firm.

He was the seventh of eight children. His parents were peasants. His father died when he was very young and his mother struggled to educate the children on her own. His mother had a great influence on him. Though the family was poor, she taught them to be generous with others. Commenting on his early childhood, he said:

> I have experienced poverty; I came face to face with it in my childhood. We struggled to survive. This makes it easy for me to champion the cause of the poor. It is not my struggle; it is the struggle of a class. Struggle has been a part of my life. People in the rural areas are simple and humble; they are down to earth. I connect with them because I grew up there; I went through the same difficulties. I learnt from my mother to feel for others.

James Mwangi studied accounting at the University of Nairobi, graduating at the top of his class. He joined PricewaterhouseCoopers upon graduation, moved to Ernst & Young after a few years and then to Trade Bank where he rose very quickly to the position of Group Financial Controller. He was one of the most senior Kenyan bankers in the country when he left Trade Bank in 1994 to join Equity Building Society. The case writer asked him why he joined Equity. He explained:

> It was a cause that appealed to my heart and soul. I was earning 12 times what Equity could offer. I was newly married and we had one child. My wife asked me how we will bring up a family on that income. I did not rationalize my decision. At that time Equity had only 2,892 accounts. The cause spoke to my heart. This was the last indigenous institution and it was about to be shut down. I had to do something about it. So I burnt the bridges and put my career and reputation at stake. I put everything I had into Equity. The option of failure was remote.

Refocusing the Firm

Although he joined Equity as the chief financial officer and change agent, James was effectively the chief operating officer. At a time when other financial institutions were moving out of the rural areas, Equity continued to focus on providing financing to its target market – the common folk in the homesteads, villages and towns.

The Building Societies Act then in force limited the operations of the business. James saw that the business model had to change if the company was to survive. The mortgage loans which Equity gave were rarely used to build homes. Their customers needed money to expand their small businesses. They needed money to buy more cows, fertilizer, etc. In 1994, Equity applied for and was granted a licence to operate as a Micro Finance Institution (MFI).

As an MFI Equity had access to short term savings and could grant short term facilities. The loan tenure was between 6 to 12 months. And the average size of the loan was $300. To attract deposits, the entry point was reduced to zero; there was no need to deposit money to open an account. Account holders could deposit money anytime and also withdraw anytime. Ledger and account maintenance fees were reduced to a minimum. This was at a time when banks had minimum deposit requirements to open an account and withdrawals were allowed once a week.

First Steps

James soon found that not only was staff morale low (there had been no salary increases for years), discipline was poor. For a successful turnaround employees had to acquire new skills and more importantly change their attitude to work.

> During the first two years, James led like a dictator. Staff either had to uphold professional discipline or leave. There were strict deadlines, a dress code, long working hours and an uncompromising customer service. The message was: You are either for us or against us ... As the results of this hard line approach began to bear fruit, both in terms of performance and the adoption of the new culture by the staff, James shifted more towards staff training, coaching and participating rather than making all the decisions himself.[3]

None of the staff at the time had a university education and they lacked professional banking experience. James saw the need to boost the confidence of the staff and fill the skills gap. During 1994, James Mwangi and Nancy Nyambici (a training consultant) provided training for all employees. Training sessions on self awareness, marketing, customer service, etc. were conducted. The trainers used the training programme as an opportunity to communicate the strengths of the new strategic direction (which was taking shape) and to instil in the employees the hope that they could turn around the fortunes of the bank. James commented on his first actions:

> I spent a lot of time with people; I became a trainer. Even today, I am spending a whole day with the branch leadership. The interaction infuses and induces the right culture. Efforts were made to build a culture of client service and team work. These training sessions also created opportunities for coaching and mentoring.

Clarifying the Mission and Vision

After the initial training sessions, management saw the need to define the firm's mission and vision. A consultant was brought it to facilitate the process. All employees were encouraged to participate in the formulation of the mission and vision (see Exhibit I for the mission, values and vision statement). The new vision and mission became James' mantra. He instilled hope in the employees. From a moribund organization, they were going to become a successful institution and a voice for the *mwananchi*. In a very short time, every member of staff knew the mission and vision and could recite them. The process was lengthy but 'by the middle of 2005 everyone within Equity knew, and had bought into, the institution's plan and understood the roles they played in achieving it…'. In the words of one assistant manager, 'before… we just went to work to work. Now we are going to work to achieve goals.'[4]

Building the Customer Base

Between 1984 and 1993, Equity Building Society had two products: a savings and a mortgage product. James and his team set out to build the customer base through aggressive one-to-one selling. '[I]n addition to mobilizing staff members, Equity persuaded influential customers to promote the institution. Equity's Board members, executive directors, management and staff spent vast amounts of time at formal gatherings, factories, shopping centres, offices and public meetings, creating awareness of the institution and its products and services with religious zeal.'[5]

An old member of staff who is now a branch manager commented on those times:

> We fought for survival. We went on marketing drives and sometimes met our competitors there. We were ignored by our colleagues in the industry. Our name was not even on the programme of events for the function. If we were lucky, we were asked to greet the people at the end of the meeting. We were snubbed because we were considered a village bank. The humiliations our marketing teams suffered in the market brought us closer together. We kept our focus on our customers; how to serve them better and retain them. When we got back to the branch we told the entire team our experience and we strategized…. I think this is the genesis of our family spirit. We did not lose our focus on how to find new customers and retain them.

Performance improved between 1994 and 2003 (see Exhibit II). However, growth brought new challenges, one of which was the need to increase the capital base. In 1997, Equity invited its customers to convert their deposits into shares. Many of them took advantage of the offer and the number of shareholders grew from 10 to 2,500. When it became necessary to shore up the share capital again in 2003, Equity attracted $1.4 million from the African Micro Finance Fund. The Fund gained control of 16 per cent of the firm.

By 2003, Equity had metamorphosed from a building society to a successful micro finance institution. However, the micro finance model was not without its limitations. As Equity's customers grew their businesses, their needs changed. Some customers were effectively running small and mid-sized enterprises. As a MFI, Equity could not provide its customers with chequing accounts, bank guarantees or trade finance, nor carry out foreign exchange transactions on their behalf. It was clear that another change was necessary: Equity had to become a commercial bank. The management focus shifted towards developing the capacity to operate as a commercial bank. James Mwangi was to lead the institution into the future but this time as managing director.

James Mwangi Takes Charge

James Mwangi became the managing director of Equity in 2004 following the retirement of John Mwangi. At the time, the firm had become very profitable. The number of deposit accounts had grown from 12 in 1994 to 252,000 by the end of 2003 while value of deposits had increased from 115 million in 1994 to 3,368 million KSh. Equity had established itself as a micro finance institution serving the *mwananchi* – the common folk.

Entering the Premier League: Aligning with the Mission

One of James Mwangi's first tasks as managing director was to articulate the mission and values of the firm. Senior and middle level managers participated in the process which was facilitated by a group of consultants. By the end of 2004, seven critical success factors for the mission and vision had also been identified. They included: an organizational culture that values people, enhances performance and supports people; a customer focused organization, high quality asset portfolio, efficient and effective operations and execution of strategically planned expansion. Throughout the first half of 2005, the mission, values, vision and critical success factors were communicated to the whole organization. The organization was focused on the critical success factors; everyone in the organization now had the template against which to evaluate their role and contribution. Goals, targets and measures as well as activities were agreed for each of the critical success factors. In 2008 brand protection and customer experience was added as a critical success factor.

Building Organizational Capacity

Corporate Governance

Equity Building Society was set up by a few friends. As the firm's performance worsened in the early 1990s, some of the shareholders lost interest and pulled out. Between 1994 and 2000 Peter Munga, John Mwangi and James Mwangi were the only members of the board. During these years, the survival of the company was their primary concern. They got very involved in the day-to-day activities of the firm.

In 2000, the trio invited four successful professionals and businessmen to the board. One of them was one of the earliest clients of Equity. A new era began in which board meetings were held regularly and for the first time, 'Board minutes reported ... heated debates on the projections presented by management. In the minutes of subsequent meetings, one sees signs of differing opinions, discerning questions, diversity of perspectives and a strong grasp of economic, financial and strategic issues.'[6]

The British American Investments Company got a seat on the board with their purchase of a substantial stake in the firm. In 2003, Africap (funded by DFID, IFC, and others) joined the board having bought 16 per cent stake in the institution. Finally, Helios EB, a private equity fund, joined the board in 2007 with the acquisition of 24.99 per cent shareholding. The CEO of the Nations Group (the largest media group in Kenya) was a member of the board. In February 2009, the board had 14 members, 12 of whom were non-executives. All board members signed Equity Bank's 86-page document which detailed the Code of Corporate Practices and Conduct (see Exhibit III for the Statement on Corporate Governance).

Leadership

James Mwangi realized that without a strong leadership team the organization would stagnate. He explained:

> We have three generations working in the Bank today. The pioneers set up Equity Building Society. As the firm grew, we realized that we needed a new set of skills. The pioneers were not prepared to lead the transformation. To give them the same opportunity as those we were to bring from outside, we encouraged them to register for degree programmes in the local universities. Many of them were admitted and the Bank paid the fees.

In 2003, James initiated the process of recruiting people from outside into management positions. Senior level positions in marketing, human resources management, IT, finance and internal audit were filled from outside. The new recruits came from blue chip companies like East African Breweries, Safaricom, etc.

The head of credit was poached from the Central Bank of Kenya. This second generation led the transformation of Equity from a micro finance institution to a commercial bank. Many of them joined the bank at a time when it could not match their salaries. The case writer asked the MD why they agreed to join Equity. He responded:

> I have a personal gift of giving and receiving friendship. I suspect that they came because of me. I told them what I could offer but painted a graphic picture of the future. Maybe they joined the future. They found a purpose to live for. Equity is not about banking; it is a cause. The whole organization is aligned to the cause. It is difficult to fit into Equity without seeking a meaning in your life. The organization is not about money, it is about championing a cause; about being the voice of the voiceless. It is a movement.

James Mwangi believed that consultation and involvement in decision making make people feel bound to the decision. However, although he sought opinions widely, he did not lack the courage to take decisions. While he delegated authority and responsibility, he performed a very strong oversight function. The IT platform gave him access to real-time information on performance. Customers also called him to make suggestions or lay their complaints.

Leadership development programmes were organized regularly for managers. The senior team had attended the Advanced Management Programme organized by the Strathmore Business School in collaboration with IESE Business School. Apart from regular training programmes, job shadowing was often used for staff development.

The case writer asked James to elaborate on his style:

> We de-emphasize hierarchy. Everyone is addressed by his or her first name. We do not respect positions. We want people to behave as human beings. We look for people who are independent. We have no room for mimicry or sycophancy. We want to sift through our collective knowledge and come up with great solutions.
>
> I am a coach. I have an intuitive sense of when someone needs me to coach them. I respect my team and I am willing to lead it. I think I am known to give room to people to perform. I listen to advice. I ask questions. I allow people try so people feel they can learn, and learn from their mistakes too. I may guide the decision but they know it is their decision.

A few managers commented on James leadership style:

> James is a visionary leader. He shares the vision, ensures that the objectives are understood and then allows you run with it. He gives you the resources you need to deliver, and then he demands results. You know he is there

for you; you can consult him if you need help. He also consults a lot. He is always looking for new insights so he talks to people a lot. He values consultants.

A branch manager commented:

> I am on ground. I take decisions. New issues come up all the time; we deal with very poor people. I throw up the issues to the head office. They fine tune my suggestions, process the information, etc. I talk to James, to Alex. I tell them I am in a fix. I tell them what I have tried and they make suggestions.
>
> New challenges come up everyday. For example, a customer walks in to open an account. We find out he has no National Identity Card. We tell him how to get one – the name of the agency, the address, etc. One customer came to withdraw money from his deceased daughter's account and he had no death certificate. We help them find solutions. We are in touch with the Registration Bureau, etc. We solve the problems.

A senior manager commented on James' power of persuasion:

> We wanted to buy a new IT package some time ago. The initial investment was for $10m. The executive team thought it was too expensive. James convinced us and the Board to spend even more than that. He said we will see the results in 3 years, and we did.
>
> In 2004 when there were only 700 members of staff he knew all of them. The Bank has grown tremendously since then so it is difficult for him to know everybody now. He gives members of staff surprise calls to ask questions about the results he is looking at on the screen. Once he called up a branch manager and said, 'I see you have opened many new accounts today. What is going on?' James is in touch with the people and the business. He knows what is happening. He wants an explanation for success as well as failure. Customers call him up too. It is sometimes embarrassing for senior managers; a general manager may not have heard of a complaint that James received from a customer.

Organizational Structure

When James Mwangi became MD in 2004, the positions and reporting relationships were as shown in Exhibit IV. In preparation for the transformation of Equity into a commercial bank, a general manager level was added to the structure. The positions of general manager, business growth and development, customer service, information technology services, and legal services and company secretary were created. The general managers reported to the managing director.

In 2007, a new layer was once again added to the structure: the director (see Exhibit IX). General managers reported to the directors who in turn reported to the managing director. In 2008, the position of Director, Customer Service was created. The new positions were filled from outside. No member of the executive team had been with the bank for longer than four years (except the managing director). A number of managers who reported directly to the managing director in 2004 were now three or four levels below the managing director.

Building the Culture

When he became change driver and finance director in 1994, James Mwangi focused on building a culture of customer service and teamwork. Through training programmes, clear targets and personal example, James taught the staff the importance of discipline, teamwork, and uncompromising customer service. The culture is that of a caring bank. A lot of value is placed on humility, listening, and partnering.

According to the Director of Strategy:

> Our culture is built on humanity. It is easy to embrace our core values. Creativity, teamwork and unity of purpose are all pertinent values in a movement. Our people are passionate about what they do. This is because of the DNA of the bank.

James Mwangi elaborated on the bank's culture:

> Friendliness and humility are important to us. We are a very humble brand. Our people have to be humble and down to earth. I interact a lot with the staff. I spend 80% of my time with the staff. I champion the DNA of the bank. I cascade the vision. My role is to live the mission and vision; to set the example, to the best of my ability. I never do anything even subconsciously that goes against the mission and vision. Our mission and vision have remained the same over the years. What we have done is give it a wider geographical space, scale it up, use words that reflect the changing times. The spirit has not changed. We built the culture over time. I pushed it till it acquired a life of its own. I never in my actions or behaviour contradict the culture.

The bank has an open door policy. The branch managers' offices are located close to the entrance door. Customers are encouraged to see the branch manager if they so desire. One branch manager explained:

> I attend to over 50 customers each day. I cannot lock my door. I come in early and close late to get my paper work done. At the end of the day, I can say: Yes, I was working.

In 2005, corporate culture was identified as one of the key success factors for the bank's mission. As the bank grew and became more successful, James was concerned that the culture was not lost. Promoting from within was not a viable option as new skills were required. To manage the possible negative impact of the rapid growth in staff numbers on the culture, Equity appointed some of the older members of staff as culture ambassadors. They told anecdotes of the beginnings and related customer success stories emphasizing the role Equity played in these successes.

Operations

Between 1993 and 1999 Equity's customers grew from about 3,000 to 50,000. All transactions were carried out manually and no new branches were opened. The result was crowded banking halls and very long queues. Customers waited for over an hour to be served. Although procedures and processes had been optimized and standardized, the increase in the volume of business exacerbated the operations. In 2000, Equity launched computerized banking software, Bank 2000. It took only four months instead of the estimated 24 months to install the system. Managers and employees spent weekends in the office to facilitate a smooth transfer from the manual system to the new system. The results were impressive. Transaction time was reduced to 5 minutes; the number of active savings accounts per staff member grew by 59 per cent in 2001 compared to 11 per cent the previous year[7].

Although 21 new branches had been established since the software was introduced, the number of customers grew so fast that a lot of pressure was put on the infrastructure (see Exhibit V). The business model of high volume, low margins put a lot of pressure on operations especially after Equity became a bank in January 2005. The number of customers and the value of deposits doubled. Account activity also increased. Long queues returned crowding the banking halls. It soon became clear that the capacity of the banking software, which was installed in 2000 and subsequently upgraded, was limited in terms of the number of accounts and transactions it could handle and also the management information it could provide. Resources were strained and it was feared that customer satisfaction would dip.

Mwangi convinced his management team and the board to invest about US$10 million in Finacle by InfoSys. The new system could handle 35 million accounts, 5000 ATMs, thousands of point of sales, etc. By December 2005 the system had been deployed. The bank also began to install ATMs more aggressively.

Following the listing of Equity Bank on the Nairobi Stock Exchange in August 2006, the number of new accounts increased from about 1,200 per day to 2,400 per day. To handle the increase in volume, more ATMs were established and customers were encouraged to use them. By December 2008, the bank had 3.3 million customers, 97 branches, 500 ATMs (Visa branded) and 2500 points of sale.

Winning and Delighting Customers

The customer is at the heart of Equity Bank's activities. While competitors discouraged frequent account withdrawals and required minimum account balances as well as minimum deposits to open an account, a customer could open an account with Equity Bank without money. No minimum account balance was required. There were no limitations on access to money in the account, no limit on the amount and frequency of withdrawal and account maintenance was free.

The provision of innovative and value adding products to the *mwananchi* was considered central to Equity Bank's strategy. There were products for farmers, fishermen, women, the youth, etc. A customer of the bank who is a small business owner told the case writer:

> They have many products. They are now selling insurance. The other day I went to my branch and found that they now give loans to enable people buy water tanks and septic tanks! Can you believe it? All that you require is a pay slip; no collateral! Everyone in Kenya will soon own a plastic tank.

To drive innovation and unearth the real needs of customers, the bank regularly conducted market research. Surveys and focus groups were used to understand and delve deeper into customer expectations, customer complaints, etc. The findings of these research projects sometimes challenged management thinking and beliefs about customer expectations. James Mwangi commented on the first market survey which was carried out in 2000/2001:

> with market research things that we never thought were true, and things that we held so dearly as true, were challenged... Armed with the findings of the market research on what the market segment wanted, we refined our products.[8]

Customer surveys are conducted regularly and action plans are communicated to customers. For example, after the second survey in 2002, the bank sent 200,000 personalized letters and SMS messages to its clients communicating the changes to be made in the organization as a result of the listening exercise.

Customers regularly gave feedback to the bank through personal visits and phone calls. Some customers went to the head office to talk to James Mwangi personally. One senior manager commented:

> If something happens in one of the branches the MD hears of it from a customer within 48 hours. Customers sometimes call to advise him to terminate the appointment of officers who do not fit the Equity culture.

Customers also made complaints and suggestions by completing the customer feedback forms available in the banking halls. An older member of staff in one of the branches commented of the feedback process:

> We ask for their contact details in the suggestion forms so we can visit them and listen to them more closely. Sometimes, we do not have a solution to the customer's problem, but we give them hope. Hope is important.

A recent customer survey showed that about 75 per cent of the customers were first time users of banking services. A large majority said they liked the fact that the members of staff were warm and friendly. One of the things they said they did not like was the congestion at the branches. As one customer put it: 'Equity is not like the other banks. If I have a problem, I can see the Branch Manager and he will listen. They care about their customers and offer loans to us when other banks never would. Equity is my bank, even if I have to queue for an hour to get my salary right now, I know they are working to change that – because they care.'[9]

Customers were grateful to the bank for changing their lives. Many have been able to educate their children, pay hospital bills, etc. They benefited a great deal from the basic business training Equity Bank provides for its customers. An officer in the Naivasha branch elaborated:

> We want our customers to be the role models in their community. We help them succeed. We feel it is our duty to listen to our customers. No matter how busy we are, if a customer stops any of us in the banking hall, we listen and respond to the customer. This has helped our customers a lot. Some of them are illiterate and they have never used a bank before. After listening, we make suggestions to management and this helps us serve our customers better.

A credit officer who has been with the Bank for 9 months said: 'We go out to meet the customers. We sit with them on stools or stones and discuss one on one. This cements the relationship with the customer. The farmers tell you their stories. Before they had nothing, with loans from Equity they now have a few cows, they send their children to school, etc. They appreciate. As a credit officer, I have freedom to do my job so long as I follow the procedure. I can consult anybody if I have a problem. People support you, they guide you.' Some of the older customers called the branch manager their son. The branch manager commented: 'this encourages me to treat them as my parents. A bond develops. This bond links me with my colleagues; who become my brothers and sisters. This is a family. We help one another; if a cashier has a problem, we help him or her find a solution.'

The case writer asked a new customer about her experience with Equity Bank. She responded:

> I am a sukumawiki farmer. I came because I want to plan ahead. My children are growing and I want to save for their school fees. Someone told me to go to Equity because they do not ask for money to open the account. I can also use any of their branches. There are no monthly charges. There were very many people but the lady was fast. She explained to me that I can

put money into my account every day from my daily sales. She helped me draw up a plan for saving for my children. I am going to deposit a little money every day.

The employees and the bank also helped customers through unexpected situations. A customer may walk into a branch to cash some money from his account and find that he has no money because the wholesaler has not paid for the milk or tea he supplied. Sometimes, the customer has no money for the fare back home. The bank gives him the fare (about 100 Ksh) without documentation. The customers always pay back.

Many of the customers especially those in the rural areas felt they were owners of the bank. They talked about their membership number and not their account number. They took pride in the success of the bank. When in 2004 they knew that Equity wanted to become a commercial bank, they expressed their fear that Equity may behave like other banks and forget the *mwananchi*. James was careful during its re-branding to communicate its commitment to the common folk. In a recent survey, 78 per cent of customers said that only death will make them leave Equity Bank.

The bank has grown through word of mouth advertising. Customers introduce their friends and relatives. They act as guarantors for those who want loans. Equity Bank also uses public relations events to increase its brand awareness. Two of such events were the acquisition of a banking licence and the listing on the NSE. Such public relations events were held in prestigious hotels and long term customers were invited. The press coverage of these events provides free advertisement for the bank. The fact that Equity Bank is a successful Kenyan institution is emphasized at these events. The managing director was also frequently in the news. The many awards won by the bank as well as presentations by the managing director at the African Business Leaders' Forum and G8 Gleneagles were presented in the media as achievements of an indigenous institution.

When customers were asked what they did not like about Equity the response was, congestion of the banking halls. To solve the problem, management had set up new branches, ATMs had been installed but the congestion problem persisted. One of the very congested branches was located next to the Nairobi City Hall. To decongest the branch, a new branch was opened within a few metres of the first and ATMs were installed. Management soon realized that the ATMs were not being used and congestion in the first branch continued while the new branch built its clientele. Customers would go to the branch with their ATM cards in their pockets and queue to see the cashier. One customer explained: 'This is our branch. We like it here. The man at the counter makes me happy.'

To encourage customers to use the ATMs, management hired 100 street hawkers (young boys who sold recharge cards and other items on the road). They were trained and then sent to the branches to convince customers to use the ATM machine and teach them how to use it. The hawkers mixed with the customers on the long queues. They explained the convenience and cost effectiveness of the ATMs to the customers. They also helped customers use the machines for the first time. Within one month, many of the customers started using the ATMs. The Director of Strategy compared their strategy with that of other banks:

> Some banks introduced a stiff penalty for cash withdrawals from the counter. Instead, we sold the convenience and value to our customers. Today, 80% of our transactions are done with the ATM.

A major challenge for Equity as it grew was how to serve its customers whose businesses had become very successful. A number of these customers had annual turnover of between 10 to 20 million US$. Their needs had changed. They wanted trade finance, SME banking, foreign exchange and VISA cards. By 2006, Equity Bank was one of the most capitalized banks in Kenya. It was doing better than the multinationals. It could do big ticket transactions but should the focus change? Could the Bank serve the *mwananchi* and the mid-sized companies?

The Director of Strategy explained:

> We are a micro finance institution. We focus on the poor. But should we lose customers we have worked with over the years? Are we an incubator for other banks? No, we are not. So we decided to set up a few prestige branches and created a corporate banking unit to serve these customers. Today, we have four of these branches. We never advertise this aspect of our business. The prestige branches are by invitation only. All the customers who use these branches are our old customers. However, these customers invite their friends, business partners, etc. so the branches are growing.

People Management

James Mwangi was convinced that people were critical to the realization of the bank's mission. The number of staff had grown substantially over the years (see Exhibit VI). A lot of effort was made to recruit and retain people who fit the bank's culture. In his own words:

> We are a very disciplined and militant organization. The culture repulses those who are opposed to it. It is like blood transfusion. Any member of staff who is not humble, not down to earth is under pressure. He or she is swimming against a strong current. On the other hand, if the personality fits the culture, it is like swimming downstream. We never lose people at the leadership levels. Once you have stayed with us for one year, it is difficult to leave. About 80% of those who leave voluntarily do so within the first six months of employment.

The organizational culture was a very effective social control mechanism. New recruits who did not share the values came under a lot of pressure to conform. Those who do not fit leave within a few months.

Recruitment

The bank attracted people who are caring, humble, and down to earth. People were not hired into a job role: their principal responsibility was to contribute to the achievement of the purpose. A manager who had been with the bank for four months commented: 'Equity Bank does not just give you a job; it is a calling. I used to work for a foreign bank. There were days I did not look forward to going to work. I felt stifled. At Equity, decision making is fast. We ask the key questions: does it fit with our strategy? Can we do it? Which resources are required? And we move. A relative of mine, who is a customer of Equity Bank, told me about the Bank before I joined. She was very enthusiastic about the Bank. After I joined, I found that all what she told me about Equity was true.'

Performance and Reward Management

Expectations were clearly communicated and resources were provided to enable people achieve set objectives. James Mwangi explained:

> Entrepreneurial spirit is important but you need much more otherwise you have a rail and no trains. People need resources in order to deliver. Our assets have increased over 30 times in the last four years. We cannot have achieved that with entrepreneurial spirit. We provided the resources and found competent people who believe in the course.
>
> You cannot empower people with rhetoric. Maybe I am the only entrepreneur in this bank. Entrepreneurs dream but the dreams must be operationalized and executed. It is execution that counts and there is nothing entrepreneurial about execution.

Performance was carefully managed at the bank. The process began with goal setting. The Director of Strategy elaborated:

> At the Managers' Congress every quarter, they (the managers) let us know what they want to achieve. There is a spirit of competition. If one manager sets a target for himself that others think is low, they question him: 'Why is your target so low? You have many tea farmers in the area. Don't they need our services?' At the end an agreement is reached.

During the year, performance was monitored and managed. The appraisal system was recently changed to an open and collective system. James believed that open and transparent appraisals were better suited to the mission of the institution. 'This is not a bank', he emphasized; 'this is a movement. We are all members of a movement. We should all know what each one is contributing.'

Managers on the same level sat down with a senior executive, usually the MD, to discuss their performance. Each colleague contributed to the debate. They asked questions and rated each other's performance. The views of subordinates were also taken into consideration during the appraisal sessions. If a manager's performance was below expectation, a team made up of his colleagues was given the task of coaching him and helping him succeed. All the members of staff were encouraged to ask for help whenever they needed it.

Sometimes, a decision was taken to demote a member of staff. The MD explained:

> We tell the person with performance problems: Look we gave you a general's position but you are not delivering so you should go to a captain's position and let's look for a general for this job. From the top management team of 1993, not one of them is in the executive management. We have brought in layers of management and hired people from outside to fill these positions. Today, there are 4 or 5 people who can succeed me. We all want to be led by the best person; the one who will generate the most value for the Bank.

The case of the IT manager is illustrative. He was the head of IT and reported directly to the MD before 2004. As the bank grew and a new IT platform was required, a general manager was poached from another bank to head the department. Today, the IT manager is about 4 layers below the MD. Recently, he became a shareholder of the bank.

Practically all the staff who had been demoted still worked with the Bank. The Director of Strategy explained:

> We let people know why they have to go back and we ensure that everyone reports to someone who is better experienced, knowledgeable, etc. Everyone sees their role; their contribution. They recognize that the better the leader, the better for everybody. They know they have built the institution and they can see their role. They also realize that the institution is growing and new skills are required. We are a team. Glory goes to the team; awards are given to the team. If we see you are not a good striker, we find where you will contribute best and put you there. She concluded: 'If things don't go right in your home, you don't leave your home.'

A branch manager commented on the appraisal system:

> There are no arguments. The appraisal is on numbers. You were supposed to handle say 300 transactions, why did you deal with 200? What are your

challenges? The review is to help the member of staff to succeed. The Team provides advice, mentoring, etc. to those that need help to reach their goals.

I attend the appraisal sessions for branch managers. I have access to the figures for all the branches. It is a transparent system. Branch managers ask each other for help. I sometimes call up other branches 'my brother how are you handling this?' At the appraisal we critique each branch's performance and proffer solutions to problems they are having. It is not humiliating. At the branch level it is the same. The Key Performance Indicators (KPIs) and performance against them are on the intranet. Anyone of us can access them. We track many things. There are no arguments. We work through the numbers and ask questions.

Performance was rewarded. For performance levels between 8 and 10, the bonus was three times the person's salary. Employees who had a performance rating of 2 or below were asked to leave the bank. In 2007, 18 people left on account of poor performance.

There was a salary structure and each employee had access to information on how bonuses were calculated, how much her earnings would be, etc.

Pay is competitive. We all have individual and branch targets. For example, each cashier is expected to handle say 300 transactions a day; no credit officer should have more than 2% of loans outstanding unpaid. We earn a quarterly bonus which is based on the KPIs,' explained a branch manager.

Social Responsibility

The bank started a pre-university sponsorship programme in 1998. The male and female students with the best scores in the national examination (KCSE) in each of the districts where Equity Bank has a presence are awarded scholarships to university. The programme was formally launched in 2007 by the Minister of Education, Prof. George Saitoti. In 2008, the bank spent 112 million KSh on 186 students.

The students were invited to work as interns in the branch of Equity in their district. A branch manager shared his experience with the programme:

This branch serves two districts so we get four interns every year. We encourage the interns to save during the time they spend with us. A number of them pay for the education of their siblings with some of their savings. Most of them go on to university and come back to work with us during the vacation period. During this time they are exposed and get to understand our culture. When they graduate, we give them employment in the district. I have a few of them in my branch. They are serving their community.

Equity Bank was involved in a host of social projects including the lighting of slums in Nairobi. Most of these projects were suggested by the members of staff in the community.

Moving Ahead

James Mwangi sat at his desk in his office on the 14th floor of the NHIF Building. The new head office building of the bank can be seen from one of the windows and one can make out the Nairobi Park and the Ngong Hills. But James' thoughts were not on the beautiful scenery; he was taking stock and looking ahead. A new mission and vision had been agreed upon in 2008 (see Exhibit VII); there was so much to be done.

He had no doubt that the institution had been transformed. By the end of 2008, Equity Bank had become a one-stop financial services firm. It provided insurance services, and had received a licence from the Capital Markets Authority and the Retirement Benefits Authority to provide custodial services. The bank was listed on the Nairobi Stock Exchange on the 7 August 2006 at an initial value of 6.3 billion KSh. By 31 December 2008, its market capitalization was over 65 billion KSh. It was the only stock that returned positive shareholder value during 2008 at the Nairobi Stock Exchange (see Exhibit VIII for financial results).

The shareholding was well diversified. No individual owned more than 6 per cent of the shares. Institutional investments owned about 40 per cent of the bank. Helios EB Investors became the largest single shareholder with their investment of US$180 million in the bank. British–American Investments Company (Kenya) Limited was the second largest shareholder with about 11 per cent of the shares. Both Africap and Equity Bank Employees held about 4 per cent of the stock each. Over 7000 shareholders held about 31 per cent of the stock.

Results of surveys in East Africa showed that only 35 per cent of Ugandans have access to finance. During 2008, Equity bought Uganda Micro Finance now Equity Bank Uganda Limited. This added 31 branches to the branch network almost overnight. A managing director had already been appointed for the green-field operation in southern Sudan. Equity had entered a new phase in its history; the Equity Group had been born. James wondered whether the executive team could lead the bank through this new phase.

An additional source of concern was competition. The success of Equity Bank had drawn attention to the wealth at the bottom of the pyramid. Competitors were falling over each other selling products to the *mwananchi*. Could the other banks copy Equity's strategy successfully? Maintaining the tempo was not going to be easy.

James Mwangi wondered if the bank could continue to meet the expectations of the customers and the employees.

The public owns this institution. Seventy-eight per cent of our customers told us in the last survey that only death could make them leave Equity. This is good, but are their expectations realistic? Some of them want us to go beyond the socio-economic mission. They see us as a panacea so they bring all their problems to us. Can we meet these expectations? Should we?

For 15 years, we have not confronted failure. For many years, employees have not known hard or lean times. We expect and see smooth curves, no shocks; we are constantly growing. What will happen if there is a huge set-back? Does the Bank have the capacity to manage failure?

EXHIBIT I Mission and vision statements

MISSION STATEMENT 1995

'We, Equity Building Society, will mobilize savings and term deposits for the timely provision of loan facilities to generate sufficient and sustainable profits. This will enable us to contribute to the members' (clients') welfare and to the national economy. Equity recognizes the importance of staff members and their contribution to the institution and will avail them of opportunities for growth and job security.'

Vision: To become the biggest microfinance provider in Kenya in terms of funding, loan portfolio and profitability.

MISSION STATEMENT 2007

We mobilize resources and offer credit to maximize value and economically empower the micro-finance clients and other stakeholders by offering customer-focused quality financial services.

VISION STATEMENT 2001–2005

To be the dominant microfinance provider in Kenya by the year 2005.

VISION STATEMENT 2005–2020

To become the microfinance provider of choice in Kenya and the region.

Core Values

Professionalism
Integrity
Creativity and Innovation
Teamwork
Unity of Purpose
Respect and dedication to customer care
Effective Corporate Governance

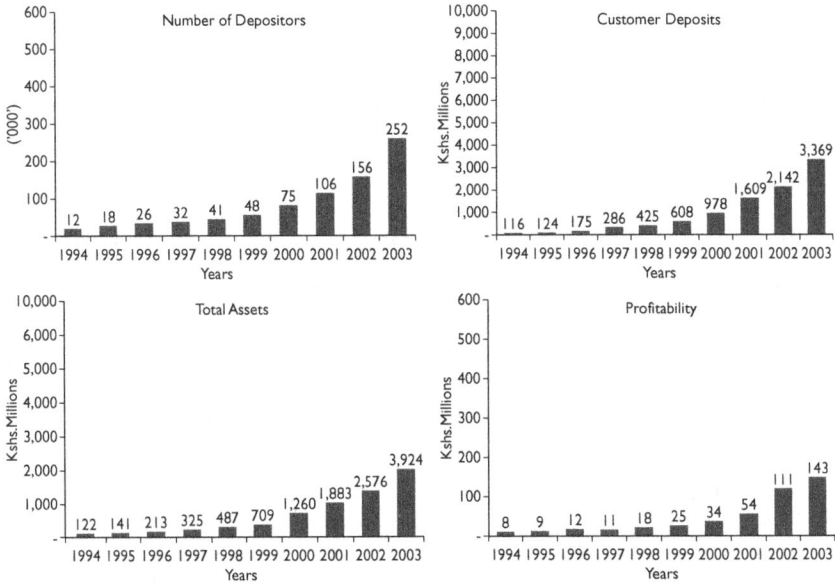

EXHIBIT II Summary of Equity Bank performance 1994–2003

Source: Equity Bank information memorandum, 3 July 2006

EXHIBIT III Statement on Corporate Governance

Equity Bank's corporate governance is a culture built on the bank's core values. The Bank is managed by a Board of Directors that is responsible for the long term strategic direction to ensure maximization of economic value to stakeholders. This Bank incorporates high standards of corporate governance and business ethics. It is also characterized by transparency and openness, good corporate citizenship, fairness, compliance with regulatory and prudential requirements.

The bank has an elaborate governance structure comprising Shareholders, Board of Directors and Board Committees together with an effective management structure that enhances the separation of duties and dual control system.

Oversight Role of the Board of Directors

Over the years, the Board of Directors has supervised the delivery of dramatic growth with the bank continuing to deliver strong financial performance. It has also provided leadership to the Bank resulting in the bank being able to take its services to the furthest reach of the Kenyan society and generate great shareholder wealth.

The Board has attracted directors who have shown great commitment and enthusiasm in involving themselves in the affairs of the Bank and who have demonstrated the spirit and ethos of the organization. In line with maintaining international standards, the Board commissioned and successfully completed a self evaluation exercise in year 2007. The evaluation focused on the role and responsibility of the Board, structure, composition, functions and processes, information, meetings, among other critical areas.

Board Committees

The Board has established seven committees which are all governed by Charters.

Audit Committee: It ensures that the bank has and adheres to the sound policies, processes and procedures that deliver business strategic plans effectively. It also reviews the financial performance of the Bank, internal controls, performance and findings of internal auditors.

Credit Committee: Reviews and oversees the overall lending policy of the Bank, it ensures lending systems and procedures are adequate and adhered to.

Risk Management Committee: Ensures the quality, integrity and reliability of the Bank's management. It also discharges duties relating to corporate accountability and associated risks in terms of management assurance and reporting. The committee also monitors compliance with the Bank's risk policies and procedures and reviews regularly the adequacy of the Risk Management framework in relation to the risks faced by the Bank.

Strategy and Investment Committee: It supervises the development of corporate strategy and monitors the implementation of the same. It manages the process of resource allocation to increase shareholder value in pursuit of the vision of the bank. It also reviews and considers the proposed strategic investments, makes recommendations to the Board and advices the management accordingly.

Tendering and Procurement Committee: Oversees and keeps the Board appraised on issues pertaining to the tendering and procurement of goods and services for the bank including regularly reviewing the tendering and procurement procedures.

Governance, Board Nominations and Staff Remuneration Committee: Ensures implementation and compliance with Human Resource Policies, makes recommendations to the board for policy on executive and senior management remuneration formulated to attract and retain high calibre staff and motivate them to implement the bank's strategy. It also ensures the board appointments maintain a good mix of skills, experience and competence in various field of expertise.

Board Executive Committee: It provides coaching and mentoring for the chief executive and provides the link between the board and the management. The committee provides a first line of support and response to management.

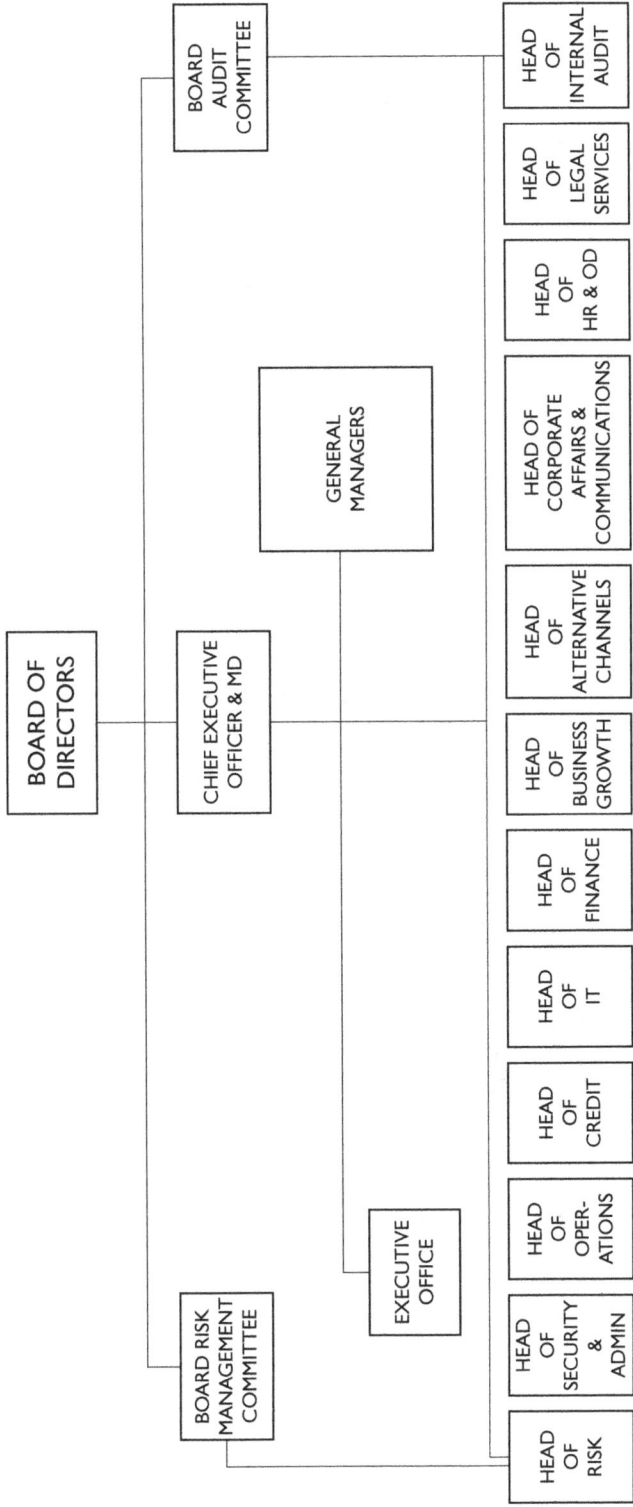

EXHIBIT IV Equity Bank organization structure 2004

Source: Equity Bank Prospectus 2006

GROWTH IN CUSTOMER NUMBERS
Ukuaji katika idadi ya wateja

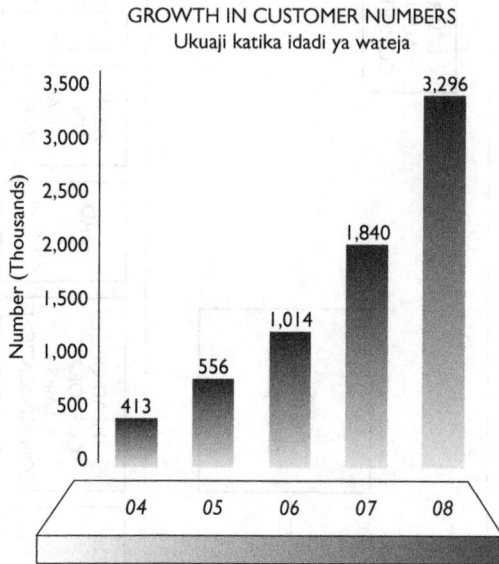

GROWTH IN CUSTOMER DEPOSITS
Ukuaji katika akiba za wateja

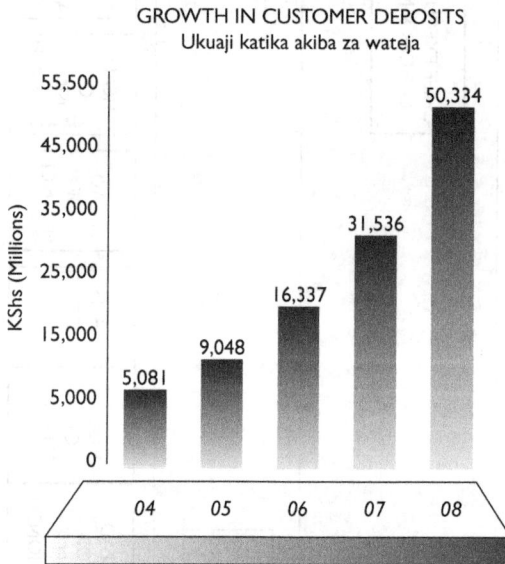

EXHIBIT V Growth in number of customers and deposits 2004–2008

Source: Equity Bank 2008 annual report and financial statements

EXHIBIT VI Growth in numbers of staff at different levels in Equity 1995–2006

	'95	'96	'97	'98	'99	'00	'01	'02	'03	'04	'05	'06
Board level	3	3	3	3	3	7	7	7	8	7	10	9
Executive management	2	2	2	2	2	2	2	2	3	12	14	15
Branch/assistant branch managers	6	6	10	13	15	18	22	24	30	49	61	71
Senior managers at Head Office	2	2	2	1	1	2	3	3	7	10	23	63
Administrative support staff	4	4	1	5	5	4	7	15	22	24	24	152
Credit staff	6	8	10	12	16	17	36	28	51	86	149	297
Savings staff	25	34	31	47	72	72	81	108	205	360	591	692
Management information systems staff	1	1	—	1	1	1	3	5	8	13	33	48
Finance/accounting staff	3	2	1	3	1	4	6	7	11	7	14	17
Marketing staff	—	—	—	1	—	—	5	10	12	10	10	22
Internal audit staff	—	—	—	—	—	—	2	3	5	4	5	9
Total	50	62	60	86	116	124	176	210	360	530	884	1,395

Source: *MicroSave* 2007

EXHIBIT VII Mission and vision statements 2008

Purpose

We exist to transform the lives and livelihoods of our people socially and economically by availing them of modern, inclusive financial services that maximize
their opportunities.

Our Vision

To be the champion of the socio-economic prosperity of the people of Africa.

Mission Statement

We offer inclusive, customer focused financial services that socially and economically empower our clients and other stakeholders.

Positioning Statement

Equity provides Inclusive Financial Services that transform livelihoods, give dignity
and expand opportunities.

Tagline

Your listening, caring partner.

Our Motto

Growing together in trust.

EXHIBIT VIIIa Income Statement Sheet 2004 – 2008
PROFIT AND LOSS ACCOUNT **FOR THE YEAR ENDED 31 DECEMBER**

In millions of Kenya Shillings	2008	2007	2006	2005	2004
Interest income	7,169	3,155	1,635	948	459
Interest expense	−1,217	−495	−127	−82	−64
Net interest income	**5,952**	**2,660**	**1,508**	**866**	**396**
Fee and commission income	1,308	562	1,863	937	640
Net fee and commission income	1,308	562	—	—	—
Trading income	734	246	—	—	—
Other operating income	3,562	2,353	—	—	—
Total operating income	**11,556**	**5,821**	**3,371**	**1,803**	**1,036**
Impairment loss on financial assets	875	−25	—	—	—
Personnel expenses	2,584	1,469	1,856	1,040	563
Operating lease expenses	357	182	—	—	—
Depreciation and amortization	712	423	280	138	84

Provision for bad and doubtful debts	—	—	133	124	171
Other expenses	2,271	1,409	—	—	—
Total expenses	**6,799**	**3,458**	**2,269**	**1,302**	**818**
Profit before tax	**4,757**	**2,363**	**1,103**	**501**	**218**
Share of profit of associate	34	15	—	—	—
Profit before income tax	4,791	2,378	—	—	
Income tax expense	−1,038	−488	−350	−156	−82
Profit for the year	**3,753**	**1,890**	**753**	**345**	**136**
Earnings per share (KShs)	10.25	7	8	3.8	5.43
Dividend per share (KShs)	3	2	—	2	2

Source: Equity Bank annual reports (2003–2008)

EXHIBIT VIIIb Balance Sheet 2004–2008
BALANCE SHEET **AS ON 31 DECEMBER**

In millions of Kenya Shillings	*2008*	*2007*	*2006*	*2005*	*2004*
Assets					
Cash and cash equivalents	12,018	11,996	2,691	13,061	790
Loans and advances to customers	40,857	21,836	10,920	5,524	2,874
Government securities	—	—	1,651	1,254	—
Treasury bonds	—	—	—	—	578
Investment securities	12,151	13,543	11	11	11
Placement and balances with other banking institutions	—	—	2,023	2,094	1,914
Investment associate	1,156	442	—	—	—
Tax recoverable	—	—	—	—	—
Property and equipment	4,259	2,603	1,470	1,045	408
Prepaid lease	4	4	—	—	4
Intangible assets	348	224	161	90	8
Investment in subsidiary companies	2,976	—	—	—	—
Amount due from group companies	182	—	—	—	—
Other assets	3,184	2,428	1,088	126	120
Deferred tax	—	—	—	4	—
Total assets	**77,135**	**53,076**	**20,025**	**11,457**	**6,707**
Liabilities					
Deposit from customers	48,977	31,536	16,337	9,048	5,082
Current tax	514	209	147	168	12
Deferred tax liabilities	67	45	11	—	9

Continued

EXHIBIT VIIIb (Continued)

In millions of Kenya Shillings	2008	2007	2006	2005	2004
Other borrowed funds	6,167	4,521	486	—	297
Other liabilities	1,751	1,848	843	647	—
Total liabilities	**57,476**	**38,159**	**17,824**	**9,863**	**5,398**
Equity					
Share capital	1,851	1,811	452	452	91
Share premium	12,161	10,543	—	—	843
Available for sale reserve	(112)	13	—	—	—
Statutory loan reserve	308	253	—	—	—
Other reserves	—	—	1,748	1,141	(12)
Revenue reserves	—	—	—	—	299
Capital reserve	—	—	—	—	51
Retained earnings	4,340	1,754	—	—	—
Proposed dividends	1,111	543	—	—	38
Total equity	**19,659**	**14,917**	**2,201**	**1,594**	**1,309**
Total liabilities and equity	**77,135**	**53,076**	**20,025**	**11,457**	**6,707**

Source: Equity Bank annual reports (2003–2008)

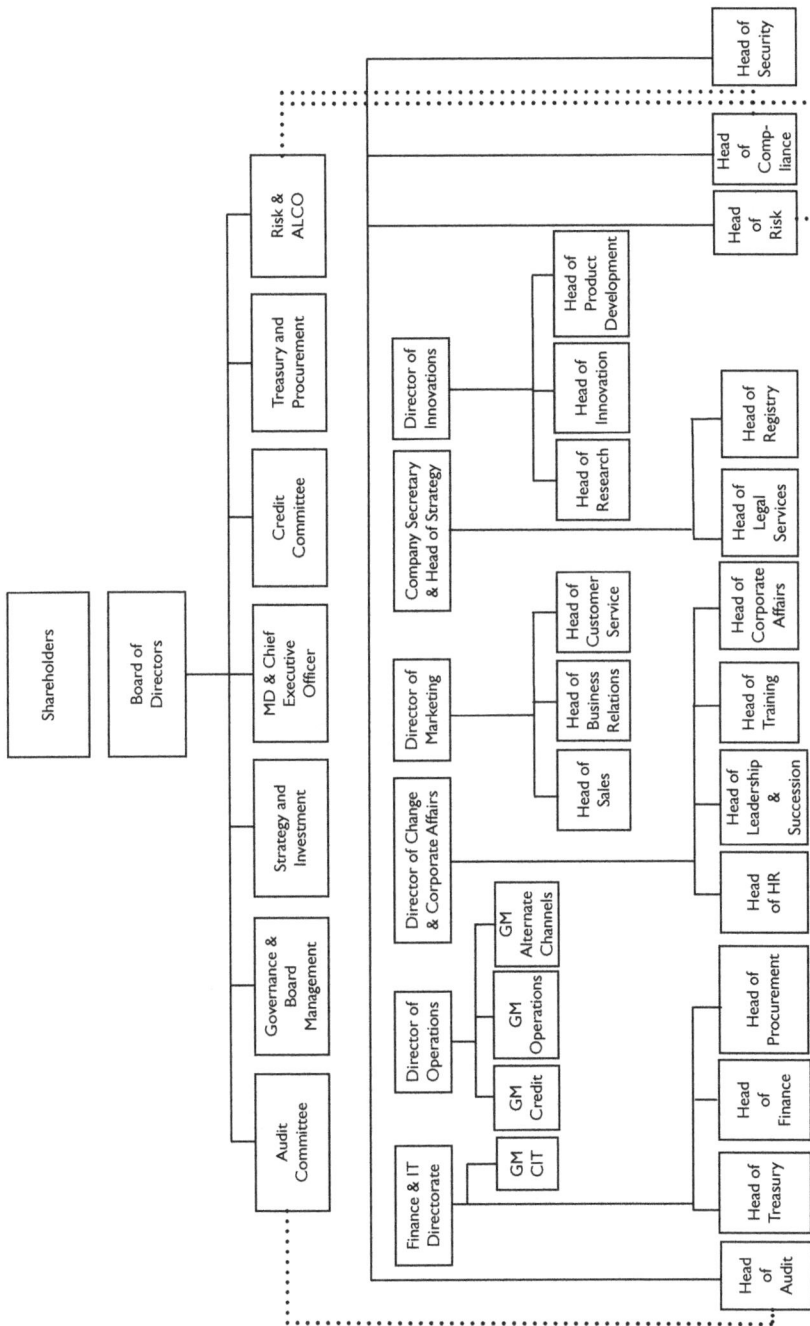

EXHIBIT IX Organizational structure 2007

Notes

1 *MicroSave Africa* 2002: 4.
2 Coetzee *et al.*, p.2.
3 *Microsave* 2002.
4 *MicroSave* 2007: 5.
5 *MicroSave Africa* 2002: 11.
6 Coetzee *et al.* (cited in MicroSave 2007: 15).
7 *MicroSave* 2002: 42.
8 *MicroSave* 2007.
9 *MicroSave* 2007: 11.

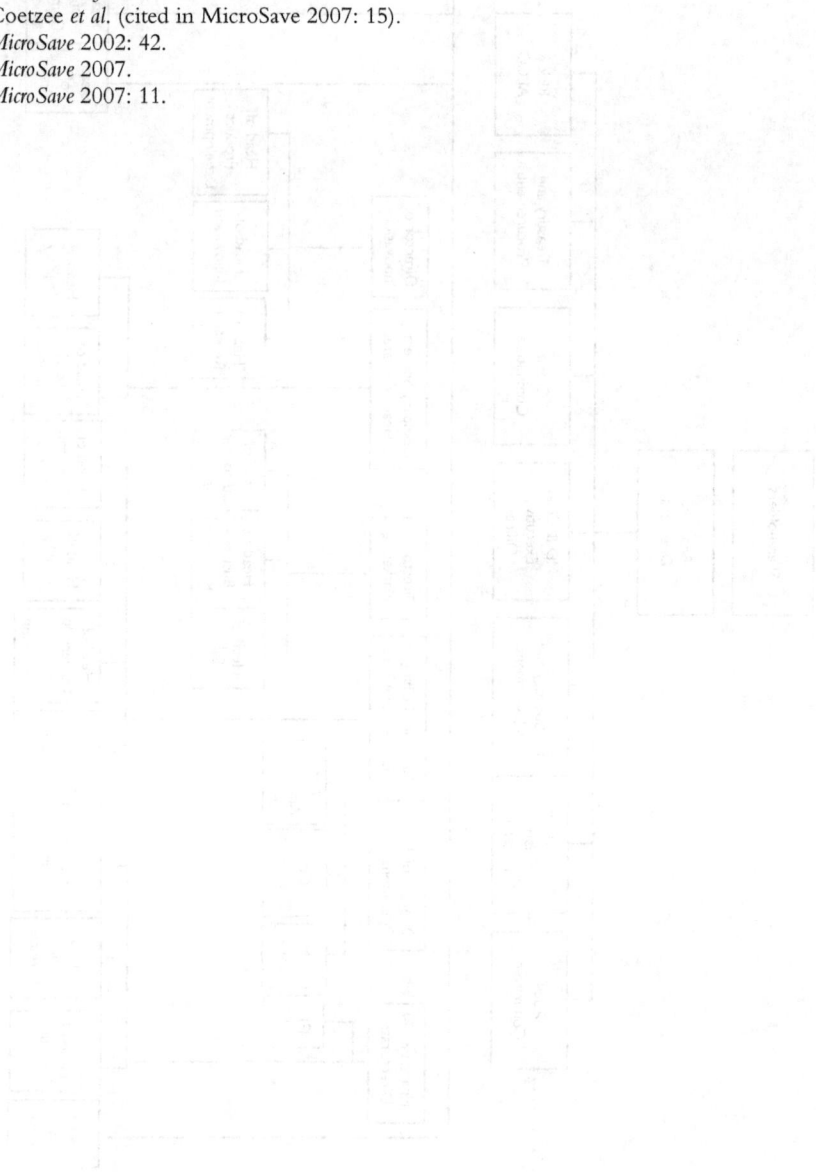

BIBLIOGRAPHY

Lions on the Move: the Progress and Potential of African Economies (2010). McKinsey Global Institute: 7.

AfDB (2010). *African Economic Outlook 2011.*

African Telecommunication/ICT Indicators 2008: at a crossroads. The International Communications Union. www.itu.int/ITU-D/ict/.../africa/2008/index.html. Retrieved 15 August 2011.

Akunyili, D. (2004). Public Sector Performance – The Case of NAFDAC. Paper presented at the Lagos Business School Breakfast Club Meeting. 6th July 2004.

Albert, S. (1995). 'Towards a Theory of Timing; An Archival Study of Timing Decisions in the Persian Gulf War'. *Research in Organizational Behavior,* 17: 1–70.

Amabile, T. M. (1997). 'Motivating Creativity in Organizations: On Doing What You Love and Loving What You Do'. *California Management Review,* 40(1): 39–58.

Amis, J., Slack, T. and Hinings, C. R. (2002). 'Values and Organizational Change'. *Journal of Applied Behavioral Science,* 38(4): 436–65.

Amis, J., Slack, T. and Hinings, C. R. (2004). 'The Pace, Sequence and Linearity of Radical Change'. *Academy of Management Journal,* 47(1): 15–39.

Andriopoulos, C. and Dawson, P. (2009). *Managing Change, Creativity & Innovation.* London: Sage.

Armenakis, A. A., Harris, S. G. and Mossholder, K. W. (1993). 'Creating Readiness for Organizational Change'. *Human Relations,* 46(6): 681–703.

Armenakis, A. A., Harris, S. G. and Feild, H. S. (1999). 'Making Change Permanent: Institutionalizing Change Interventions', in Pasmore, W. A. and Woodman, R. W. (eds), *Research in Organizational Development and Change,* Vol. 12, Stamford, CT: JAI Press: 97–128.

Atkinson, A. A., Waterhouse, J. H. and Wells, R. B. (1997). 'A Stakeholder Approach to Strategic Performance Measurement'. *Sloan Management Review,* Spring: 25–37.

Avolio, B. J., Bass, B. M. and Jung, D. I. (1999). 'Re-Examining the Components of Transformational and Transactional Leadership Using the Multifactor Leadership Questionnaire'. *Journal of Occupational and Organizational Psychology,* 72: 441–62.

Babarinde, O. A. (2009). 'Bridging the Economic Divide in the Republic of South Africa: A Corporate Social Responsibility Perspective'. *Thunderbird International Business Review*, 51(4): 355–68.

Barney, J. B. (1991). 'Firm Resources and Sustained Competitive Advantage'. *Journal of Management*, 17(1): 99–120.

Baum, J. R., Locke, E. A. and Kirkpatrick, S. A. (1998). 'A Longitudinal Study of the Relation of Vision and Vision Communication to Venture Growth in Entrepreneurial Firms'. *Journal of Applied Psychology*, 83: 43–54.

Beer, M. and Nohria, N. (2000). *Breaking the Code of Change*. Boston, MA: Harvard Business School Press.

Beer, M., Eisenstat, R. A. and Spector, B. (1990). 'Why Change Programs Don't Produce Change'. *Harvard Business Review*, 68(6): 158–66.

Beitler, M. A. (2006). *Strategic Organizational Change. A Practitioner's Guide for Managers and Consultants*. Greensboro USA: Practitioner Press International.

Bennigson, L. A. and Swartz, H. (1987). 'The CEO's Change Agenda'. *Strategy & Leadership*, 15(3): 12–19.

Bennis, W. (1993). *An Invented Life, Reflections on Leadership and Change*. Reading MA: Addison-Wesley.

Berson, Y., Shamir, B., Avolio, B. J. and Popper, M. (2001). 'The Relationship between Vision, Strength, Leadership Style, and Context'. *Leadership Quarterly*, 12: 53–73.

Bigsten, A. and Durevall, D. (2008). 'The African Economy and Its Role in the World Economy'. *Current African Issues*, no. 40. The Nordic Africa Institute.

Blunt, P. and Jones, M. L. (1992). *Managing Organizations in Africa*. Berlin: Walter de Gruyter.

Bouckenooghe, D. (2010). 'Positioning Change Recipients' Attitudes toward Change in the Organizational Change Literature'. *The Journal of Applied Behavioral Science*, 46(4): 500–31.

Brain, M. (2000). *How Compasses Work*. http://www.howstuffworks.com/compass.htm. Retrieved 24 March 2009.

Bridges, W. (2003). *Managing Transitions, Making the Most of Change*, 2nd edn. Cambridge, MA: Persus Books Group.

Brown, S. L. and Eisenhardt, K. M. (1995). 'Product Development: Past Research, Present Findings, and Future Directions'. *Academy of Management Review*, 20: 343–78.

Brown, S. L., and Eisenhardt, K. M. (1997). 'The Art of Continuous Change: Linking Complexity Theory and Time-Paced Evolution in Relentlessly Shifting Organizations. *Administrative Science Quarterly*, 42: 1–34.

Buchanan, D. A. (2003). 'Demands, Instabilities, Manipulations, Careers: The Lived Experience of Driving Change'. *Human Relations*, 56(6): 663–84.

Buchanan, D. and Boddy, D. (1992). *The Expertise of the Change Agent: Public Performance and Backstage Activity*. Englewood Cliffs, NJ: Prentice-Hall.

Buchanan, D., Fitzgerald, I. L., Ketley, D., Gollop, R., Jones, J. L., Saint Lamont, S., Neath, A. and Whitby, E. (2005). 'No Going Back: A Review of the Literature on Sustaining Organizational Change'. *International Journal of Management Reviews*, 7(3): 189–205.

Burke, W. W. (2002). *Organization Change*. Sage Publications.

Burke, W. W. (2011). *Organization Change:Theory and Practice*, 3rd edn. Thousand Oaks, CA: Sage.

Burke, W. W. and Litwin, G. H. (1992). 'A Causal Model of Organizational Performance and Change'. *Journal of Management*, 18(3): 523–45.

Burnes, B. (2004). *Managing Change*. Essex: Pearson Education Limited.

Caldwell, R. (2003). 'Models of Change Agency: A Fourfold Classification'. *British Journal of Management*, 14: 131–42.

Carnall, C. A. (1999). *Managing Change in Organizations*, 3rd edn. Harlow England: Prentice Hall.

Child, J. and Tsai, T. (2005). 'The Dynamic Between Firms' Environmental Strategies and Institutional Constraints in Emerging Economies: Evidence from China and Taiwan'. *Journal of Management Studies*, 42(1): 95–125.

Clawson, J. G. (2007). *Buy-In*. Darden Business Publishing, UVA-OB-0924.

Clegg, C. and Walsh, S. (2004). 'Change Management: Time for a Change!' *European Journal of Work and Organizational Psychology*, 13(2): 217–39.

Collins, J. C. and Porras, J. I. (1985). 'Building a Visionary Company'. *California Management Review*, 37(2): 80–100.

Collins, J. C. and Porras, J. I. (1991). 'Organizational Vision and Visionary Organizations'. *California Management Review*, 34(1): 30–52.

Conner, D. (1992). *Managing at the Speed of Change*. New York: John Wiley.

Dawson, S. (1986). *Analyzing Organizations*. London: Macmillan.

de Caluwe, L. and Vermaak, H. (2003). *Learning to Change: A Guide for Organizational Change Agents*. Thousand Oaks: Sage Publications.

Denis, J., Lamothe, L. and Langley, A. (2001). 'The Dynamics of Collective Leadership and Strategic Change in Pluralistic Organizations'. *Academy of Management Journal*, 44(4): 809–37.

Densten, I. L. (2002). 'Clarifying the Relationship between Inspirational Motivation and Extra Effort'. *Leadership and Organization Development Journal*, 22: 40–4.

Di Virgilio, M. E. and Ludema, J. D. (2009). 'Let's Talk: Creating Energy for Action through Strategic Conversations'. *Journal of Change Management*, 9(1): 67–85.

DiMaggio, P. J. and Powell, W. W. (1983). 'The Iron Cage Revisited: Institutional Isomorphism and Collective Rationality in Organizational Fields'. *American Sociological Review*, 48(2): 147–60.

Dirks, K. T. and Ferrin, D. L. (2002). 'Trust in Leadership: Meta-Analytical Findings and Implications for Research and Practice. *Journal of Applied Psychology*, 87(4): 611–28.

Dixon, S. E., Meyer, K. E. and Day, M. (2010). 'Stages of Organizational Transformation in Transition Economies: A Dynamic Capabilities Approach'. *Journal of Management Studies*, 47(3): 416–36.

Doing Business 2013 Fact Sheet: Sub-Saharan Africa. International Finance Corporation & The World Bank. www.doingbusiness.org

Doyle, M. (2002). 'From Change Novice to Change Expert. Issues of Learning, Development and Support'. *Personnel Review*, 31(4): 465–81.

Doyle, M., Clayton, T. and Buchanan, D. (2000). 'Mixed Results, Lousy Process: The Management Experience of Organizational Change'. *British Journal of Management*, 11(3): S59–80.

Du Toit, A. S. A. (2003). 'Competitive Intelligence in the Knowledge Economy: What is in it for South African Manufacturing Enterprises?' *International Journal of Information Management*, 23(2): 111–20.

Duck, J. D. (1993). 'Managing Change: The Art of Balancing'. *Harvard Business Review*, 71(6): 109–18.

Dunphy, D. C. and Stace, D. A. (1988). 'Transformational and Coercive Strategies for Planned Organizational Change: Beyond the O.D. Model'. *Organization Studies*, 9(3): 317–34.

Dunphy, D. C. and Stace, D. A. (1993). 'The Strategic Management of Corporate Change'. *Human Relations*, 46(8): 905–20.

Dutton, J. E. and Ashford, S. J. (1993). 'Selling Issues to Top Management'. *Academy of Management Review*, 18: 397–428.

Dutton, J. E., Ashford, S. J., O'Neill, R. M. and Lawrence, K. A. (2001). 'Moves that Matter: Issue Selling and Organizational Change'. *Academy of Management Journal*, 44(4): 716–36.

Eisenhardt, K. (1989). 'Making Fast Strategic Decisions in High-Velocity Eenvironments'. *Academy of Management Journal*, 32: 543–76.

Elrod, P. D. II and Tippett, D. D. (2002). 'The "Death Valley" of change'. *Journal of Organizational Change Management*, 15(3): 273–91.

Epitropaki, O. and Martin, R. (2004). 'Implicit Leadership Theories in Applied Settings: Factor Structure, Generalizability, and Stability over Time'. *Journal of Applied Psychology*, 89(2): 293–310.

Equity Bank's Market-Led Revolution. Micro Save. March 2007.

Fontrodona, J. (2002). 'Management in the Service of the Person. A New Attitude for a New Millennium'. *LBS Management Review*, 7(1): 65–80.

Foster, R. D. and Akdere, M. (2007). 'Effective Organizational Vision: Implications for Human Resource Development'. *Journal of European Industrial Training*, 31(2): 100–11.

Foster, R. N. and Kaplan, S. (2001). 'Creative Destruction'. *McKinsey Quarterly*, Issue 3: 41–51.

Gabarro, J. J. (1987). *The Dynamics of Taking Charge*. Boston: Harvard Business School Press.

Galbraith, J. R. (1995). *Designing Organizations*. San Francisco: Jossey-Bass Publishers.

Gardner, W. L. and Avolio, B. J. (1998). 'The Charismatic Relationship: A Dramaturgical Perspective'. *Academy of Management Review*, 23: 32–58.

Garvin, D. (2000). *Learning in Action: A Guide to Putting the Learning Organization to Work*. Boston: Harvard Business School Press.

Gersick, C. (1994). 'Pacing Strategic Change: The Case of a New Venture'. *Academy of Management Journal*, 37(1): 9–45.

Ghemawat, P. (1991). *Commitment: the Dynamic of Strategy*. New York: The Free Press.

Gill, R. (2003). 'Change Management – or Change Leadership?' *Journal of Change Management*, 3(4): 307–18.

Goffee, R. and Jones, G. (2000). 'Why Should Anyone be Led by You?' *Harvard Business Review*, September–October: 63–70.

Golembiewski, R. T., Billingsley, K. and Yeager, S. (1976). 'Measuring Change and Persistence in Human Affairs: Types of Change Generated in OD Decisions'. *Journal of Applied Behavioural Sciences*, 12, 133–57.

Goodman, P. and Rousseau, D. (2004). 'Organizational Change that Produces Results: The Linkage Approach'. *The Academy of Management Executive*, 18(3): 7–16.

Grant, A. M. (2010). 'It Takes Time: A Stages of Change Perspective on the Adoption of Workplace Coaching Skills. *Journal of Change Management*, 10(1): 61–77.

Gravenhorst, K. M. B., Werkman, R. A. and Boonstra, J. J. (2003). 'The Change Capacity of Organisations: General Assessment of Five Configurations'. *Applied Psychology: An International Review*, 52(1): 83–105.

Greenwood, R. and Hinings, C. R. (1988). 'Organization Design Types, Tracks and the Dynamics of Strategic Change'. *Organization Studies*, 9(3): 293–316.

Greiner, L. E. (1972). 'Evolution and Revolution as Organizations Grow'. *Harvard Business Review*, 50(4): 37–46.

Grobler, P. A., Warnich, S., Carrell, M. R., Elbert, N. F. and Hatfield, R. D. (2011). *Human Resource Management in South Africa*, 4th edn. Hampshire: Cengage Learning EMEA.

Grove, A. S. (1983). 'Breaking the Chains of Command'. *Newsweek*, October 3.

Grove, A. S. (1996). *Only The Paranoid Survive: How to Exploit the Crisis Points that Challenge every Company and Career*. New York: Currency Doubleday.

Hailey, V. H. and Balogun, J. (1998). 'Diagnosing Context: A Key Step in Successful Change Implementation'. Paper presented at the British Academy of Management Conference.

Hall, G. E. (2013). 'Evaluating Change Processes: Assessing Extent of Implementation (Constructs Methods and Implications)'. *Journal of Educational Administration*, 51(3): 264–89.

Hamel, G. and Prahalad, C. K. (1994). *Competing for the Future*. Boston: Harvard Business School Press.

Harris, L. C. and Ogbonna, E. (2002). 'The Unintended Consequences of Culture Interventions: A Study of Unexpected Outcomes'. *British Journal of Management*, 13: 31–49.

Harris, S. G. and Cole, M. S. (2007). 'A Stages of Change Perspective on Managers' Motivation to Learn in a Leadership Development Context'. *Journal of Organizational Change Management*, 20(6): 774–93.

Hatum, A., Pettigrew, A. and Michelini, J. (2010). 'Building Organizational Capabilities to Adapt Under Turmoil. *Journal of Change Management*, 10(3): 257–74.

Hawkins, J. and Dulewicz, V. (2009). 'Relationships between Leadership Style, the Degree of Change Experienced, Performance and Follower Commitment in Policing'. *Journal of Change Management*, 9(3): 251–70.

Hempel, P. S. and Martinsons, M. G. (2009). 'Developing International Organizational Change Theory Using Cases from China. *Human Relations*, 62(4): 459–99.

Heneman, R. E. and Tansky, J. (2002). 'Human Resource Management Models for Entrepreneurial Opportunity: Existing Knowledge and New Directions'. In: J. A. Katz and T. M. Welbourne (eds) *Advances in Entrepreneurship, Firm Emergence and Growth*, Vol. 5, Greenwich, CT: JAI Press Inc.: 55–81.

Higgs, M. and Rowland, D. (2000). 'Building Change Leadership Capability: The Quest for Change Competence'. *Journal of Change Management*, 1(2): 116–31.

Higgs, M. and Rowland, D. (2001). 'Developing Change Leaders: Assessing the Impact of a Development Programme'. *Journal of Change Management*, 2(1): 47–64.

Higgs, M. and Rowland, D. (2005). 'All Changes Great and Small: Exploring Approaches to Change and its Leadership'. *Journal of Change Management*, 5(2): 121–51.

Hofstede, G. (1994). *Cultures and Organizations*. London: HarperCollins.

House, R. J., Hanges, P. J., Javidan, M., Dorman, P. W. and Gupta, V. (2004). *Culture, Leadership and Organizations. The GLOBE Study of 62 Societies*. Thousand Oaks: Sage Publications.

Howell, J. M. and Higgins, C. A. (1990). 'Champions of Technological Innovation'. *Administrative Science Quarterly*, 35: 317–41.

Huy, Q. N. (2001). 'Time, Temporal Capability, and Planned Change'. *Academy of Management Review*, 26(4): 601–23.

Hwang, A., Khatri, N. and Srinivas, E. S. (2005). 'Organizational Charisma and Vision Across Three Countries'. *Management Decision*, 43(7/8): 960–74.

IMF (2012). World Bank Financial Surveys. Regional Economic Outlook. Sub-Saharan Africa October 2012.

Ituma, A., Simpson, R., Ovadje, F., Cornelius, N. and Mordi, C. (2011). 'Four "Domains" of Career Success: How Managers in Nigeria Evaluate Career Outcomes. *The International Journal of Human Resource Management*, 22(17): 3638–60.

Jackson, T. (2004). *Management and Change in Africa*. London: Routledge.

Jick, T. D. (1989). *The Vision Thing*. Technical Note: N9-490-019. Boston: Harvard Business School.

Jick, T. D. (1990). *The Challenge of Change*. Technical Note 9-490-016. Boston: Harvard Business School.

Jick, T. D. (1991a). *Implementing Change*. Technical Note 9-191-114. Boston: Harvard Business School.

Jick, T. D. (1991b). *Note on the Recipients of Change*. Technical Note 9-491-039. Boston: Harvard Business School.

Jick, T. and Peiperl, M. (2003). *Managing Change: Cases and Concepts*. McGraw-Hill/Irwin.

Judge, T. A., Thoresen, C. J., Pucik, V. and Welbourne, T. M. (1999). 'Managerial Coping with Organizational Change: A Dispositional Perspective'. *Journal of Applied Psychology*, 84(1): 107–22.

Kamoche, K. (2011). 'Contemporary Developments in the Management of Human Resources in Africa'. *Journal of World Business*, 46: 1–4.

Kanter, R. (1983). *The Change Masters*. New York: Simon & Schuster.

Kanter, R. M., Stein, B. A. and Jick, T. D. (1992). *The Challenge of Organizational Change*. New York: The Free Press.

Kanter, R. M., Stein, B. A. and Jick, T. D. (2003). *The Challenge of Organizational Change: How Companies Experience it and Leaders Guide it*. New York: Free Press.

Katz, D. and Kahn, R. L. (1978). *The Social Psychology of Organizations*. New York: John Wiley.

Kaufman, H. (1975). 'The Natural History of Human Organizations'. *Administration & Society*, 7: 131–49.

Kendra, K. A. and Taplin, L. (2004). 'Change Agent Competencies for Information Technology Project Managers'. *Consulting Psychology Journal: Practice and Research*, 56(1): 20–34.

Kessler, E. H. and Chakraharti, A. K. (1996). 'Innovation Speed: A Conceptual Model of Context, Antecedents and Outcomes'. *Academy of Management Review*, 21: 1143–91.

Kim, C. W. and Mauborgne, R. (1992). 'Parables of Leadership'. *Harvard Business Review*, 70(4): 123–8.

Kim, C. W. and Mauborgne, R. (2004). 'Blue Ocean Strategy'. *Harvard Business Review*. 76–88.

Kolb, D. A. (1984). *Experiential Learning: Experience as the Source of Learning and Development*. Eaglewood Cliffs: Prentice Hall.

Kotter, J. (1990). *A Force for Change: How Leadership Differs from Management*. New York: Simon & Schuster.

Kotter, J. P. (1995). 'Leading Change: Why Transformation Efforts Fail'. *Harvard Business Review*, 74(2): Reprint No. 97506.

Kotter, J. P. (1996). *Leading Change*. Boston, MA: Harvard Business School Press.

Kotter, J. P. (2007). 'Leading Change'. *Harvard Business Review*, 85(1): 96–103.

Kotter, J. P. and Heskett, J. L. (1992). *Corporate Culture and Performance*. New York: The Free Press.

Kotter, J. P. and Cohen, D. S. (2002). *The Heart of Change*. Boston: Harvard Business School Press.

Kotter, J. P. and Schlesinger, L. A. (1979, 2008). 'Choosing Strategies for Change'. *Harvard Business Review*, July–August: 1–11.

Kouzes, J. and Posner, B. (1988). *The Leadership Challenge*. San Francisco: Jossey Bass.

Kraiger, K., Ford, J. K. and Salas, E. (1993). 'Application of Cognitive, Skill-Based, and Affective Theories of Learning Outcomes to New Methods of Training Evaluation'. *Journal of Applied Psychology*, 78: 311–28.

Lau, C. M. and Woodman, R. W. (1995). 'Understanding Organizational Change: A Schematic Perspective'. *Academy of Management Journal*, 38(2): 537–54.

Lawrence, S. A. and Callan, V. J. (2011). 'The Role of Social Support in Coping during the Anticipatory Stage of Organizational Change: A Test of an Integrative Model'. *British Journal of Management*, 22(4): 567–85.

Lawson, E. and Price, C. (2003). 'The Psychology of Change Management'. *McKinsey Quarterly*, 2: 30–40.

Lawson, J. G. (2011). *Level Three Leadership: Getting Below the Surface*. Upper Saddle River, NJ: Prentice Hall.

Levin, I. M. (2000). 'Vision revisited'. *The Journal of Applied Behavioral Science*, 36(1): 91–107.

Levy, A. (1986). 'Second Order Planned Change: Definition and Conceptualization'. *Organizational Dynamics*, Summer: 5–20.

Liguori, M. (2012). 'The supremacy of the Sequence: Key Elements and Dimensions in the Process of Change'. *Organization Studies*, 33(4): 507–39.

Lyons, J. B. and Schneider, T. R. (2009). 'The Effects of Leadership Style on Stress Outcomes'. *The Leadership Quarterly*, 20: 737–48.

McCall, M. W. Jr. (2010). 'Recasting Leadership Development'. *Industrial and Organizational Psychology*, 3(1): 3–19.

McGahan, A. M. (2004). 'How Industries Change'. *Harvard Business Review*, 82(10): 86–94.

Magretta, J. (2002). 'Why Business Models Matter'. *Harvard Business Review*, 3–8.

Mangaliso, M. P. (2001). 'Building Competitive Advantage from Ubuntu: Management Lessons from South Africa'. *Academy of Management Executive*, 15(3): 23–33.

Margolis, S. L. and Hansen, C. D. (2003). 'Visions to Guide Performance: a Typology of Multiple Future Organizational Images'. *Performance Improvement Quarterly*, 16(4): 40–58.

Mento, A. J., Jones, R. M. and Dirndorfer, W. (2002). 'A Change Management Process: Grounded in Both Theory and Practice'. *Journal of Change Management*, 3(1): 45–59.

Meyer, A. D., Brooks, G. R. and Goes, J. B. (1990). 'Environmental Jolts and Industry Revolutions: Organizational Responses to Discontinuous Change'. *Strategic Management Journal*, 11: 93–110.

Meyer, M. and Botha, E. (2004). *Organisation Development and Transformation in South Africa*, 2nd edn. South Africa: LexisNexis.

Miller, D. (2002). 'Successful Change Leaders: What Makes Them? What Do They Do That is Different?' *Journal of Change Management*, 2(4): 359–68.

Mintzberg, H. (1990). 'The Manager's Job: Folklore or Fact'. *Harvard Business Review*, March–April: 163–76.

Montgomery, C. A. (2008). 'Putting Leadership Back into Strategy'. *Harvard Business Review*, January: 54–60.

Nadler, D. A. and Tushman, M. L. (1980). 'A Model for Diagnosing Organizational Behavior'. *Organizational Dynamics*, Autumn: 35–51.

Nadler, D. A. and Tushman, M. L. (1989). 'Organizational Frame Bending: Principles for Managing Reorientation'. *Academy of Management Executive*, 8(3): 194–304.

Nadler, D. A. and Tushman, M. L. (1990). 'Beyond the Charismatic Leader: Leadership and Organizational Change'. *California Management Review*, 32(2): 77–97.

Nelson, L. (2003). 'A Case Study in Organizational Change: Implications for Theory'. *Learning Organization*, 10(1): 18–30.

Nikolaou, I., Gouras, A., Vakola, M. and Bourantis, D. (2007). 'Selecting Change Agents: Exploring Traits and Skills in a Simulated Environment'. *Journal of Change Management*, 7(3/4): 291–313.

Nohria, N. (1993). *Executing Change: Three Generic Strategies to Implementing Change*. Technical Note NG-494-039, Harvard Business School.

Nohria, N. (1995). *Note on Organizational Structure*. HBS 9-491-083. Harvard Business School.

Nutt, P. C. (1987). 'Identifying and Appraising how Managers Install Strategy'. *Strategic Management Journal*, 8(1): 1–14.

Nutt, P. C. and Backoff, R. W. (1997). 'Facilitating Transformational Change'. *Journal of Applied Behavioral Science*, 33(4): 490–508.

Ostroff, F. (2006). 'Change Management in Government'. *Harvard Business Review*, 84(5): 141–7.

Ovadje, F. (2002). 'How CEOs Get in the Way of Organizational Change and What They Can Do About It'. *The Lagos Business School Management Review*, 7(1): 55–64.

Ovadje, F. (2006). *CMC Connect: The Challenge of Realizing the Company Vision*. Lagos Business School Case.

Ovadje, F. (2009). *The Transformation of Equity Bank*. Lagos Business School Case.

Ovadje, F. (2011). *Seven Seas Technologies (C)*. Lagos Business School Case.

Ovadje, F. (2012). 'Manager–Subordinate Trust Relationships in West Africa'. In: Cardona, P. and Morley, M. (eds) *Manager–Subordinate Trust A Global Perspective*.

Ovadje, F. and Utomi, P. (2007). *Dora Akunyili at NAFDAC: The Challenge of Changing a Government Agency*. LBS Case Study.

Ovadje, F. and Cardona, P. (2011). 'Show Me You Trust Me: Trust in the Boss–Subordinate Relationship. Paper presented at the Inaugural Conference of the African Academy of Management, San Antonio, Texas.

Parish, J., Cadwallader, S. and Busch, P. (2008). 'Want To, Need To, Ought To: Employee Commitment to Organizational Change'. *Journal of Organizational Change Management*, 21(1): 32–52.

Pellettiere, V. (2006). 'Organization Self-Assessment to Determine the Readiness and Risk for a Planned Change'. *Organization Development Journal*, 24(4): 38–43.

Peng, M. W. (2003). 'Institutional Transitions and Strategic Choices'. *Academy of Management Review*, 28: 275–96.

Peng, M. W., Lee, S. H. and Wang, D. Y. L. (2005). 'What Determines the Scope of the Firm Over Time? A Focus on Institutional Relatedness'. *Academy of Management Review*, 30(3): 622–33.

Peng, M. W., Wang, D. Y. L. and Jiang, Y. (2008). 'An Institution-Based View of International Business Strategy: A Focus on Emerging Economies'. *Journal of International Business Studies*, 39(5): 920–36.

Peréz López, J. A. (1993). *Fundamentos de la Dirección de Empresas*. Madrid: Rialp.

Peters, T. J. and Waterman, R. H. (1982). *In Search of Excellence: Lessons from America's Best-Run Companies*. New York: Harper & Row.

Peterson, S. J., Walumbwa, F. O., Byron, K. and Jason, M. (2009). 'CEO Positive Psychological Traits, Transformational Leadership, and Firm Performance in High-Technology Start-up and Established Firms'. *Journal of Management*, 35(2): 348–68.

Pettigrew, A. (1975). 'Towards a Political Theory of Organisational Interventions'. *Human Relations*, 28: 191–208.

Pettigrew, A. (1985). *The Awakening Giant*. Oxford: Blackwell.

Pettigrew, A. M. (1988). University of Warwick. Centre for Corporate Strategy and Change. *The Management of Strategic Change*. Blackwell.

Pettigrew, A. and Whipp, R. (1991). *Managing Change for Competitive Success*. Wiley-Blackwell.

Pettigrew, A. M., Woodman, R. W. and Cameron, K. S. (2001). 'Studying Organizational Change and Development: Challenges for Future Research'. *Academy of Management Journal*, 44(4): 697–713.

Pfeiffer, J. (2005). 'Producing Sustainable Competitive Advantage through the Effective Management of People'. *Academy of Management Executive*, 19(4): 95–105.

Porras, J. and Silver, R. (1991). 'Organizational Development and Transformation'. *Annual Review of Psychology*, 42: 51–78.

Porter, M. E. (1979). 'How Competitive Forces Shape Strategy'. *Harvard Business Review*, 57(2): 137–45.

Porter, M. E. (1980). *Competitive Strategy*. New York.

Post, J. E., Preston, L. E. and Sachs, S. (2002). 'Managing the Extended Enterprise: The New Stakeholder View'. *California Management Review*, 45(1): 5–28.

Prochaska, J. O., DiClemente, C. C. and Norcross, J. C. (1992). 'In Search of How People Change: Applications to Addictive Behaviors'. *American Psychologist*, 47: 1102–14.

Quinn, R. E. (1988). *Beyond Rational Management: Mastering the Paradoxes and Competing Demands of High Performance*. San Francisco: Jossey-Bass.

Reisner, R. A. F. (2002). 'When a Turnaround Stalls'. *Harvard Business Review*, 80(2): 45–52.

Romanelli, E. and Tushman, M. L. (1994). 'Organizational Transformation as Punctuated Equilibrium: An Empirical Test'. *Academy of Management Journal*, 37(5): 1141–666.

Rune, L., Marcus, S., Bjarne, E. and Johansen, S. T. (2005). 'The Production of Trust during Organizational Change'. *Journal of Change Management*, 5(2): 221–45.

Rune, T. (2005). 'Organizational Change Management: A Critical Review'. *Journal of Change Management*, 5(4): 369–80.

Sadler, P. (2001). *Management Consultancy*. London: Kogan Page.

Saunders, M. N. K. and Thornhill, A. (2003). 'Organisational Justice, Trust and the Management of Change: An Exploration'. *Personnel Review*, 32(3): 360–75.

Schein, E. H. (1969). 'The Mechanisms of Change'. In: Bennis, W., Benne, K. and Chin, R. (eds.) *The Planning of Change*. New York: Holt, Rhinehart & Winston.

Schein, E. H. (2004). *Organizational Culture and Leadership*, 3rd edn. San Francisco, CA: Jossey-Bass.

Schein, E. H. (2010). *Organizational Culture and Leadership*. John Wiley.

Schneider, B., Brief, A. P. and Guzzo, R. A. (1996). 'Creating a Climate and Culture for Sustainable Organizational Change'. *Organizational Dynamics*, 24(4): 6–19.

Scott, R. (1992). *Organizations*. Englewood Cliffs: Prentice Hall.

Scott, W. R. (2001). *Institutions and Organizations*, 2nd edn. Thousand Oaks, CA: Sage.

Self, D. R., Armenakis, A. A. and Schraeder, M. (2007). 'Organizational Change Content, Process, and Context: A Simultaneous Analysis of Employee Reactions'. *Journal of Change Management*, 7(2): 211–29.

Senge, P. M. (2006). *The Fifth Discipline. The Art & Practice of the Learning Organization*. Doubleday.

Shamir, B., House, R. J. and Arthur, M. B. (1993). 'The Motivational Effect of Charismatic Leadership: A Self-Concept Based Theory'. *Organization Science*, 4: 577–94.

Shelton, C., John, Y. and Qian, L. (2005). 'Managing in an Age of Complexity: Quantum Skills for the New Millennium'. *International Journal of Human Resource Development & Management*, 5(2): 127–41.

Simon, H. (1976). *Administrative Behavior*. New York: The Free Press.

Skinner, D. (2004). 'Evaluation and Change Management: Rhetoric and Reality'. *Human Resource Management Journal*, 14(3): 5–19.

Smith, M. (2003). 'Changing an Organisation's Culture: Correlates of Success and Failure. *Leadership & Organization Development*, 24(5/6): 249–61.

Smollan, R. K. (2006). 'Minds, Hearts and Deeds: Cognitive, Affective and Behavioural Responses to Change'. *Journal of Change Management*, 6(2): 143–58.

Smollan, R. K., Sayers, J. G. and Matheny, J. A. (2010). 'Emotional Responses to the Speed, Frequency and Timing of Organizational Change'. *Time & Society*, 19(1): 28–53.

Solomon, E. (2001). 'The Dynamics of Corporate Change: Management's Evaluation of Stakeholder Characteristics'. *Human Systems Management*, 20(3): 257–65.

Stace, D. A. and Dunphy, D. C. (1991). 'Beyond Traditional Paternalistic and Developmental Approaches to Organizational Change and Human Resource Strategies'. *The International Journal of Human Resource Management*, 2(3): 263–83.

Stace, D. A. and Dunphy, D. C. (1992). 'Translating Business Strategies into Action: Managing Strategic Change'. *Journal of Strategic Change*, 1(4): 203–16.

Steven, K. (1975). 'On the Folly of Rewarding A, While Hoping for B'. *Academy of Management Journal*, 18(4): 769–83.

Stewart, J. and Kringas, P. (2003). 'Change Management: Strategy and Values in Six Agencies from the Australian Public Sector'. *Public Administration Review*, 63(6): 675–88.

Strange, J. M. and Mumford, M. D. (2002). 'The Origins of Vision: Charismatic Versus Ideological Leadership. *Leadership Quarterly*, 13: 343–77.

Strickland, F. (1998). *The Dynamics of Change: Insights into Organizational Transition from the Natural World*. London: Routledge.

Suhomlinova, O. (2006). 'Toward a Model of Organizational Co-Evolution in Transition Economies'. *Journal of Management Studies*, 43(7): 1537–58.

Sverre, S. (2009). 'Organizational Brilliance: On Blinding Visions in Organizations'. *Journal of Organizational Change Management*, 22(4): 373–38.

Tan, V. and Tiong, T. N. (2004). 'Change Management in Times of Economic Uncertainty'. *Singapore Management Review*, 27(1): 49–68.

Teagarden, M. B. (2009). 'Sub-Saharan Africa at a Key Inflection Point'. *Thunderbird International Business Review*, 51(4): 317–18.

Terence, J. (1999). 'Managing Change in South Africa: Developing People and Organizations'. *The International Journal of Human Resource Management*, 10(2): 306–26.

Tichy, N. W. (1982). 'Managing Change Strategically: The Technical, Political and Cultural Keys'. *Organizational Dynamics*, Autumn: 59–80.

Tichy, N. and Devanna, M. (1986). *The Transformational Leader*. New York: John Wiley.

Trompenaars, F. and Hampden-Turner, C. (1998). *Riding the Waves of Culture*. New York: McGraw-Hill, p. 162.

Turner Parish, J., Cadwallader, S. and Busch, P. (2008). 'Want To, Need To, Ought To: Employee Commitment to Organizational Change'. *Journal of Organizational Change Management*, 21(1): 32–52.

Tushman, M. and O'Reilly, C. (1996). 'Ambidextrous Organizations: Managing Evolutionary and Revolutionary Change'. *California Management Review*, 38(4): 8–30.

Tushman, M. and O'Reilly, C. A. (1997). *Winning Through Innovation*. Boston: Harvard Business School Press.

Utomi, P. O. (1998). *Managing Uncertainty: Competition and Strategy in Emerging Economies*. Ibadan: Spectrum Books Limited.

van Emmerik, I. J. H., Bakker, A. B. and Euwema, M. C. (2009). 'Explaining Employees' Evaluations of Organizational Change with the Job-Demands Resources Model'. *Career Development International*, 14(6): 594–613.

Van Knippenberg, D. and Sitkin, S. B. (2013). 'A Critical Assessment of Charismatic–Transformational Leadership Research: Back to the Drawing Board?' *The Academy of Management Annals*, 7(1): 1–60.

Waddell, D. and Sohal, A. S. (1998). 'Resistance: a Constructive Tool for Change Management'. *Management Decision*, 36(8): 543–8.

Walumbwa, F. O. and Lawler, J. J. (2003). 'Building Effective Organizations: Transformational Leadership, Collectivist Orientation, Work-Related Attitudes and Withdrawal Behaviours in Three Emerging Economies. *International Journal of Human Resource Management*, 14(7): 1083–101.

Weick, K. (1979). *The Social Psychology of Organizing*. Reading, MA: Addison-Wesley.

Weick, K. E. (1995). *Sense-Making in Organisations*. Thousand Oaks, CA: SAGE.

Weick, K. E. (2011). 'Reflections: Change Agents as Change Poets – On Reconnecting Flux and Hunches'. *Journal of Change Management,* 11(1): 7–20.

Westley, F. and Mintzberg, H. (2005). 'Visionary Leadership and Strategic Management'. *Strategic Management Journal*, 10: 17–32.

Whelan-Berry, K. (2005). 'Change Visions and the Organizational Change Process a Cross-Case Multi-Level Analysis. Paper presented at the Academy of Management, Honolulu, HI, August 2005.

Whelan-Berry, K. S. and Somerville, K. A. (2010). 'Linking Change Drivers and The Organizational Change Process: A Review and Synthesis'. *Journal of Change Management*, 10(2): 175–93.

Young, M. and Dulewicz, V. (2006). 'Leadership Styles, Change Context and Leader Performance in the Royal Navy'. *Journal of Change Management*, 6(4): 383–96.

Zaccaro, S. J. and Banks, D. J. (2004). 'Leader Visioning and Adaptability: Bridging the Gap between Research and Practice on Developing the Ability to Manage Change'. *Human Resource Management*, 43: 367–80.

Zaltman, G. and Duncan, R. (1977). *Strategies for Planned Change*. New York: John Wiley.

INDEX

CPSIA information can be obtained at www.ICGtesting.com
Printed in the USA
LVOW05s2158301014

411364LV00013B/250/P

9 780415 819237